More Advance Praise for

Judge Sentences

TALES FROM THE BENCH

"Meagher's writing is insightful and compassionate; the muscular prose laced with an attractive self-deprecatory wit. Keenly and sympathetically observed, the characters and their stories, like life in the courts, are never tidy, frequently carrying a disquieting, thought-provoking edge. An excellent, absorbing read."

LAVANYA SANKARAN, author of *The Red Carpet*

§ § §

"Irish wit and a painter's eye for the human comedy (of every social class) that washes up in the lower courts of Boston. This is what it feels like to be a judge—this judge, Dermot Meagher, who ends up being the best character in a book filled with people you won't forget. Hilarious, one-of-a-kind and deeply intelligent."

ANDREW HOLLERAN

§ § §

"The bench's gain was literature's loss, as Judge Dermot Meagher proves with this addictive collection. Judge Meagher is a born raconteur. The court system seems to be the closest thing we have in twenty-first–century America to the Circus Maximus, and Judge Meagher plumbs this world with an Ovidian eye. Often moving, and always engaging and pithy, these true tales from behind the bench will delight all, with no prejudice toward either defendant or plaintiff. A highly recommended, deeply pleasurable read!"

J. G. HAYES,
author of *A Map of the Harbor Islands*

"The stories in *Judge Sentences* are short, each involving a case or a character, observed from the point of view of the judge; not the cartoon version of judges seen on daytime television and crime shows but a workaday judge in the daily grind of a big urban court system. Again and again in these stories one gets the sense of a deeply humane man trying to thread the law through the needle of human misery. This judge is empathic but he is not naive. He is worldly but he is never cynical—he is what used to be called *civilized*. I loved the stories and I am inspired by Judge Meagher, as a lawyer and as a human being."

MICHAEL NAVA,
novelist and attorney

§ § §

"Beautifully written and irresistibly entertaining, *Judge Sentences* reveals the workings of a busy urban court through the eyes of a very perceptive and very humane judge. Meagher has a flair for the understated insight, and a profound understanding of human nature. His self-deprecating sense of humor, compassion, and intelligence shine on every page."

HELEN FREMONT,
author of *After Long Silence: A Memoir*

Judge Sentences

DERMOT MEAGHER

JUDGE Sentences

TALES FROM THE BENCH

NORTHEASTERN
UNIVERSITY
PRESS
Boston

§

Published by
University Press of New England
Hanover and London

NORTHEASTERN
UNIVERSITY PRESS
Published by
University Press of New England
One Court Street, Lebanon NH 03766
www.upne.com

Manufactured in the United States of America
Designed by Eric M. Brooks
Typeset in Quadraat and Spontan by Passumpsic Publishing

University Press of New England is a member of the Green Press Initiative. The paper used in this book meets their minimum requirement for recycled paper.

Names and other identifying information in these stories have been changed. Some situations have been conflated. Otherwise these stories are true.

Library of Congress
Cataloging-in-Publication Data
Meagher, Dermot, 1940–
Judge sentences: tales from the bench / Dermot Meagher
ISBN 978-1-55553-715-9
(cloth: alk. paper)
1. Meagher, Dermot, 1940–
2. Massachusetts. Supreme Judicial Court—Biography. 3. Judges—Massachusetts—Biography. 4. Justice, administration of—Massachusetts—Anecdotes. I. Title.
KF373.M39943A3 2009
347.744'014092—dc22 2009035926

5 4 3 2 1

The following portions of this book have been previously published: "The Blue Jay Feather," "Justice Will Prevail," "Emergency Duty," "Restraint," "Attorney O'Leary," and "Jury Duty" first appeared in *DoubleTake*. "Casey Quinn," "The Russian Steam Room Invader," "The Armani Scam," and "The Nude Descending" first appeared in *Boston* magazine. "Joey Ryan" was published in slightly different form as "The Steak Knife Kid" in *Boston* magazine.

The Supreme Court and the Courts of Appeal will take care of themselves. Look after the courts of the poor, who stand most in need of justice. The security of the republic will be found in the treatment of the poor and the ignorant. In indifference to their misery and helplessness lies disaster.

§

CHARLES EVANS HUGHES,
Chief Justice of the U.S. Supreme Court (1930–1941), in a speech to the New York Bar Association, 1919

CONTENTS

INTRODUCTION

*So various and subtle are the impulses toward decision.**

This book is a compendium of first-hand reportage of courtroom proceedings from arguably the most important and impartial person in the judicial process: the (hitherto silent) judge, who hears the case, guides its presentation, and often decides the case.

The judge sits up high and sees everything that happens in the courtroom. For practical and symbolic reasons, we make the judge the best observer. There have been many partisan books by lawyers, and even some by parties in a dispute, about what happens during a trial, but books from the trial judge's point of view are almost nonexistent.

Trial judges are not permitted to write about how they arrived at their decisions, and in many cases they don't have to say any more than "guilty" or "not guilty," or "for the plaintiff in the sum of X dollars," or "for the defendant." A recent appellate decision disbarring a leading trial lawyer in Massachusetts stated, "Probing the mental processes of a trial judge, that are not apparent on the record of the trial proceeding, is not permissible."** In addition, judges don't want to be overturned on appeal for deciding a case based on what is not in the record (the transcript and papers). "The less you write, the less trouble you can get into," one salty, esteemed Massachusetts trial judge advised. "Keep your mouth shut . . . and do what you want," he added.

Then there's Martin Lomasney's old Massachusetts political

*From the remarks of Massachusetts Supreme Judicial Court Justice Benjamin Kaplan at the memorial sitting for Justice R. Ammi Cutter, 418 Mass. 1603(1994).

***Glenn v. Aiken*, 409 Mass. 699, 703, 704 (1991), cited with approval in the Matter of Gary M. Crossen, Supreme Judicial Court Advance Sheets, February 6, 2008.

maxim, which applies to trial judges as well: "Don't write when you can speak; don't speak when you can wink; don't wink when you can nod."

Finally, trial judges don't write about how they make decisions because they aren't accustomed to verbalizing how or why they do what they do. That's a little too "touchy feely," therapeutic, and introspective for most of them.

§ § §

Although the cases that I heard over seventeen years as a trial judge in Massachusetts were often short, they were important events in the lives of the people who stood before me. The cases always contained at least one basic story. The problem is that there were lots of gaps in the stories over or around which judges and writers have to leap or navigate. A judge doesn't have the luxury of making decisions with the economist's ideal of complete information. In fact, usually at least one side is trying to keep information from the judge. In most cases, if the judge were given information before the trial, he would have to disqualify himself. A judge is supposed to determine facts based on the evidence presented at trial, relying on common sense and life experience. The judge is then supposed to apply those facts to the law to see if the result sought by the person bringing the case should occur. Further complicating the situation, judges are not supposed to ask a lot of questions during a trial. That is the task of the opposing sides in an adversary trial system of justice such as ours.

I created these stories from a few of the many cases that have come before me over the years. Plausible or otherwise, they are not typically the stories presented in court by one side or the other; more often they're a combination of both sides' stories, filtered through my own experience, including events that occurred far from any courtroom. I hope that the stories allow the reader to peer inside my head as I navigated "the various and subtle impulses toward decision," in Judge Kaplan's fine words.

These stories interest me because of one or more of their characters or because of the situation being litigated. Some of my responses were ideological—I believe in the Constitution, for example. Most of the time I was just smiling and saying to myself, *What a privilege and honor it is to have this job.*

{ i }

GOD WRITES IN CROOKED LINES

When I was in college I heard a Dominican monk named Brother Antoninus read some poems from his book titled *Crooked Lines of God*. I do not remember much about the poems, but I thought about the title while rereading the three stories that follow.

These three cases are about somebody's faith. The deity being invoked in each has a different name, I suspect. In spite of the odds against the parties, I believe that just results occurred. As for my part, the notion that I might have been "guided" only occurred to me some time later, when I was writing the stories.

JUSTICE WILL PREVAIL

Just keep on praying

§ § §

It was a small courtroom, and I could hear everything in it. There were only four rows for spectators, and each row seated four people uncomfortably. This day, the only spectators were two African American women in the next-to-last row. One was young and plump with two sets of gold earrings as big as hood ornaments. One set was oversized Claddagh rings, the Irish betrothal ring of two hands holding one crowned heart. If worn on the right-hand ring finger with the heart facing out, the ring means that one is available; if worn facing in, it means one's heart is taken. God knows what it means hanging from the ears, and God bless America that a young black woman would be wearing an Irish symbol of romance. She also wore a black down jacket and a reversed baseball cap.

The other woman was old and tiny, with big glasses that slipped down her nose. She wore an old brown coat and a little, well-worn, black felt hat. She was identified by the defendant's lawyer as the grandmother of Kelvin Miller, who was also small and was slouched sullenly in the defendant's chair, in a black hooded sweatshirt, baggy jeans, and elaborate new sneakers.

I had just announced that I was reserving judgment and requested supplemental memoranda from the lawyers. We had heard the evidence, and now I wanted the lawyers to give me the relevant law in light of their separate versions of the evidence.

I was getting off the bench when I heard the younger woman say to the older one, "What happened? What'd he do? What's he doing?" The older woman, in a weary voice, said, "We just have to keep on praying."

I went out the side door with the court officer; the women went out the back door. Unintentionally, we met in the hallway at the corner, and the grandmother said again, to no one in particular this time, "Just keep on praying; Justice will prevail."

What I had been hearing was a motion to suppress the drugs that had allegedly been found on Kelvin Miller after a car in which he was the backseat passenger was stopped in Park Square for a defective taillight—or perhaps, as one esteemed appellate judge said, "on suspicion of being black."

Kelvin Miller's lawyer, a zealous young man, argued that the trooper, Patrick Owens, had no right to order anyone out the car, least of all Kelvin Miller, the passenger in the backseat; the most the trooper should have done for this non-arrestable offense was give the driver a citation for the defective taillight and tell him to get it fixed. Because the search had been illegal and unconstitutional, the lawyer said, the evidence (in this case, the drugs) should not be used against Kelvin Miller. If I were to suppress the drugs, declaring them to have been illegally seized, there would be no evidence to convict Kelvin Miller, the accused, in his pending criminal trial. Such pre-trial suppression hearings are common in criminal cases, and in drug cases especially. The case can rise or fall on the judge's decision regarding the motion to suppress.

Trooper Owens was tall, athletic, and clean-cut. He was impressive in his jodhpurs and boots. But for a gap between his two front teeth, he could have been the poster boy for the state police. He said he had been patrolling in downtown Boston, near the Transportation Building in the theater district, when he saw a car with a defective taillight and followed it to Park Square, where he stopped it. Mirabile dictu, he found three young black men in the car, reeking of freshly burned marijuana. He asked the driver to step out of the car; discovering him to be without a license or registration, he placed him under arrest and ordered him into the backseat of the cruiser.

Trooper Owens then removed Kelvin Miller and another young man who had been sitting in the front passenger seat. He discovered nothing on Mr. Miller after a pat frisk but then searched the car "incident to the arrest" of the driver. Trooper Owens testified that he then found, under the driver's seat toward the rear passenger seat where Kelvin Miller had been sitting, a two-inch cigar butt full of marijuana, known on the street as a stubbie. Based on this discovery, Trooper Owens decided to search Mr. Miller again, more closely this time, and found a bag of marijuana in his sock. According to the trooper, Mr. Miller then ran down the street and discarded another bag containing crack cocaine.

This story was a little too neat for me. I spent a lot of time researching the applicable law and found that, indeed, the scenario fit the then most recent iteration of the so-called automobile exception to the constitutional mandate that all searches require a warrant. The automobile exception went something like this: because automobiles are mobile, the requirement of obtaining a warrant before a search should be relaxed. There often isn't time to obtain a warrant for a car, which can be moved quickly and cannot always be kept stopped until the procedures to obtain the warrant have been followed.

It didn't please me to know about the automobile exception or the way these facts just fit it. I continued researching, looking for an exception to the automobile exception, but none was forthcoming by the day I received the supplemental memoranda.

Both memoranda stated facts that were not consistent with my memory or notes of the trooper's testimony. Both lawyers' statements of the facts were reiterations of the facts stated in Trooper Owens's police report, which had been written right after the arrest. It seemed that neither lawyer had really listened to the testimony of the trooper on the stand. That sometimes happens with young lawyers during a hearing because they are too busy trying to think of their next question to take note of the information that came from the previous answer.

According to the police report, the trooper discovered the bag of marijuana under the backseat and found fragments of marijuana on the floor in front of the front-seat passenger. The stubbie was on the center console between the front seats, not, as the trooper testified under oath, under the front seat near Kelvin Miller, the fortunate grandson of the prayerful grandmother.

After a couple of days trying to figure out which version of the facts was "true," I realized that this quest was impossible. Because the trooper's testimony belied his police report, and his police report contradicted his testimony, neither should be believed. The Commonwealth of Massachusetts had failed to show that anything the trooper said or wrote about the search was believable. I therefore suppressed all the physical evidence, leaving the Commonwealth with no case.

Kelvin Miller's grandmother was right. Justice will prevail.

THE BLUE-JAY FEATHER

A tennis-playing lawyer and random acts of kindness win the day

§ § §

I bought my first drawing of a blue-jay feather in 1978 at the Massachusetts College of Art Christmas Fair. I bought another the next year at the same place without realizing I'd bought the first. The third one started the collection because I bought it conscious of the two before it.

One day the next August, before his daily swim off the rocky beach at Jamestown, Rhode Island, my brother-in-law, Michael, drew a pastel of seashells, blue-jay feathers, and stones that he'd found there. So, of course, I had to have that, too. Later at one of the early AIDS Support Group auctions, I bought two homemade wooden blue jays that had belonged to a friend who had just died.

In my backyard, the lord of the trees is the blue jay. There are lots of other birds—robins, grackles, and sparrows, even sometimes a cardinal—but the boss is the blue jay. Furthermore, it seems that whenever I'm in trouble I look up and there's a blue jay.

Timmy, who takes care of my yard, says that each of us has a bird that is attached to us, that guides us. He says his is a crow. "And yours," he says, "must be the blue jay. You didn't know about this?"

I say that I didn't but that I am glad to know now. "However," I say, "I don't like to think of myself as quite as pushy as a blue jay."

"Well, maybe you are," says Timmy with that big smile as he walks away.

§ § §

The judges in the Boston Municipal Court hear a variety of cases. The largest number of cases are criminal—all misdemeanors and all but the most serious felonies. Next are civil—personal-injury, property damage, and contract cases. Then there are appeals from certain state agencies, like the Division of Employment Security, requests for restraining orders, and mental-health civil commitments.

I dread mental-health civil-commitments. This day there were two. They're always sad. The first one wasn't too hard to decide. The man was quite troubled. He had beaten up people on the street and beaten up the staff once he got to the hospital. It was his fifteenth commitment since turning eighteen.

Between the cases, when I walked out of the mental-health center's law library, which was being used as the hearing room but which also served as a storage room and perhaps a lunchroom, there was a young man wearing a visitor's pass, sitting in the hall. He was about five foot eight, kind of chunky, with thick black hair and a thin beard along the edge of where he would have liked his jaw to be. I wondered who he was. I knew from the visitor's badge that he wasn't a patient. He didn't have a suit jacket on, so he probably wasn't a doctor testifying for the defense. And the state's doctors didn't wear passes.

When I returned to the library, the respondent in the second case, Robert Fortier, was brought in. He looked like the man in the hall: thick black hair but no beard. He was very neatly dressed. His haircut was rather old-fashioned, a pompadour in fact, and his clothes were dated too, a neat plaid shirt and khaki pants, unlike the rumpled baggies worn by most of the young men I see in court. He looked around the room with no particular reaction even after Marilyn McKay, the experienced and professional clerk who had come down with me from the courthouse, formally called the case.

Two burly guards came in with the respondent; the bigger one leaned forward onto the table and watched the hearing as though it were a tennis match.

The lawyer representing both patients that day was Albert Lehane. Mr. Lehane is a character; he works at being a character. He's Irish from Cambridge, and he went to Harvard on a scholarship for local boys. He's got a year or two on me, which put him at the time around sixty-one. He always talks about Harvard. Sometimes we make bets, the court officer and the clerk and I, about how many times he'll mention Harvard in any one conversation. During a three- or four-minute chat, it's usually seven or eight times. Lehane also loves to play tennis, and he won't let the court continue cases to certain days when he has matches planned. He often pulls a half-eaten apple out of his pocket and chaws on it. When he talks to you, he stands with his arms tightly crossed on his upper chest and gives you a puss.

Lehane thinks he's got me on two counts: I'm Irish and I went to Harvard as well. Anti-Irish Catholicism was the liberals' anti-Semitism in our day, even among the Catholics, many of whom would have had you believe they just stepped out of *Brideshead Revisited* rather than *Long Day's Journey Into Night*. Nevertheless, most of us Irish Catholics tended to feel the familiar bond of oppression at the secular, if no longer Protestant, school. But unlike Lehane, I wasn't in Pi Eta, the Irish-Catholic boy's club at Harvard where Lehane had been a member, although he assumes I was. Our lives must connect at some points, but not those he talks about.

And Lehane talks a lot. At first it appears to be nonsense, but I suspect he's trying to find out what I "had for breakfast that day," as the jurisprudes say. One theory of jurisprudence says that what judges do in a case on any given day depends on what they had for breakfast—in other words, on their mood. According to this theory, there really is no ideology of decision making.

Anyway, although some people think he's too garrulous, Mr. Lehane was masterful in this case. (As I write this, a blue jay has appeared in the backyard. I can hardly believe it. He's on the hammock chain. He likes that. Sometimes he's even on the hammock chain when I'm in the hammock.)

The same doctor testified in both cases, introducing himself with, "My name is Doctor Harold Wallace Harris." *Funny, I didn't know "Doctor" was a first name*, I thought. "The respondent, Robert Fortier, was found wandering around the Arsenal Mall with a patched suitcase, acting bizarrely," he testified.

Doctor Wallace Harris gave no further description of the event that had led to Robert Fortier's confinement in the mental-health center for the past month. From the mall, Mr. Fortier was taken to a local hospital, and from there to the mental-health center. He refused medications, refused an electroencephalogram, and refused psychological tests.

One day he'd been seen meditating over something he had made in the center's art-therapy class, "as if it were a relic or some sacred object." Another time, Mr. Fortier paced the hall so rapidly that he had to be forcefully medicated with Risperdol, an antipsychotic drug. After that he willingly took the drug and became more "responsive." The doctor believed that he was an "extreme risk of harm to himself" and that he was "nonresponsive to environmental cues," whatever that meant.

On cross-examination, the doctor admitted that Mr. Fortier had appeared too frightened to speak to the hospital staff. The doctor determined that Mr. Fortier had never been hospitalized before.

"Who wouldn't be frightened?" Mr. Lehane asked the doctor rhetorically. "Have you ever sat down with Mr. Fortier and talked to him for about an hour or so, like I did yesterday?"

The doctor responded with only slightly veiled agitation, "I have nine patients in four hours on Thursdays and twenty-four patients on the unit. Some are very sick."

In the court petition, the document that had been presented to begin this proceeding, the doctor and the hospital director requested that I order that Mr. Fortier forcibly be given Risperdol, Haldol, Ativan, Klonopin, and other medications if he was not willing to take them voluntarily and that he be committed to the mental-health center for six months.

The petitioners rested their case after Dr. Wallace Harris finished testifying.

Mr. Lehane asked to have the respondent's brother, Richard, enter the room to testify. He was the man I'd seen in the hallway, with the pencil-thin beard and the visitor's pass. I had suspected they were brothers when I first saw Robert, but I didn't know whose side Richard would be on; sometimes family members seek their relative's commitment, and sometimes they have reason.

Richard testified that until the previous July Robert had made frequent visits to the family home, but had stopped coming by in August or September. In September, Robert walked into a family christening, announced that he no longer wanted to have anything to do with the family, and left.

Throughout his testimony, the brother talked about "us," meaning his parents, his brother, and himself. It was obvious that there had been closeness and that the brother was sad that it had been broken. Richard had gone to Robert's apartment to see him in early November, but there had been no contact over the holidays. "It was the first Thanksgiving without him," Richard said. He believed something had been bothering Robert extremely.

On cross-examination, Richard said that Robert was the more sociable of the two brothers, that Robert had studied jujitsu, that when Robert went to college he had partied the first year and not done too well, and that he had been put on academic probation but pulled himself together. The brothers grew up in Texas and moved to Boston in 1980. Their father taught French and Latin and now worked with computers. Robert had problems getting a job when he first got out of college—he received close to five hundred rejection letters—so he joined the Peace Corps and liked it. He was in Africa for two-and-a-half or three years. He wrote home once or twice a month.

"We never fought. We've always been the best of friends," said Richard wistfully. "He remained with us, but he was different after the Peace Corps. He'd incorporated the culture of Mali. He also had taken a malaria drug, which had visual effects." Nothing more was said about the malaria or the drug. "He was open and friendly and closed at the same time."

Robert had worked at a bookstore but kept looking for something in his field, mechanical engineering. He had almost gotten a job at General Electric, but they'd chosen another person. "He wanted to get out of the house; he wanted to be independent. Basically, he told us, 'It's my business, I'll take care of myself.' The failure to get a job hit him hard," the brother said.

Robert himself then testified. I was surprised. This is not the usual occurrence. In most civil-commitment cases, the lawyer tries to keep the client off the stand lest he start talking about hearing voices through his dental fillings or something else that would keep him locked up. And a patient cannot be compelled to testify.

At first, Robert seemed innocent, almost naïve—too relaxed, considering the possible consequences of his testimony. He sounded as if he accepted the reasonableness of the doctor who would have me keep him medicated and hospitalized for the next six months. There didn't appear to be a lot of fight in him. But somehow as he went on, the telling of his story made him strong.

He told us that he was twenty-nine and had last lived on Commonwealth Avenue in Allston. He had graduated from the Boston Latin School and Worcester Polytechnic Institute. After college, he interned near Washington, D.C., but couldn't find a job in his field. He last worked as a designer of fire-protection systems for buildings but had recently gone on unemployment.

"I was shy," he said, laughing to himself. I was not sure what he meant. This little private revelation was disturbing, and the laugh after it was not helpful in explaining it. Perhaps "shy" was the word others used by others to describe him and his behavior, and perhaps the laugh indicated that he knew the problem went deeper than that.

Robert had entered the Peace Corps in February 1992 and was sent to Mali, where he taught English as a second language to seventh graders. "I liked it a lot," he said. He also distributed eyeglasses to people in the area: "New Eyes for the Needy from New Jersey," he said with a little smile. He was in the Peace Corps for two-and-half years, after which he traveled to Morocco and then to Paris. At the end of his tour, he had approximately $1,500 saved up. His student loans were deferred but still existed. He looked for work at bookstores and considered teaching in city schools, but held back the applications because he found an engineering job. That lasted only four months, however. He decided to move out of his parents' house because as a result of being in the Peace Corps he was used to having independence.

"I didn't intend for things to work out this way," he said. "I needed some time for myself. I didn't give up, but I didn't accomplish much. I felt that I needed more time for myself." Regarding his behavior in the mental hospital, Robert said, "I preferred not to take psychological testing. I'd never been in a hospital before. I can't be in isolation." As for his resistance to taking medications, he said, "I don't even take aspirin."

On cross-examination, when asked about the incident at the Arsenal Mall and the empty suitcase, he said he had been shopping: "I needed something to carry things in."

He was then asked about his meditating over the object from the art therapy class.

"It is a dreamcatcher, like a mandala," he responded. "It's Native American. It will catch good dreams and let bad ones pass through. I made it. It's a hobby. I've been making them since I was a kid. I had to look at it to get ideas for the next dreamcatcher I'm going to make."

Mr. Lehane asked for a recess, and I needed one. When I returned, Robert was holding a blue-jay feather in one hand and looking at an embossed leather disk about six inches in diameter on the table. I wondered where they had come from but saw no harm in their being there. I hoped the attendants wouldn't take them from him.

Robert said, "Wow, they're beautiful."

The disk must have come from his brother, I thought. I recalled that Richard had been holding something like it all through his testimony. I hadn't seen the feather before. I assumed it was from the brother as well.

After we went back on the record, Mr. Lehane said, "We have an agreement, Judge. We'd like to continue this matter for a month. Robert agrees to take the medication he's taking now, Risperdol, and the hospital will try to get him into another facility, a less restrictive facility."

"I agree," I said, as sagely as I could, trying to mask my relief. "It seems like a wise decision."

On the walk back to the courthouse, I said to Ms. McKay, the clerk, who has been around the courts and these hearings much longer than I have, "That was a very kind thing for Richard to give Robert the disk and the blue-jay feather."

"I gave him the feather," she replied. "They use feathers in dream-catchers. My nephew makes them. I love birds. I'm a member of the Audubon Society. I pick up feathers wherever I go. I found two blue-jay feathers this morning. After that hearing, I figured he could use one. I'm glad he liked it so much."

"Was it okay to do that?" she asked disingenuously. "Would you like the other one?"

"Yes, I would. Thank you."

THE RESCUE OF RAYA STENETSKY

They thought the old lady was crazy

§ § §

Early in my career at the Boston Municipal Court I was sent to the Massachusetts General Hospital to hear a request for the civil commitment of an allegedly mentally ill person. I had never before been to the Mass General, as it is called in Boston, to hear this type of case.

The Mass General had just built an expensive new psychiatric ward. In a wide hallway, over a button at the side of a door, was a sign labeled PLEASE PRESS FOR ADMISSION. I pressed. The door hummed open, and I walked down a white corridor, passing people in what was to be my "courtroom." It was a cold modern room with walls that were ice blue and too bright; I was to sit in an uncomfortable plastic chair at a table in front of a large window overlooking the Charles River, facing the participants and the audience.

In front of me to the right was Mr. Cooley, a tall man in his fifties, the lawyer for the subject of this hearing. On the left was Ms. Aaron, a short, very well-dressed woman who was the lawyer for the petitioner, the hospital. She came from a large firm, perhaps one of the corporate law firms retained by the hospital.

Seated in the other rows were a number of young people whose presence had not been explained to me. I requested that they identify themselves, which did not make them happy. They were residents and medical students, and to them this was just another class. They occupied the good chairs, which I asked three of them to surrender for myself, the clerk, and the court officer, us worker bees.

Minutes later, an elderly woman with long, wild, white-and-gray hair pulled back behind her ears, was escorted into the room. She was about the size of my mother, maybe a little taller—five foot one, perhaps—and she was bright-eyed and eager, like my mother. Her cheeks were very pink. She wore two cardigan sweaters, also like my mother, and carried in her arms a large plastic bag filled with documents. She sat to the right of Mr. Cooley. Her name was Raya Stenetsky.

Raya Stenetsky had been discovered on a cold December night on the porch of a house belonging to someone she did not know in Chelsea, a nearby city, which has seen better days. She was holding a package of frankfurters, and she had some dried fruit in her coat pocket. The Chelsea police took her to the Mass General emergency room. She ended up in this bright, shiny mental ward.

The doctor, a young woman psychiatrist, had not been able to find out much because Ms. Stenetsky refused to talk to the doctor or to anyone else; she sat in her room most of the time, reading a book. She was a "Canadian national," the doctor kept saying. As recently as two years ago, Ms. Stenetsky had traveled all over Europe: Berne, Paris, Rome, Amsterdam, London. When not traveling, she lived in Montreal. From some source never revealed, the doctor claimed that Ms. Stenetsky was in the United States because she had seen some black people in the Montreal airport, heard them talk about Washington, D.C., and had come to help them. Somehow she had worked her way up to Boston. Nobody knew the details.

In the Orwellian tautological way these mental health people sometimes talk, the doctor decided that because Raya Stenetsky would not cooperate with the hospital—she believed that she had been kidnapped by the police and kept to herself—she must be crazy. Did they think that she should welcome being locked in a ward and questioned, with the possible consequence of being confined and drugged for six months? The hospital was seeking a six-month commitment, as well as what is called in the parlance a "substituted judgment" that would require me to substitute my judgment for Ms. Stenetsky's (because they said she was not competent) and decide that it was in her best interest that she be forced to take Haldol, Ativan, Valium, Xanax, Prozac, Thorazine, lithium, Klonopin, or some combination of the preceding.

Although Mr. Cooley was eloquent in his defense, he did not give me an alternative to commitment. He did indicate that all Ms. Stenetsky wanted to do was go to Israel.

I noticed that Ms. Stenetsky had taken a book from her plastic bag during the hearing.

"What is she reading?" I asked her lawyer.

I was told that it was a Hebrew book, which apparently mystified the psychiatrist, whose last name was Levy. Dr. Levy would have me find that that book was another indicator of Ms. Stenetsky's insanity. I kept my counsel, which is another way of saying I kept my mouth shut, and let everybody talk on. Ms. Stenetsky followed each speaker intently with her eyes although she still held the book open on her lap.

After the psychiatrist's testimony, Ms. Stenetsky tried to give me a manila envelope stuffed with papers, but her lawyer leaned in and whispered to her as he grabbed her arm. He advised her against it, and he intercepted the envelope en route.

Ms. Stenetsky had also refused to be examined medically. The psychiatrist thought that she might have lupus, because of her rosy cheeks. *It couldn't be hanging out in the cold on a porch in Chelsea*, I thought silently.

Early in the hearing I had decided that I would take advantage of one of the more useful tools in my box—reserving judgment. I would not decide the case until I returned to my office. I was not impressed with the doctor's speculation about either the facts of Raya Stenetsky's life or her alleged mental illness. The standard of proof was high: beyond a reasonable doubt. That is the same standard that is used in a criminal case and rightly so. A finding against Raya Stenetsky would deprive her of her liberty, just as if she were to be sent to jail.

When I returned to the courthouse, I committed Ms. Stenetsky for four months or until she had improved, in the hope that she could be kept warm for the rest of the winter. But I did not allow the substituted judgment for the drugs. The hospital would not be able to give her drugs against her will. I hoped that the food was as good as the facility was clean and that there were more books for her to read. I knew that the hospital would probably appeal.

A few weeks later, Dr. Garfield, a wise and helpful man who has worked at the Boston Municipal Court for years providing a variety of psychiatric and medical services, stopped me in the corridor and said, "You dealt with an old Jewish woman at the Mass General? Mr. Cooley called me about this case, and I went to talk to her."

"Oh, is that so?" I said noncommittally.

He said, "Yes, it was a very difficult case. She wouldn't talk to me; she wouldn't talk to anybody. However, eventually I talked to her in Yiddish. My sister came with me, and she speaks Yiddish too. We both talked with her. It turns out that she'd been in a concentration camp and then moved to Canada upon gaining her freedom. At first she didn't trust me, but I kept talking. She used to be a Hebrew teacher."

That explained the book.

"She lived in Montreal and in Israel," Dr. Garfield continued. "In addition, she has two cousins in Miami who could keep her for a week or so and then help her get on a plane to Israel."

"That's nice of them," I said.

"Your decision was appealed to the Superior Court, but upheld by Judge Hogwood. Now we're trying to see if we can't get her out altogether. We have to go back to Judge Hogwood."

It's no wonder she thought she was being kidnapped, I thought.

Dr. Garfield added, "After we finished talking, she wanted to give me two hundred dollars. She said it was Chanukah, and she was so happy to have talked to me. I told her I couldn't take it, and she told me I had to take it. In addition, she has twenty-seven hundred dollars that she's hiding in the Hebrew book."

I had to have a little faith that Judge Louise Hogwood would do the right thing or, more to the point, that God would do the right thing for the long-suffering but ever-strong Raya Stenetsky. A little faith would get us both through.

The case was sent back to me by Judge Hogwood for my reconsideration, but I did not hear it. My father's death intervened, and I was out the day the rehearing was scheduled. Having heard Dr. Garfield's view of this situation, I would have had to disqualify myself in any event. One of my colleagues heard the returned case.

I was told that during the rehearing, which was in a courtroom in the Suffolk County Courthouse rather than at the hospital, Raya Stenetsky appeared alert and presentable. Nevertheless, the hospital was eager to keep her. The doctor who spoke on the hospital's behalf, Dr. Levy again, had never testified in one of these cases before in court. Dr. Garfield, on the other hand—he who had interviewed Ms. Stenetsky with his sister and who was an old hand around the courthouse—told her story quite dramatically, with frequent references to the fact that she had been in a concentration camp. He opined that she no longer needed to be committed or forcibly medicated. (Apparently Raya Stenetsky had decided to take some medications at Dr. Garfield's urging.)

The judge was convinced by Dr. Garfield and by Raya Stenetsky's story, and he released her. It turns out that she has a guardian in Canada and about $75,000 there. She was planning to go to Miami to visit her cousins and then to Israel. A man in the courtroom, a friend of Dr. Garfield, an elderly widower engineer who also spoke both Yiddish and Hebrew, was going to accompany her.

{ ii }

DISORDERLY CONDUCT

Almost all of the conduct described in this book is disorderly, but some instances are worse than others. In the first three stories in this section, one of the parties is the problem, but in the last the whole courtroom loses it under the stimulation of the television camera.

A specific prohibition against disorderly conduct is contained in one of the oldest statutes in Massachusetts. The same statute also punishes "common streetwalkers and nightwalkers." It used to forbid "loitering," but that crime was declared "void for vagueness." In the court where I served, the statute was most often invoked against prostitutes because catching the prostitute in the actual act of taking money and offering sex was too difficult and time consuming. However, the statute was also called on when the authorities did not have anything more specific to cite.

The characters in these next four stories were engaged in disorderly conduct in the more commonly understood sense. The court was being called on to stop it. Sometimes it did so successfully, sometimes not, never permanently.

CASEY QUINN

She never knew what hit her

§ § §

My introduction to Casey Quinn occurred shortly after I became a judge. She had been arrested for being a "common nightwalker," one of the many young women in spandex shorts and fishnet stockings picked up at three o'clock in the morning while prowling around the so-called Combat Zone, a neighborhood in downtown Boston that had been set aside for seediness in the 1960s.

A few weeks after I first saw her, she was arrested again for the same thing, but during that incident she bit the young, recently married police officer who brought her in and then told the cop that she had AIDS. She later recanted, but her recantation was, as we say, not reliable. For the next six months, the officer and his bride would have to wait and worry until the virus incubated sufficiently to reveal itself on a test. However, one of my colleagues managed to persuade Ms. Quinn that it was in her best interests to get tested. She proved to be HIV negative, much to everyone's relief.

Casey was still in her early twenties, small with brownish-black hair and bright, dark eyes. She traveled in a pack, the only girl with four or five bedraggled male neo-hippies in tow. At first glance she looked like a modern-day Wendy from *Peter Pan*. A longer view revealed that she was tougher than any of the boys and had not an ounce of maternalism. I'd seen her a couple of times marching down one of the streets on the back side of Beacon Hill, her sorry retinue straggling behind.

In our last case together, a couple of policemen came upon her outside the package store at the corner of Charles and Mount Vernon streets, the base of Beacon Hill, just as she was about to deck her boyfriend, who she had pushed up against the wall. One of the rookie officers asked Ms. Quinn, "Can we help you?"

She turned and said, "Fuck you! Get the fuck out of here!"

The policemen were not deterred. Again one asked, in a stronger voice, if they could help her.

Casey said, "Fuck you! We'll take care of this."

Her captive nodded in agreement or terror or both.

Casey was arrested for disorderly conduct. She was lucky because she was assigned Attorney Kenneth Katz, one of the best of the appointed counsel working in the court. Mr. Katz moved to dismiss the case, arguing that Casey could not be found guilty of disorderly conduct for saying "fuck you" to a policeman.

Casey stood in the dock as Mr. Katz argued, raising her shackled fists and muttering "right on" at all his good points. I allowed the motion to dismiss and released her.

Some months later about eleven o'clock on a summer Saturday night, I was standing in front of Spiritus Pizza in Provincetown. Spiritus is Provincetown's Via Veneto, its St. Mark's Square, the place to see and be seen on a summer night. I ran into a guy I knew, Andy, a social worker who, coincidentally, had worked with Casey Quinn. He looked sad and upset.

"I was just watching the ten o'clock news," he said. "Casey Quinn was killed, hit by a bus in Copley Square."

He was obviously distraught and needed to talk to someone who could connect to this information. And there I was. As if she were laid out in front of us at a wake, he began to reminisce about the deceased.

He had met Casey Quinn at the drop-in center for runaway kids at the Arlington Street Church, a progressive Unitarian Universalist church—the Vatican of Unitarianism, as a matter of fact. On his first night as director she came in like a fury, sat on his lap, and said, "Oh, another faggot! You and I are going to get along just fine."

More than anyone else he worked with, Andy told me, Casey was bent on self-destruction. She'd been a heavy drug user and went with kinky tricks whom other, saner prostitutes avoided.

I asked what drugs she used, and he said, "Everything, but she really liked crack cocaine."

He told me of a night Casey didn't want to go to a shelter or out to trick. So she walked across the street to Shreve, Crump & Low, Boston's fanciest jewelry store, broke a window, and waited for the cops to come arrest her.

"Well, she's in heaven now," said Andy, looking up. "It's because of her that I'm down here in Provincetown selling exotic Asian tchotchkes to rich gay couples. It was too hard up there in the city. I had to get out. I couldn't take it anymore."

Neither could Casey, it seems.

OBSESSION

Love is strange and can send you back to Cincinatti

§ § §

My introduction to Harriet Rose was at a hearing to revoke her probation. Ms. Rose had previously been found guilty of making harassing phone calls and had been put on probation. The probation officer, who had given up on her, was asserting that she had violated the terms of her probation and wanted me to send her to the House of Correction.

When people are put on probation, they agree to general terms such as "the defendant agrees to obey all state and federal laws," and sometimes other, more specific terms are imposed. In this case, one of the more specific terms was that "the defendant, Harriet Rose, will not contact Rocco Sacco in any way."

Ms. Rose sat in the chair reserved for defendants, looking like the social worker she once had been, neat, dull, and plain. She came from Ohio but had lived in Boston since her graduation from Boston University, where she had been both an undergraduate and graduate student. She had worked for the Welfare Department but was now unemployed. She had lived in the North End for ten years. She was in her late thirties, with mousy hair too tightly curled, and she wore good, dated-but-clean autumn-colored clothes—light brown slacks, a light green blouse, and a dark brown shapeless jacket. She rarely lifted her head except to scan the courtroom.

Eventually her eyes locked on Rocco Sacco. Mr. Sacco was seated behind and to the left of her, perhaps ten feet away, with his mother, his girlfriend, Maria Laurano, and another attractive woman who was his sister.

Rocco Sacco was called to the stand. He was about twenty-five and had thick dark hair, light eyes, and a body by Bernini. He was wearing a beautiful soft, dark-tweed Italian sports jacket, a dark green shirt without a tie, dark pants, and tasseled Italian loafers. He told his sad story.

"Judge, this is the fourth time we've been here with this woman. I live in the North End; my mother lives in the North End; my father lives in the North End; my grandmothers are in the North End. We've always lived in the North End. And this woman is making our lives miserable. I can't take it anymore, Judge." Mr. Sacco was awfully upset. Agitated though he was, he still looked like a movie star. One of my colleagues said he looked like the young Clark Gable or Tom Selleck.

"Start at the beginning, Mr. Sacco," I said avuncularly, leaning over the bench.

"One night I went to the laundromat, and this woman was there," he said, nodding toward Ms. Rose, who still did not look up. "She asked me if I could change a dollar. I did. I gave her four quarters. Then she asked me if I had any extra soap. I did, and I gave it to her. She went away and then asked me if I had any bleach. I said I did, and I gave some to her. As I was leaving, she said, 'bye now.' I walked a block and noticed she was following me. The next day there was a Valentine slipped through the door addressed to me. I don't know how she got my name. Maybe she just looked on the door, but maybe she saw the tag on my gym bag, which I was using to carry my laundry. I thought that was kind of cute. The Valentine was signed 'Harriet.' The next day there were two Valentines, and the next day there was a letter. Here's the letter."

The letter steamed. "You are my reason for living. . . . I long to climb all over your body. I imagine the hair on your chest and want to follow it down, down, down with my finger and then with my tongue. . . . I saw the way you looked at me yesterday, and I will never forget it. I know that you could not talk to me because she was there, but soon we'll be together and you will never forget me."

Mr. Sacco went on, "I saw her once outside my building, and I told her to please stop sending me things. It was very flattering, but I had a girlfriend—not this girlfriend, but another girlfriend I had before. She said, 'Oh—oh, okay.' I didn't see her for about a week, but then I saw her again. When I looked out my window, I saw her looking up. I started to get more letters. I had an unlisted phone number, but I started to get phone calls, heavy breathing. And then I'd get phone calls with nothing, sometimes in the middle of the night. The letters were typed; they weren't signed. I finally had a tracer put on my phone, and the calls were traced to her. We brought a case, and I thought it was all taken care of. She said she wouldn't do it again. I thought she was found guilty, but it's something else; I don't know what it was."

I looked at the probation officer.

"A continuance without a finding, Your Honor," said the probation officer.

"So, after that it started again, and there was a second case. Then she was found guilty and put on probation. I don't want the woman to go to jail, but I want her to leave me alone. And she hasn't left me alone. So it gets worse now, Judge."

I looked at the papers and found that there had been a finding of guilty with probation for two years.

"The letters have started again. The calls have started again. I changed my number, and two weeks ago this was put through my mail slot." From a brown paper bag he poured out onto the shelf in front of the witness stand a pair of pink panties.

Harriet Rose looked down even further toward the floor. I had no idea what to do. The defense lawyer chose not to cross-examine Mr. Sacco, which gave me no time to think. With great solemnity I ordered a court-clinic evaluation.

The probation officer informed me that there had already been two court-clinic (i.e., psychological) evaluations.

I said as sagaciously as I could, "Well, I think we need another" and left the bench.

Of course, the court-clinic report came back as expected, with a diagnosis of obsessive-compulsive disorder and recommended outpatient treatment. By the time the report was received, there was another case against Harriet Rose for similar activity against Rocco Sacco.

On that case she was held in jail pending trial by one of my colleagues. My colleague, a feminist, said, "She's ruining the life of that young man and his family."

Finally, another of my wiser colleagues managed to persuade her lawyer that she ought to go home to her parents in Cincinnati, Ohio.

She has not reappeared.

ASH WEDNESDAY

The answering machine fortuitously kept them both in the USA

§ § §

On Ash Wednesday the first year that my office in the Boston Municipal Court's judges' lobby was in the Old Building of the Suffolk County Courthouse, a nineteenth-century copy of the Hotel de Ville in Paris, a burly priest who worked two floors down in the Juvenile Court and wore his Roman collar askew (presumably to show that he was a regular guy) came barreling down the corridor as I was heading to my courtroom in my robe (which showed that I am not a regular guy). I was accompanied by Franny Cooney, the court officer, who exclaimed, "Jesus, Mary, and Joseph, what do we have here, Padre Pio?" as the priest rubbed his right thumb into his left palm and then aimed the thumb at my forehead.

Not realizing what he was doing, and thinking that he was going to put out my one good eye, I ducked, and he reached off into the air like a wide receiver who had missed a pass. I heard later that he tagged one of the two Jewish judges as well as Dr. Garfield, the court physician, also Jewish, and most of the Protestants on our floor. I am sure that it did them no harm to be reminded that "ashes thou art and to ashes thou shalt return," but I doubt they felt that way.

"Now wasn't that a constitutional crisis of separation of church and state!" I exclaimed.

Nobody else thought that it was out of order, however. They told me the priest did this every year, just like Dr. Garfield gave the flu shot to all the employees every year.

Franny Cooney, the court officer accompanying me, also got hit. However, he knew what was coming, and he stood there, closed his eyes, and took it like a confirmation candidate waiting for the bishop's slap. The priest then hustled into the judges' lobby itself, sacred territory supposedly forbidden to outsiders. As there were not as many practicing Catholics as there had been on the court, I wondered how he'd be received.

Franny and I continued our walk to the courtroom. I wasn't sure how pious Franny was, so I resisted the wisecrack and kept my mouth shut en route, except to ask, "What have we got down there?"

"Domestic violence—a restraining order—two women."

There were three women in the courtroom. None of them looked over thirty. They were all good-looking and well-dressed. Two were together at the defense table. Inez Garcia, who had long, thick, dark hair and wore a stylish brown dress, was the respondent, the person against whom the restraining order was being sought. The woman next to her, a sandy-haired blonde in a pale blue suit and glasses, was her lawyer.

At the front table was a blonder blonde, in black slacks and a white shirt, who was the petitioner. She was Svetlana Ribik.

She had come to court the week before and claimed that Inez Garcia, her former lover, broke into her house and harassed her on the previous weekend. Another judge listened to her story and issued a temporary restraining order. Today, after Ms. Garcia had been notified, I was supposed to decide whether a permanent order should issue. Even though Ms. Ribik had written up an affidavit detailing her grievances against Ms. Garcia, it was important that I hear those grievances on the record at this hearing and that they be repeated for Ms. Garcia's edification (even though her lawyer had probably already read the affidavit before this hearing.) Ms. Garcia's lawyer had to be given the opportunity to question Ms. Ribik about her allegations.

Ms. Ribik began, "Since I broke up with Inez a year and a half ago, she has been begging me to be her friend. For over one and half years she has gotten angry and threatened me. Two weeks ago I saw her on the street. I was with my new girlfriend. Later that evening there was a loud banging on my door. I opened the door, and Inez threw me to the wall, screaming. I asked her to get out of my house, and she began beating my new girlfriend, who was visiting. She never before attacked me physically, ever. However, I am scared of her. I can't trust her. I find myself looking around all the time to see if she's behind me. I never hurt Inez, ever."

On cross-examination, Svetlana testified that she and Inez had gone together for two years but that "everyone knew that [they] had broken up." She also added that on the night of the incident in the apartment, Inez Garcia demanded the television, the radio, and some kitchen supplies. Ms. Ribik did not deny that they belonged to Ms. Garcia. However, she was in shock that Inez could behave this way.

Inez Garcia then testified. She was thirty years old. She had trained as a psychologist in Argentina and was at Boston University as a visiting research scholar on a visa that had expired the day before.

Ms. Garcia had seen Svetlana with her new girlfriend on Boylston Street, although she did not know that the other woman was the new girlfriend. Svetlana had introduced her only as "a friend." After introducing the "friend," Svetlana said, "I'll call you tomorrow." That same Saturday afternoon and evening there were three phone calls from Svetlana to Inez. This was not unusual. Even though they had broken up, they were in touch by phone every day. They had even been "intimate" a few times since the breakup. Inez had not been home so the calls were left as taped messages on Inez's message machine.

Inez's lawyer, Ms. Howe, stood up and requested permission to play the tapes of the phone messages. She had even known to bring a tape player. (The court has one that a litigant left behind in 1980, but it is more than a little unreliable.)

The first message, received at three-thirty in the afternoon, was fairly perfunctory: "Hello Inez, how are you? It was good to see you today. I like that outfit. I'll call tomorrow."

The second, received at 9:04 PM, was different: "Inez, I love you, love you, love you. You are the only one. When I bumped into you I felt awkward introducing you to Alice as my best friend."

The third call, ten minutes later, pulled out all stops. "This is Svetlana. Where are you? It is ten-fifty. I love you; I will always love you. I'll call you at eleven-fifty."

When Inez returned home, she called back because the voice had seemed to get more desperate with each call. Inez knew that Svetlana was worried about an upcoming surgery, and Inez was worried about her. On the phone, Svetlana sounded as if she were in trouble. Inez asked Svetlana if she had been drinking. Svetlana replied, "A little."

Inez called a cab and went over to Svetlana's apartment. It was about 11 PM. Inez, who still had a key, knocked, got no response, and then opened the door. The apartment opened onto a hall leading to the living room. Svetlana, who was in the living room, saw Inez and approached her tipsily.

Svetlana said, "Don't leave. Come here." Inez grabbed Svetlana because she was afraid that Svetlana would fall.

Inez said, "I came here to see you. I was worried after those calls." Svetlana was not alone. Alice was there as well. They both were almost naked.

Inez continued, "We all started screaming. Alice started laughing. Svetlana said, 'This is my girlfriend.' Alice denied it and started laughing at us. Svetlana grabbed me and threatened me. She scratched me. After I got out of jail, I went to the doctor and . . ."

That was the first I had heard about jail. If Inez had gone to jail, criminal charges must have been brought. If criminal charges had been brought, there would be immigration problems for Inez Garcia. That was why she was represented today and fighting the restraining order. The problem was not the restraining order in and of itself, but the criminal charges. *And what if Inez Garcia beat the criminal charges?* I wondered. *What does the Immigration and Naturalization Service think about lesbians?* I knew they used to deport gay men.

Ms. Howe jumped up and said, "Judge, I'd like to introduce the doctor's report."

Svetlana did not have a lawyer to object, so I had to take her possible objection into account. It is difficult for a judge to deal with people who are unrepresented by lawyers. The system is built for lawyers. That sounds very undemocratic and elitist these days, but it's true. In court administration this is called the *pro se* problem. There are Bar Association committees pondering it. Judges may appoint lawyers only in criminal cases; in civil cases, judges are further limited because they may not substitute themselves for the nonexistent lawyer. On the other hand, they are obligated to be fair and not let the lawyer for the other side run over the pro se party.

I said, "Please let Ms. Ribik see the report." I waited a little bit and then said to Svetlana Ribik, "Do you have any objection to my seeing that report?"

She didn't. I read it. Indeed, Inez had received scratches and bruises, whether from Svetlana or Alice or the police, the report could not say. It was smart of Inez to have documented her injuries.

"I just wanted to sit down and talk," said Inez. "The new girlfriend kept calling her friends, laughing and making fun of us. We all ended up screaming at each other.

"Alice snuck into the other room and called the police. But I invited them in when they came to the door. I told them I wanted my things back. They said they didn't have time to listen to my 'personal problems.' I reminded them that it was their job to sort these things out. They tried to get me out of the house.

"I told the police, 'I'm not leaving until I get my personal belongings.' And I listed what was mine: the TV, the VCR, the radio, the kitchen stuff, and my toothbrush.

"The police arrested me because Alice was making fun of the situation. I told her, 'Just shut up!' I pushed her back onto the couch because she stood right next to me, in my face. She was trying to choke me with her hands, but," Inez added sarcastically, "the police did not see that. "The police threw me against the other sofa. I kicked towards Svetlana because she was coming after me. But I didn't touch her."

"Do you have any questions of Ms. Garcia, Ms. Ribik?" I asked.

"No, no," Svetlana Ribik said sheepishly. "I had no idea about those tapes. I hadn't heard them before. I don't remember them."

"Do you wish to make a closing argument, Ms. Howe?" I asked reluctantly.

She was entitled to make a closing, but if she did, Svetlana could argue too. Lay people like Svetlana Ribik don't usually understand that a closing argument is supposed to be a summary of the evidence presented in the light most favorable to them. Lay people usually see closing arguments as another opportunity to repeat their testimony, to add what they forgot earlier or to give a tirade.

Ms. Howe argued very wisely. She opposed the restraining order because of her client's delicate immigration status. She thought that Ms. Garcia would be acquitted on the criminal charges but that her visa might be in trouble if the restraining order were granted and if the facts behind the restraining order were revealed. "This was a complicated romantic situation that got out of hand," Ms. Howe said.

That was it: very neat, candid, brief, and, best of all, not incendiary.

Svetlana Ribik started off slowly. She was still in shock and looked worried. "I don't recall those phone calls. I had no idea that I said those things to Inez. I had been drinking a lot, but I didn't think I had blackouts. I am also here on a visa. I am a nurse. Inez's friends started calling me and threatening me. I was scared. I don't remember those phone calls. No."

I denied the petition for a restraining order.

MS. LARRY LIN

Appearances can be deceiving

§ § §

My introduction to Larry Lin occurred in 1989, a few months after I was made a judge. She had been doing business, and getting arrested for it, since 1979. Although she was born in Portland, Maine, in 1960, she had an Asian accent. She was very thin and wore women's clothes well, especially miniskirts with very high heels. She didn't appear to think of herself as a man dressed as a woman. Her voice was high as were her heels.

One of my more progressive colleagues instructed me that she, the judicial colleague, always asked transvestites how they wanted to be called—"mister" or "miz"? My colleague said that was the least we could do. They had not only been arrested in full drag but were now being paraded in court in a rumpled outfit with five o'clock shadow and smeared makeup. It must be pretty humiliating. That made sense to me, so I asked Larry Lin how she wanted to be addressed.

She looked at me blankly. She hadn't understood.

I then asked, "Would you like to be called 'mister' or 'miz'?"

She looked up at me as if to say *Are you serious?* and then said, "Miz," with a slight smile.

One day, close to lunch, she appeared in the first session courtroom for soliciting two dumpy older detectives. Unlike some of the women prostitutes, Larry Lin hadn't learned to look at the shoes. Most detectives, particularly the older ones, wore regulation thick-soled, black shoes. Most prostitutes wouldn't go near them after having checked the shoes, but not Larry Lin. She had been arrested so often I almost wanted to find someone to give her the tip.

After I released Larry Lin on her own recognizance, her promise to appear at the next court appearance, she preceded me out of the courthouse down the steps to Boston's City Hall Plaza. At the curb she lifted her left calf behind her as she hailed a cab with her right hand, just like Mary Tyler Moore or a Revlon commercial of the busy young professional woman off to the next business meeting. For Larry Lin, unlike for most of her "sisters in sin," it appeared that the magic of being a career girl did not wear off in the morning, even after a night in the Tombs. Her look was quite believable. In fact it's hard to believe that Larry was biologically a man.

The second time Larry appeared in front of me, we received a request via one of the court officers not to send her to the Deer Island House of Correction, *please*, because she had infected half the population with gonorrhea during her previous visit.

§ § §

My introduction to transvestites occurred on Halloween in 1958, when I was a freshman in college. I had just turned eighteen, had just arrived at college a month before, and was more than a little overwhelmed by Boston, freshman year, and my classmates.

The great-grandson of a former president of the United States, a handsome six-foot-two juvenile-squash champion, and I piled into a dark blue Volkswagen station wagon that belonged to a man in my dormitory named Richard, who I had met on the steps of Memorial Hall in line to register for classes a few weeks before. We were headed to Boston to see the Halloween celebration in the city. I was thrilled to be in such sophisticated company. We were too young to get into the bars, but we wandered the streets of Boston's Combat Zone and Bay Village, four scrub-faced white boys in khaki pants, tweed jackets, and rep ties.

It took seven tall, overdressed women before we realized that we were seeing men in women's clothes. That epiphany occurred only after the seventh tallship sailed past us on the arm of a shorter man in a bad tuxedo and said, in a very deep voice, "Take your hands out of your pockets, boys, or you'll never get laid." We thought that remark was so risqué that it became an inside joke. After that, as we approached each other in the Yard or in the lunch line at the freshmen dining hall, one of us would say, "Take your hands out of your pockets . . ." and we'd laugh conspiratorially.

A year or two later, Richard—who has since died and who was the only one of the three classmates I kept up with—dropped out to live in Greenwich Village and dye his hair blond. When he returned to college, his hair restored to a respectable brown, he gave me an introduction to the law of transvestitism. He said that legally in Massachusetts men may only dress up as women on Halloween. On the few occasions when I pondered this information over the next forty-plus years, I assumed Richard's nugget of legal information was apocryphal—until a few months after seeing Larry Lin, when I asked an older colleague who'd been a prosecutor in Boston in the sixties if it was true. He told me that that had been the law, believe it or not. The prohibition against cross-dressing, like other Massachusetts laws against pleasure in most of its myriad forms, was one of the Puritans' blue laws. And like many of the other blue laws, it was repealed in the seventies.

§ § §

One day in the first criminal session the most interesting case involved two wholesome-looking white men in their early thirties who had encountered a prostitute in the Combat Zone and followed her into a parking lot. They crowded her a little too much behind a truck and frightened her. Well, she might have been frightened when one of them pulled out a badge, which belonged to him as a former police officer in a sleepy little town on Cape Cod. Not only did he flash the badge, but he also pulled a pistol from his belt while his friend told the prostitute how much they wanted to "play with her pussy."

The men's arraignment for assault with a dangerous weapon, threats, and soliciting—a felony and two misdemeanors—was interesting for many reasons. Not only had one of the defendants recently been a policeman, but the assigned lawyer for the non-cop was an ardent feminist. Nevertheless, she argued, "Judge, it just seems that these guys got a little too exuberant with this girl after a few drinks, and she panicked at their come-on."

The "girl" in question, of course, was Larry Lin, who the previous night had called herself "Courtney Wright." It seems that upon hearing the solicitation, not being able to deliver on her prospective clients' expectations, and seeing the gun, she ran up to a Transit Authority policeman on Washington Street, who didn't know her. She explained her plight, but was arrested for soliciting by the efficient officer, who sent his colleagues after Larry's assailants.

Up to this point in the hearing, Larry had been held for her own protection in the "Cage," a holding area near the first session courtroom but separate from the regular dock and the usual, presumably tougher, defendants. The Cage was for those who were trouble, who might cause trouble, or who would attract trouble. Who went into the Cage was decided by the chief court officer for criminal business, who had been doing his job very well for over twenty-five years. (Because transvestites were men, albeit dressed in women's clothes, they could not be put in the women's dock.) The Cage sat in the middle of a corridor with floor-to-ceiling wire mesh at either end. Once the door was opened to the room with the cage, its occupants were much more visible than those in the holding cell next to the dock, where other defendants who had been arrested stood while being arraigned. But in the first criminal session there is some inflexible and time-honored rule that all people arrested in the same "transaction" have to be arraigned together, no matter what the offense. It was not always a good idea.

Nevertheless, Larry Lin was brought out of the Cage so she could stand below and to the right of the dock, which held her two admirers from the night before. I don't think that her admirers, or their lawyers, realized until then that Courtney Wright was a man.

Larry Lin/Courtney Wright slinked along the wall from the Cage to the dock with her jacket pulled up to cover half her face, as if she were Jackie Kennedy trying to stymie the paparazzi. Larry held the jacket up with her handcuffed hands throughout the arraignment, peering over its collar with well-mascaraed eyes.

It was all a performance. There were hardly any spectators left in the audience except three Latino men, one of whom whistled until a court officer gave him a chilling look. There were no cameras in the courtroom; there rarely are. There was something charming about Larry's pretending that there were cameras. It made us look glamorous in a ditzy way—like we were in a Weegee photo from the thirties.

I set a small bail of $100 cash because Larry Lin was on probation and was facing a revocation of that probation as well as the new charge, even though I suspected that neither charge would go anywhere. The only evidence of soliciting was Larry's statement to the Transit policeman about what had happened behind the truck in the parking lot. The ex-cop and his pal were not going to testify against her, or she against them. All three would exercise their Fifth Amendment right against self-incrimination. If the soliciting charge against Larry Lin fell, the revocation of her probation would have no basis and that would fall as well.

Even though, according to her lawyer, Larry Lin had a job as a waiter at a Chinese restaurant in Everett, a blue-collar suburb of Boston, she was not able to put up the $100 immediately, and she was returned to the Cage to await transportation to the jail. Because of the alleged threats, I set larger cash bails for her suitors.

At the end of the session, as I passed through the corridor that contained the Cage, Larry Lin was curled up in a ball on its only bench. I have not seen her since, although some of my colleagues reported that they had. I heard recently that she died of AIDS, but nobody knows for sure.

TV POISONING*

The camera distorts everyone

§ § §

It was a Monday morning in the summer, and the first criminal session's list was long: lots of weekend arrests who had not been able to post bail. I knew before I arrived that the list would be long; there had been a full moon on Saturday night.

When I walked into the lobby, not so fresh from a weekend at the Cape, I saw three television cameramen, three still photographers, and a couple of officious, good-looking young women with lacquered hairdos and bright suits.

"Judge, these people are looking for you," Milly, the receptionist, announced unhelpfully. Until she alerted them that I was the one they were looking for, "the media," as they call themselves, hadn't had a clue. I could have passed for any middle-aged, chunky Irish guy in a suit—in other words for one out of every three judges in Massachusetts. Now their heads turned toward me in unison, like ballerinas in *Swan Lake*.

Couldn't she have at least waited until I got into the lobby? I thought. Milly was a good scout, but she would have been more discreet if anyone other than these people had been looking for me. She deflected lawyers, defendants, and irate citizens all day long. *C'mon, Milly,* I thought, *give me a chance to put down my bag, please.*

I nodded toward the Fourth Estate, muttered, "I'll be with you in a minute," and went into the inner lobby to search for the rule

* Maureen Dowd, *New York Times*, June 10, 1998, referring to Monica Lewinsky's lawyer, William Ginsburg; also called "Judge Ito Disease," referring to the judge in the first O. J. Simpson Trial.

regarding cameras in the courtroom. For some reason, in those days this rule was included in the *Canon of Judicial Ethics*, the implication being that judges who failed to follow the rule would be taken before the Judicial Conduct Commission and punished. *Such is the power of the press these days*, I thought while thumbing through the canons. The pertinent rule said that only one still camera and one video camera have to be admitted into a courtroom. That solved some of the problem—two of the still cameras and two of the TV cameras could be kept out.

I put on my robe, to add the authority of the office to the bad news I was about to deliver, returned to the outer lobby, and invited the eight of them in. Although the reporters were dressed appropriately, even glamorously, the cameramen and photographers were dressed like defendants—sweatshirts and blue jeans. They carried their cameras into the library where each of the judges had a stall. I feared that my colleagues would think it was either a raid or *Sixty Minutes*. The media ogled the inner lobby and my colleagues in their stalls as we passed through the first old courtroom, which had been converted fifty years ago into eight tiny cubicles used as judges' offices. Some of us judges call it the "ward," others the "stable." With the patina of age, it had become an almost pretty room, albeit run on direct current and completely lacking in privacy, which is why I could not talk to them there. It is photogenic, however, and I could see the cameramen and photographers framing shots.

We went through to the passageway between the lobby and the library, where the law clerks work, and sat down at a long table. They were not happy when I read them the rule and told them they would have to flip coins to see which TV camera and which still camera could enter the courtroom. One of the two reporters asked if the rule meant she could not come into the courtroom.

"Of course you can come into the courtroom, but you'll have to leave that thing behind," I said, pointing to the microphone she was clutching—as a symbol of *her* authority, I assumed. "Only one of us can talk in the courtroom at a time. The rule only applies to cameras.

This," I added pedantically, "is America. The Constitution guarantees freedom of the press."

She looked crestfallen; I think that she thought she could talk from the back of the courtroom, like Cokie Roberts at a congressional hearing.

I also told them that the camerapeople could not be disruptive and would have to stay in the court officers' box to the right of the bench. They would have to set up before the session opened, and they could not leave until the first recess. One of the reporters (who, being a spectator, could leave whenever she wanted) asked, "When will that be?"

I responded, "I don't know. We have a lot of cases, and I am going to try to do as much as I can when I have the case files available in the courtroom. My problem today is getting the files into the courtroom; there is always a snag; they come from the police stations through the DA for screening to the clerk's office, and then they have to be coordinated with Probation. But you don't need to hear my terrible troubles. I'll let the cameras out when I can."

I escorted them out of the judges' lobby as if in a procession. Their purpose was by this time known to my colleagues in their cubicles, and one judge in her stall started to hum Cole Porter's "Another Opening, Another Show."

I grabbed my notebook and went out for the hundred-yard walk to the courtroom. As happens on Monday mornings, the corridors were crowded, and the court officer escorting me had no training to protect me. Thank God that the people in the corridor did not know that. She did have a loud voice, however, and that was just as scary. She had put on lipstick for the cameras.

"Step aside, the judge is coming through! Move it, mister," she snapped at some poor lawyer regaling his clients in the middle of the corridor.

Just outside of the courtroom, a woman, later identified as the mother of the accused, and her son's lawyer were giving an interview to one of the bright suits and her attendant camera. On the other side, another camera was filming an interview with the sister of the deceased. In the little passageway just before the courtroom, two of the high school summer interns from the probation department were jumping up to see whether they could see the accused through the little barred window of the holding area. "That's him! That's him in the white T-shirt," said the younger girl.

"Get down," my escort said gruffly, and they scattered.

The courtroom was jammed. The cameras were set up. The bright suits were in the second row, notebooks in hand, one on either side of the aisle, green on starboard, red on port. One lawyer—who had nothing to do with the case and no business in the courtroom and who could rarely be found when he did have business in the courtroom—walked back and forth in front of the camera, sat down, combed his thinning blond hair, picked up a pad not his own, and walked back and forth in front of the camera again. He repeated this business two or three times.

A senior assistant district attorney from the Superior Court upstairs stood solemnly at the prosecutor's spot to the right of the bench and chatted up his juniors, who were seated and gazing up at him adoringly.

The clerk, an old-timer who had seen it all, had other plans for this posturing crowd. So caught up was I in the hullabaloo that I did not realize immediately that he was going to call the other cases first, the cameras be damned. It was his call. Perhaps it was his desire to let the courtroom calm down before calling the case of interest. However, it would have been better to get the celebrity case in and out sooner: every employee in the courthouse seemed to be curious about this case. People walked in and out, stood in the corners, behind the court officers' boxes, and in the doorways. The delay in calling the case just gave time for more people to come in and for those already in the courtroom to become restless.

The clerk called about ten of the more mundane arraignments—cocaine in the Combat Zone, solicitation for sex in front of Don Bosco Technical High School, assault at a fern bar in Faneuil Hall, and shoplifting of twenty-six bottles of Calvin Klein's Obsession at Filene's—before calling the case everyone was waiting for. The Boston Municipal Court's geographical jurisdiction extended from Massachusetts Avenue in the West through the South End and Back Bay to Beacon Hill, the Financial District, the Retail District, the Leather District, the Combat Zone, Chinatown, Faneuil Hall, the North End, and the Waterfront in the East—ensuring that Mondays were never slow.

People continued to come in, and only a few had gone out. I realized that I should have locked the doors when we began the session to prevent the traffic, but it was too late now.

The defendant, Alford Jackson, was brought out of the holding cell to stand at the dock to my left. A granite wall rose in front of him to just below his chest, and two or three court officers were standing in the dock as well. Their job was to bring men from the holding cell to the dock, as well as to maintain order.

Mr. Jackson was in his mid-twenties, good-looking, about six feet tall, 175 pounds, and light-skinned. He had on a very clean white T-shirt with something written on it in small red letters.

The clerk read the charge: "Alford Jackson, you are charged with the crime of murder in the first degree of Karim Brown on the twenty-sixth day of August."

At the defendant's microphone stood a young man who had only the year before been a law-student intern with the public defender's office.

What the hell is he doing here? I thought. *He's an amateur, if he's even a lawyer yet.*

The prosecutor began. He was not facing me as he talked to me. At first I wondered why he was looking at the wall, then I realized it was to give the camera a profile. It would have been terrible if the TV audience had seen only his bald spot.

"Your Honor, on Thursday night Karim Brown and his girlfriend, the cousin of the defendant, Cheyvonne Robinson, went to The Pixy, a nightclub on Boylston Street in the Winthrop Hotel."

The Pixy again, I thought. *That place is a bucket of blood.*

"The victim, Karim Brown, and Ms. Cheyvonne Robinson had an argument there, and Ms. Robinson returned to her apartment in the South End, on Columbus Avenue. About an hour later Karim Brown came to the apartment and knocked loudly on the door. The defendant was sleeping on the couch. He had been staying there for the prior week. He got up, went to the kitchen, retrieved a steak knife, opened the door, and stabbed Karim Brown in the chest, puncturing his heart. The victim died instantly.

"The victim had been a local basketball champion. He was all-city high scorer last year, and he had spent this year at Alabama State, where there were great hopes for him. Many people loved him, including his mother and entire family, who are sitting in the third row."

The prosecutor turned, allowing the cameras to capture his full face then pan to the victim's mother and family. Everyone else in the courtroom looked as well, including me. Unlike everyone else, however, I did not have to turn to see them.

All of a sudden the defendant shouted out from the dock, "I loved Karim too!"

The cameras flashed back to catch the court officers moving toward the defendant to keep him from another outburst—not a good shot for court administration.

It was then that I was able to read the writing on the T-shirt. It read I LOVED KARIM. I also remembered having seen on television over the weekend the circumstances of his arrest. I had paid little attention, having no foreknowledge that the matter would come before me today. In the company of his pastor, Mr. Jackson had turned himself in at Police Headquarters in front of the previously alerted cameras, carrying a bouquet of roses while saying to Televisionland, "I loved Karim."

"The Commonwealth requests that the defendant be held without bail," the assistant district attorney shouted above the din. "He has a record of convictions for larceny, assault and battery, and numerous drug offenses. As a matter of fact, he is awaiting trial in this court on a charge of distributing cocaine. No bail should be set for this most heinous crime."

Never mind that the Constitution requires bail to be set in all cases, I thought. *This is Television.*

The young man on the left, last year's intern, jumped up and began to speak.

"Sir, do you represent the defendant?" I inquired.

"Yes, Judge, I am Michael Gianoni, of Robert Shaneen's office. Mr. Shaneen is in front of the Supreme Judicial Court today and asked me to appear here for the purposes of bail."

"Are you a lawyer?

"Yes, I was admitted in May."

"Of what year?"

"This year, Your Honor."

"Who is representing the defendant?"

"Mr. Shaneen"

"Go ahead."

"My client is innocent of this charge," he said—presumptuously, in my opinion, not because he said his client was innocent but because he had previously told me that the defendant was Mr. Shaneen's client, not his. Mr. Gianoni made a flourish with his right arm toward the man in the dock. "When the truth comes out he will be acquitted. He is a good man. Although he has had a slight problem with drugs in the past, he is admired and is, in fact, a hero in South Boston, where he lives."

I found that curious because Alford Jackson did not live in South Boston, a predominantly white community that had witnessed painful racial incidents in the recent past. Yet South Boston had nothing to do with this case. Mr. Gianoni had a New York accent and apparently did not have either Boston geography or sociology down. I suspect that Mr. Shaneen knew that Alford Jackson was not going to get out, no matter what anyone said, so he sent Mr. Gianoni, the kid, to give him experience while he, Mr. Shaneen, tended to business where his considerable talents would pay off.

"He has been fighting his addiction with the help of his pastor, who is here today, as well as his mother and sisters." Now it was Mr. Gianoni's turn to do the full-face flourish. "He has been lecturing in schools about the evils of drugs and is employed by the church in its youth outreach program."

Oh, that's great, I thought and noted to myself that the most recent drug-distribution arrest had occurred less than a month before.

"I will not go into the facts of this case at this time, except to say that my client was engaged in self-defense and the defense of his cousin at the time of this unfortunate incident. His cousin would be here to tell you that but she is still too distraught to leave her mother's house."

Again from the dock, Alford Jackson shouted out, "I loved Karim!" Again the cameras zoomed in on him. This time the court officers stood still.

I set bail at half a million dollars.

Of course I watched the TV news that night, switching channels furiously. Except for the occasional appearance of my disembodied voice, I ended up on the cutting room floor, which was a good thing.

Alford Jackson was acquitted a year later by a jury. Cheyvonne Robinson, the deceased's girlfriend, testified on his behalf and said that he was protecting both her and himself. The trial was not televised.

{ iii }

ACID REFLUX

It surprises me how few cases I take home with me at night. We deal with so many cases that the mind cannot worry about them all. Furthermore, at some point a judge has to let go. Of course, that is easier if he has faith in the people who are going to pick up the case—the probation department, the rehabilitation facility, or even the prison. It would be futile to try to follow every defendant beyond the courtroom.

However, there are cases that keep me up at night. I do not mean in a benign way, making me ask myself, *How do I write this decision to make it foolproof on appeal?* The cases that really worry me rot my already bad stomach. The question they raise is, *Have I done the right thing?*

Shortly after being appointed, I and some of my judge colleagues toured the Suffolk County Jail, where defendants awaiting trial are held; the House of Correction, where we send people who are convicted; the Poly Addiction Center, where people are sent for alcohol and drug treatment; and a locked facility for those who have been convicted for the third time of driving under the influence.

Of course, our brief, sanitized views of these places are no substitute for being sentenced there. Some judges have stayed in prisons, living as inmates for short periods of time. I am not that brave. I would not want to be in any of the facilities I visited.

THE BICYCLE THIEVES

After a heated jury trial, the judge changes his mind

§ § §

The jury selection was quick. There were not many challenges from either of the defendants or the Commonwealth. Occupationally, the jury was the usual mix of blue- and white-collar citizens we see in Boston, although there were no doctors; usually we get at least one doctor.

I receive my information about the jurors from the jurors' information forms, which I may keep. The judge knows more about each of the jurors than they do about each other. I only realized that fact when I served on a jury and did not know even the first name of anyone except the foreman. Lawyers may look at the juror's information forms during jury selection but then must return them.

There were two black women; otherwise, everyone was white. Race has become important because in a case some years ago the prosecution had tried to keep all black people off a jury in the trial of a black man accused of killing a local Harvard football player in the Combat Zone. Recently, jurors' forms have begun to ask jurors to identify their race. It's a much better idea to have the juror note her or his race than to have the judge try to figure it out in this increasingly and complexly mixed America.

Three of the jurors were not married. Six of them had kids. Both defendants were white, as was the victim. Most of the jurors were under forty, except for an elderly woman from Dorchester, who had six grown children.

We pick eight jurors even though we ultimately use only six. Alternates are selected after all evidence has been heard, arguments have been made to the jury, and the judge has instructed the jury about the pertinent laws involved in the case. Cards with the names of all the jurors, except that of the already designated foreperson, are put in a small barrel. Two names are drawn for the alternates. I tell the alternates not to take their selection personally because it was made at random, and I point to the barrel the cards came out of. Often the alternates are relieved rather than disappointed that they will not have to decide the case. Sometimes they appear disappointed. They've spent all this time listening, and now they have to sit in a remote room by themselves while the other jurors deliberate.

I used to pick the foreperson at the beginning of the trial based on what I perceived to be his or her ability to resolve conflict with other people. Teachers and nurses seemed promising, as did mothers with adult children and big families. But after I picked a sleepy nurse, and after I served on a jury in a case in which the judge selected the foreperson later, I began to make my choice at the end of the trial. That delay gave me the opportunity to see the attention that the various jurors paid to the evidence, the summations, and my instructions before I chose the foreperson.

At the beginning of this trial, only the prosecutor made an opening statement, which is unusual but not unheard of. Sometimes the defendants want to find out how the prosecutor's case goes before committing themselves to a particular defense. A lot of things can happen. Witnesses do not show up, or their actual testimony differs from, or is stronger or weaker than, their anticipated testimony, or the witness folds on cross-examination. Based on the charges in this case, it was likely that the two defendants did not present a united front and did not want to reveal that to each other right at the start.

Charlie Samborski was charged with assault and battery on Thad Bartlett; assault and battery with a dangerous weapon—to wit, a bicycle—on Thad Bartlett; and larceny of property over $250, the bicycle belonging to Thad Bartlett. Fritz Farron was charged with assault and battery on Thad Bartlett.

The negative effect of deferring an opening statement until the prosecution has completed its case is that at first the jury hears only the prosecutor's interpretation of the evidence. There is a theory, based on a study no doubt, that fact-finders, both judges and jurors, make up their minds in the first few seconds of a trial and then spend the rest of the time finding reasons to ratify that judgment. With all the respect due this theory, I do not believe it, at least not about myself. My opinions about a case go all over the place in the course of a trial. Sometimes I can almost see, in my mind's eye, the decision float from one side to the other. I don't think I am alone in this regard. "So various and subtle are the impulses towards decision," said a very distinguished appellate judge in Massachusetts.

At first glance, the victim, Thad Bartlett, looked to be a hip kid. He worked hard at appearing cool and casual, but there was something about him that wasn't. Maybe this contradiction was apparent to me because I had worn a similar mask at his age. I knew that his veneer was not going to endure in the heat of a trial. It may have worked for young Thad at school, in a dormitory, or with the bigger boys, but this was a different audience. It didn't matter how cute and boyish he was. His charm was going to be removed.

Thad was a student at the Berklee College of Music, where he was studying the bass violin. He looked as though he could not even hold up a bass violin. He was about five foot six and weighed less than 125 pounds. Although a well-off kid from Connecticut, he came to court in dirty, wrinkled baggy pants and an oversized shirt—in ironic contrast to the high school–dropout defendants who wore neat slacks, white shirts, and ties.

Thad practiced five hours a day on the bass violin in addition to taking other classes. At night, he sometimes worked at a microbrewery bar. It was not my place to ask why he was doing that although at the time of the trial, five months after the incident, he was still only twenty and not of a legal age to drink. For some reason neither of the defense attorneys got into the illegality of his drinking, although they did determine how much he had had to drink on that late spring night of May 28.

Thad had ridden his bike to work about 8 PM. It was, he said, a valuable bike, a Grant ATX 780, dark blue, nineteen-inch frame; a mountain bike with twenty-one gears and, he added after a pause, "a bell." The notation of the bell was the kind of cuteness he pulled throughout his testimony. He liked performing, and at first the jury responded with smiles. The description of the bike meant little to me, except I noted that it was expensive.

His parents in Connecticut bought the bike for him when he graduated from high school. It had been stolen twice, but he had managed to get it back both times. The first time, he saw it parked unlocked inside one of the classroom buildings and took it back. The next time his six-foot-two, 220-pound roommate knocked a Spanish (his word) kid off it as the kid was speeding away from their apartment on Symphony Road. It was a good thing there were no Latinos on the jury.

On the night of the incident, as we say, Thad went to the bar where he sometimes worked as a microbrewer. He had a few glasses of beer, "just to sample," but he was not drunk "or anything like that." There were two girls in the bar, one of whom he knew "from home" and the other he "wanted to know," he said with the boyish grin, looking at the jury for approval.

After the bar closed at 2 AM, Thad and David Chase, a friend who was riding a skateboard that night and who also worked at the bar and went to Berklee as a trombone student, walked the girls up Boylston Street from the bar at Dartmouth Street to Gloucester Street. Thad pushed his bike beside him. There were a lot of kids outside the bars between Fairfield and Gloucester, but otherwise the streets were empty.

When the girls stopped to talk to schoolmates hanging around outside one of the bars, Thad and David said goodbye to them. Thad got on his bike, and David got on the skateboard. Thad pulled ahead and took a right onto Hereford Street. At Hereford and Newbury, Thad stopped to wait for his friend. Thad added that, while waiting, he was singing scat. Then, without being asked, he did a little Ella Fitzgerald riff, "bee bopp de doo, bopp biddy doo," to illustrate. We all perked up.

The next thing Thad knew, he was surrounded by three guys on bikes.

"Can you identify any of them?" asked the assistant DA.

"Yes, one was that guy with the red hair on the right, and the other was the big blond guy on the left, Charlie."

Charles Joseph Samborski was twenty-four years old, six feet, 220 pounds, a high school dropout without a GED, dishonorably discharged from the Navy, and presently unemployed, although he had worked on and off as a courier. He was husky, untidy, and dumb-looking. He seemed be in shock through most of the trial, as though the experience could not be happening to him. He should not have been surprised; he had been in court many times for similar charges, five of them, as a matter of fact, and one of them also a civil rights offense.

Such in-court identification procedures are always dramatic, but they should not be. These young men were easily visible in the seats at the table reserved for criminal defendants and their lawyers, inside the bar that separates the inner "well" of the courtroom from the audience. (Apart from criminal defendants, civil litigants, and necessary court personnel, only lawyers are permitted in the well of the court, hence the reference to lawyers as "The Bar." Judges are called "The Bench.") Prosecutors love to have victims perform this finger-pointing ritual and then solemnly add, "May the record reflect that the witness has identified Charlie Samborski and Fritz Farron." I am not sure who they are addressing; I suspect that it is me. I sometimes wonder what would happen if I said "no." I didn't do that in this case, and never have, as a matter of fact, but there are a lot of rituals that we perform in the courtroom without much thought.

The assistant district attorney stepped in: "You didn't know their names then, did you?"

"No, I didn't know them at all."

Thad continued, "What happened next was that the big blond guy told me to get off the bike."

"What did he say?"

"Can I swear here?" Thad asked, looking up at me.

"Just answer the question," I replied, getting just a bit impatient with his impishness. "We've heard most everything."

"He said, 'Get off the fucking bike, faggot!' "

"And what did you do?"

"I tried to ride through the hole between the other two guys. But the big blond guy pushed me, and I fell on the ground. Then he kicked me and called me a faggot again. He asked me where the other guy was, the guy who slashed the red Cannondale. I said, 'I don't know what you're talking about. I'm waiting for my friend on the skateboard.' "

"And then?"

"Then he, the big blond guy, Charlie, Charlie said, 'Why are you lying to me? Where's your friend, faggot?' "

"Again I said I didn't know what he was talking about."

"The redheaded guy, Fritz, said to the big blond guy, 'Don't be a jerk, Charlie. Just grab the bike and let's go.' "

"Did they get the bike?"

"Yes, but I got it back."

"How?"

"I grabbed the shirt of the guy who is not here. And he kicked me in the balls—in the groin, Your Honor." He smiled to the jury and then to me as he corrected himself. By now the jury had stopped smiling with him. "The big blond guy, Charlie, then jumped off his bike, threw me down on the ground, and started to stomp me. He broke my wrist and dented my head. I got photos."

"We'll get to the photos in a minute, Mr. Bartlett," said the assistant district attorney. "Did Mr. Farron, the redheaded man, hit you?"

"He pushed me when I tried to pull the guy who is not here off his bike after he kicked me in the . . . groin." Again a cute smile.

"After who kicked you in the groin?"

"The guy who is not here."

Now this "guy who is not here" raised problems for the progress of this case. He was a juvenile, and he would be, or had been, tried in Juvenile Court. But I could not tell the jury that. I did not expect he would show up because he could incriminate himself if he testified here if his case had not yet been tried, and maybe even if it had been.

The assistant district attorney then introduced the photos.

"This is me," Thad said, "with a cast on my broken right wrist the day after."

"This is me," he said, "with the cast after my friends jazzed it up, holding my cat, Armstrong. My girlfriend did the graffiti." He grinned.

"And this is the bump on my head, all black and blued, a week later."

There were objections to the photos. They were resolved by the prosecutor's asking after each photo, as the *Rules of Evidence* required, "Is this a fair and accurate representation of you after the assault?"

Thad answered yes and gratuitously added at the presentation of the head picture, "I was even worse than that. It was all purple and blue and yellow and mean ugly."

Oh, please, I thought, sounding like my mother in my mind. *Don't be such a shine. Don't blow this case with your hyperbole. Don't gild the lily so much that the jury ends up hating you. It's been a good case for the prosecution so far.*

Both defense lawyers were entitled to cross-examination.

The lawyer for Charlie, the big blond guy, started first. He made a big mistake. He took Thad through the whole incident again, but Thad did not waver from his story. The repetition just made Charlie's brutality look worse.

The redhead, Fritz Farron, had a smarter lawyer. He asked Thad how much he had had to drink. After first saying the proverbial "a couple of beers," Thad admitted to "four or five beers."

The lawyer then asked, "Did my client, Fritz Farron, ever hit you?"

"He pushed me away when the other guy kicked me, when I tried to grab the other guy, the guy who is not here."

At this point I had to interject.

"Does 'the other guy who is not here' have a name? Can we agree on his name?" I asked.

All the lawyers looked at each other and said nothing.

"Please come to sidebar," I said, and they walked over to the side of the bench furthest away from the jury.

I said, "This 'the other guy' or 'the guy who is not here' is very confusing for me and, I suspect, for the jury. Without trying to interfere in your trial strategies, is it too much to ask that we call him by name?"

They all looked at each other again. Mr. Farron's lawyer smiled a little and said, "Judge, I have no problem with using his name. It is Billy Goyette."

The other lawyers nodded in agreement, still not sure what the revelation of his name would do to their cases—probably nothing, but it is hard to think everything through. Nonetheless, I had some duty to make things easier for the jury.

The rest of the examination was concerned with the arrest of the defendants at the corner of Boylston Street and Massachusetts Avenue and their identification by Thad and his skateboarding friend, David Chase.

David Chase was the next to be called as a witness. He was dressed grungily like Thad, although he was bigger and blonder. He did not add much to the facts, but he did give weight to Thad's injuries. He had come upon the scene just as Charlie was "stomping" Thad. Peculiarly, the defense raised no objection to that characterization. David Chase saw Charlie and "the guy who wasn't there" ride off with Thad's $800 bike "between them, as if they were cowboys rustling a horse, each holding one side of the handlebar." He saw Thad grab the bike back and heard him screaming. He saw the defendants again at the corner of Boylston Street and Massachusetts Avenue when the cops came.

And that was the prosecution's case. It seemed peculiar to me that no police officer had testified. There is almost always a police officer for the prosecution. There was even one in the room, and her name was on the list of witnesses. *What is that about?* I wondered fleetingly, happy not to be involved in the presentation of the case and grateful that I could "move like a reed in the river," to quote one of my esteemed colleagues. Wherever I ended up was not important; the jury was going to decide this case.

I had left it up to the defense lawyers to decide who would present his case first. Fritz Farron's lawyer stood up and walked in front of the jury for his opening.

"I am going to present three witnesses: Officer Lakisha Xerxes, Billy Goyette, and my client, Fritz Farron. They will tell you that this altercation was caused by Thad Bartlett. My client's participation was minimal. Fritz Farron had just met up with Charlie and Billy Goyette in Copley Square a small rectangular park near the scene of this crime. Charlie told him they were looking for a guy who had vandalized a red Cannondale bike belonging to another messenger, a friend of my client's. My client, Fritz Farron, thought that he was on a mission to recover a bike that had been stolen earlier by someone associated with Thad Bartlett. My first witness will be Officer Xerxes."

The court officer called Officer Xerxes into the courtroom. She was a young African American woman in her thirties, about five foot five, and slim. She looked like a runner.

She and her partner, Officer Eliseo Matos, who "wasn't able to be here today," had responded to a call from Station 4 to go to the corner of Massachusetts Avenue and Boylston Street, where she saw a bruised, bleeding, and very excited Thad Bartlett. He said that he had been beaten up shortly before and that his bike had been stolen. He declined medical attention, so she put him in the cruiser to look for the assailants. On Boylston Street, on the farther side of Massachusetts Avenue, they saw the two defendants and two other young men, one of them Billy Goyette. Mr. Bartlett was very drunk. He insisted that these were the people who had tried to steal his bike and who had beat him up.

The defendants were straightforward and calmly answered the police officers' questions; they disclaimed any knowledge of Thad

Bartlett's bike. Therefore Officer Xerxes and her partner, who—she repeated—"was unable to be here today," decided that an arrest was not warranted. They took down the pertinent information—names, addresses, telephone numbers—from the defendants, should a summons be sought, and took the protesting Mr. Bartlett to the Beth Israel Hospital for treatment.

The fourth young man at Boylston Street and Massachusetts Avenue was Paul Foley, whose red Cannondale bike had been vandalized and stolen. The bike had been found pushed into a space between two stores on Boylston Street near where the four young men were standing when the police arrived. The officers saw the bike with its slashed tires and concluded that the victim was Mr. Foley, not the very drunk, albeit bruised, Thad Bartlett.

The best the prosecutor could do with the officer on cross-examination was to get her to say that she arrived after any incident that may have occurred at Newbury and Hereford streets and that she was responding to a call made by Mr. Bartlett. The idea that there could have been two victims did not occur to the police. She also acknowledged that Thad Bartlett appeared injured but that his injuries could have come from a fall. He was very drunk and did not make much sense.

Some silly discussion then ensued about whether Thad's hysteria was due to his injuries rather than his drunkenness. This line of questioning was objected to because the police officer did not have a medical degree. The objection was sustained by me, but the prosecutor would not stop. I asked the lawyers to come to the sidebar where I told the prosecutor to give it up because I was not going to let the policewoman testify as if she were a neurologist.

Fritz Farron's lawyer then called Billy Goyette to the stand, and the court officer left the room to look for him in the corridor. He returned with a pleasant-looking young man with black hair, neatly dressed in khaki pants and a polo shirt striped navy blue and red.

Mr. Goyette was sworn in by the clerk: "Do you swear to tell the truth, the whole truth, and nothing but the truth, so help you God?"

"I do," he replied. "I was in Copley Square with Charlie. Paul Foley's bike had been stolen from Copley Square over near the Trinity Church, and we went out looking for it. I found it way up on Boylston Street. The tires had been slashed. We left the bike there and went back to Copley Square to see if anybody had seen who took it. One of the skateboarders by the fountain said he saw two grunge guys; one of them was a short guy on a black bike looking at Paul's bike about an hour before. He didn't say much more except that the taller guy was touching the bike and really examining it close."

Billy continued, "Shortly after that, Fritz came by. We all know each other because we're couriers. Fritz used to be a courier, and he worked for the same company I did downtown. He knew Paul Foley from those days. Charlie and I still worked there. Charlie didn't know Fritz. Charlie started after Fritz left. Charlie talked to Fritz about what happened. I didn't hear it all, but the three of us decided to go look for the short guy on the black bike.

"We saw Thad—I didn't know his name then—in the middle of Newbury Street, standing next to a black bike up near the Boston Architectural Center. He was a short guy and looked like the skateboarder's description of the guy who was snooping around Paul Foley's bike.

"Charlie started to ask him about what he did to Paul's bike. I wasn't so sure that he was the guy, but Charlie seemed to think he was. Thad denied having anything to do with Paul's bike, and Charlie kept saying, 'Why are you lying to me?' Thad told Charlie to get out of his face and then lunged at Charlie."

The assistant district attorney began his cross-examination of Billy Goyette.

"How big is Thad?"

"He's a little guy."

"How big is Charlie?"

"He's a big guy, six foot two, 220 pounds maybe? Something like that."

"Who did what to who?"

"Thad pushed Charlie, and Charlie pushed Thad back."

There was something very young about the way Billy called everybody by their first name. It was as if this were some schoolyard fight instead of a couple of felonies for which one or both of the defendants, Charlie and Fritz, could do serious time.

"Did Thad fall down?"

"Yeah, he fell on his butt."

"Did he get up?"

"Yeah, he got up and went after Charlie again; Charlie used his bike like a shield to keep Thad away."

"Did you and Charlie try to steal Thad's bike?"

"No, the bike got thrown down the street. Nobody tried to steal it."

"What happened then?"

"Thad sat in the middle of Newbury Street and started to scream, 'They're trying to kill me! They're stealing my bike! They're trying to kill me! They're stealing my bike!' "

"Did Fritz Farron ever hit Thad?"

"No, he stood on the side, about fifteen feet away, almost on the sidewalk. He never got near Thad, or Thad and Charlie."

"Did he say anything?"

"All he said was, 'Let's get the fuck out of here! This guy's wacko,' meaning Thad."

"He didn't do anything?"

"Nothing."

"Didn't he push Thad when Thad went after you?"

"No, he never touched him."

It was 4 PM, and we adjourned for the day. I instructed the jury not to talk to anyone about the case and reminded them that they had not heard all the evidence, the summations of the lawyers, or the court's instructions on the law. I also instructed them that they were jurors, not detectives, and that they were not to snoop around at the scene of the incident or anywhere else. "The case is to be decided only on what you hear and see in court and on that alone," I added, looking directly at a juror who lived in the Back Bay, not far from Newbury and Hereford streets.

The jurors smiled when I used the word “snoop.” Perhaps one of them had already become the authority on the geography of this case, even though I had earlier admonished them not to discuss the case until it was over.

The next day Fritz Farron was called to the stand by his lawyer. Now, it is a tricky question, whether or not a defense lawyer should put his client on the stand. Early English law, whence our law comes, and even early Massachusetts law, prohibited defendants from testifying because it was assumed they would lie. That prohibition has morphed into the present privilege against self-incrimination. No inference may be drawn by the jury from the fact that a defendant does not testify. Before I served on a jury in a case where the defendant did not testify and where the judge carefully instructed us about the privilege against self-incrimination and the Commonwealth’s burden of proof, I was cynical about jurors’ ability to overlook the failure of defendants to tell their version of the story. But the jury I was on proved to be scrupulous in requiring the Commonwealth to prove the defendant’s guilt (rather than expecting the defendant to prove his innocence). It was refreshing. My service on that jury gave me new confidence in a jury’s ability to follow directions.

Fritz Farron looked like an English rugby player. He had short, bright red hair, pale skin, and light eyes. He was twenty-two years old, five foot ten, and 190 solid pounds. He stood erect and was very polite and soft-spoken. The uncanny thing was that he had a Latino accent. He had lived in Boston for three years, but before that he lived for twelve years in Puerto Rico, where his father was stationed in the Navy. Before that he had lived in Florida. He now lived in a Latino housing development in the South End called Villa Victoria with his wife and new baby. He was an apprentice carpenter and was about to get a job on the Big Dig, Boston’s giant highway construction project.

“That night, May 28,” Fritz began, “my wife had gone to spend the night at her mother's in Jamaica Plain, and I decided to take a ride on my bike. I used to be a courier, and I knew that the couriers rode around the city at night, meeting in Copley Square, by the fountain in the Common, and at Little Stevie's Back Bay House of Pizza up on Boylston Street. I hadn't been out alone since my wife got pregnant, and I was feeling restless. It was a warm night. I took a long ride along the Esplanade up to the bird sanctuary beyond Harvard by the Eliot Bridge and then back down the Cambridge side to Boston. Then I went over to the Common, but no one was there, so I went to Copley Square where I saw Billy Goyette and heard about Paul Foley's bike. Paul had been a friend when we were couriers together, and I felt bad for him. I knew that Paul didn't have much money and that it would be expensive for him to buy new tires and to get the bike repaired."

Fritz added, "I never met Charlie before but thought that it was a good thing to catch the guys who damaged Paul's bike. So I went with Billy Goyette and Charlie."

In response to his lawyer's question, Fritz said, "Yes, I saw what went on at Newbury Street. Charlie went over to this kid with a black bike and asked him where the guy who slashed Paul's bike went to. The kid said he didn't know what Charlie was talking about, and Charlie said he was lying. The kid pulled a nutty and started to scream and to attack Charlie. Charlie pushed him back, trying to protect himself, and the kid fell on the road. The kid was very drunk and just went off. We didn't try to steal his bike. I don't need another bike. The kid chased us and grabbed at Billy Goyette. He fell down again and started screaming. We just took off. I never touched him. I was off to the side near the sidewalk. Charlie was only trying to protect himself."

This gratuitous last sentence may not have been too smart. It made Fritz look like a friend of Charlie, a friend who might lie. It also presented a united front when Fritz's lawyer probably wanted Fritz to separate himself from Charlie. Witnesses on both sides of the case had testified that Charlie had, at the very least, pushed Thad. There was little doubt that Thad was seriously injured. Those injuries had to have come from somewhere, and by this time it looked like they came from Charlie.

In response to the prosecutor's questions, Fritz repeated, "I never met Charlie before that night," and, "no, we are not friends, although we have gotten to know each other a little better waiting for this trial to begin. I don't hang with him. I live in the South End. He lives in Everett. That's a long ways off. I don't even know where it is. I've never been there. And he's never been to my house."

Charlie did not testify, probably because he had a record. A prosecutor could have brought up that record, which included larcenies, other assaults, and drug cases, in front of the jury to impeach Charlie's credibility. Arguably, the assaults would have been too prejudicial to be introduced, but even without them it would be clear that Charlie was not a model citizen. In addition, he did not make as effective an impression as Fritz Farron, who seemed to have inherited a military manner. Charlie Samborski was sloppy. He was wearing the same shirt and tie on the second day of trial as he had on the first, and they did not carry over well.

The end of the testimony was rather abrupt, like a car quickly putting on its brakes. It left us at arguments and charge, or as we now say, summations and instructions. I called a recess, during which I conferred with the lawyers about my instructions to the jury. Charlie's lawyer requested that I *not* instruct on the constitutional right not to testify. I guess that he did not want to draw attention to his client's silence. However, by not letting me talk about the elephant in the living room, the lawyer lost the opportunity to have me tell the jury that they could not hold the decision not to testify against Charlie Samborski.

In Massachusetts the defense argues first.

Charlie Samborski's lawyer's argument was brief. His client was looking for the guy or guys who had vandalized Paul Foley's bicycle. He did nothing but defend himself; the victim was drunk and hysterical and fell down. This case was a vendetta.

Fritz's lawyer, on the other hand, effectively portrayed his client as the unwilling participant in the matter. He pointed out his client's credentials as a working man, a young husband, and father. He had Fritz's wife, who had been sitting in the audience for the two days of trial, stand up. She looked the part. It was not exactly proper to do that during argument, but the prosecutor did not object. Fritz's lawyer pointed out that even the victim, who was drunk and hysterical and thus not a reliable reporter, said that Fritz had only pushed him aside. He added, of course, that Fritz Farron denied even doing that, and that Billy Goyette had testified that Fritz Farron never touched Thad Bartlett at all.

The assistant district attorney, arguing for the Commonwealth, showed the pictures. That was very effective. Wisely, he did not try to refute the defense's stories. (Sometimes prosecutors start their argument trying to rebut the defense argument just presented. They sound defensive. "Focus on yourself" should be their motto.) The prosecutor also wisely pointed out the comparative sizes of Thad Bartlett and Charlie Samborski—five foot six and 125 pounds versus six feet and 220 pounds—and that it was Thad, not Charlie, who ended up in the hospital with a cast on his arm and bruises on his face.

The jury sent me two notes before they came to a verdict. The first was to ask if there were any fingerprints taken from the stolen bike. Of course, there were not. Television police shows have made juries expect more than they are given in the usual trial. The Boston police rarely take fingerprints in cases like this, but I could not tell the jury that. All I could say was, "You have heard or seen all the evidence you are going to hear or see. There will be no other evidence. You must make your decision on the evidence before you."

The second note was a request that I read the legal definition of assault and battery again. Charlie Samborski could not be located to be present for my response to the second note, and a mistrial could have been called had I answered the note in his absence. It did not matter that his lawyer was present and had been consulted on my response. All defendants had to be there. Eventually, Charlie was found at the back door smoking a cigarette with the security guard, whom he had grown up with in Everett. The result of the wait was a lot of anxiety on everybody's part.

The jury found Charlie Samborski guilty of assault and battery and attempted larceny, but not guilty of assault and battery with a dangerous weapon. They found Fritz Farron guilty of assault and battery.

Right after the jury's verdict, as is the custom in my court, I sentenced Charlie Samborski to two years in the House of Correction, with eighteen months to serve and the remaining six months suspended for four years. If, after he did the time, he again got into trouble, he could go back to jail for six months. Fritz Farron was sentenced to one year in the House of Correction, suspended for two years.

There are rules about revoking and revising a sentence. Judges can do it on their own motion within sixty days. Similarly, lawyers for a defendant have sixty days to file a motion asking for revocation or revision. These motions always go back to the sentencing judges, which can be a little difficult if the judges think they were right the first time, as judges often do. However, the standard is wonderfully broad and unusually kind. A sentence can be revised and revoked "if it appears that justice may not have been done." Sometimes I revise a sentence because I am asked to, other times because I don't sleep well at night. I get acid reflux, and I know that I should do it on my own.

In this case, the acid reflux cued me, but fortunately, Charlie Samborski's lawyer had already filed a motion to revise and revoke. He brought the motion forward about three months after the verdict and three months into Charlie's sentence. Charlie's mother and girlfriend were present at this hearing. Charlie had just been found not guilty in another court on a charge of assault and battery on his girlfriend, the mother of his child. She had refused to testify against him.

I decided that my sentence of Charlie Samborski had been too harsh. I knew that I had been carried away in the passion of the moment on the day of the verdict.

His lawyer said, "Judge, I was not as prepared as I should have been at the time of sentencing. I really thought that we would win at trial. There had been an offer from the Commonwealth that I refused before trial. It was for six months committed. I thought that we could win, so I told my client not to take the six-month offer. I thought that we could win."

The assistant district attorney was on her feet: "Judge, that offer was before trial. Now we have had a trial, and the situation is different."

The law allowed her to say that and even allowed me to take into account the fact that the Commonwealth had been forced to go to trial. But it did not say that I *had* to take it into account.

I revised Charlie's Samborski's sentence to twelve months in the House of Correction and wondered how influenced that decision was by all the bullies I had ever feared.

MATTHEW HARTNET

Not even your First Communion partner can be trusted if he's a junkie

§ § §

As we approached the end of the criminal-jury assignment session, on a not too busy day, I took count in my head of the matters remaining to be heard by looking at the lawyers left in the well (the bar enclosure). I thought that I knew who was supposed to come next because I had checked the case files the day before, and I had the list before me.

However, sitting in the bar enclosure was Attorney Matthew Hartnet. His name was not on the list. I was not unhappy to see him. Mr. Hartnet was a young lawyer who came from a neighborhood of Boston called Brighton. His father was a lawyer there as well. Matthew had learned how to practice in court at his father's side in these very courtrooms. Like his father, Mathew Hartnet always thanked the judge no matter what the result of the proceeding. The Hartnets also always thanked the clerk, which was appreciated. Perhaps they had heard the maxim, "A judge can hurt you but a clerk can kill you." Matthew Hartnet worked hard for his clients and often succeeded where less polite lawyers would have failed.

I finished calling the list; there were no more cases to be heard. Matthew Hartnet was still sitting there, so I asked, "Mr. Hartnet, what can we do for you today? I don't see you on the list."

He said, "Judge, may we have a sidebar?"

Now, the press doesn't like sidebars because reporters cannot hear what happens in conversations among lawyers and the judge at the side of the bench, not that the press is often in my courtroom. Judges don't like sidebars either. Sidebars are antithetical to the idea of a public courtroom. They got a bad rap in the O. J. Simpson trial, and most times they are not necessary. I could not imagine what the reason for this one was, but it's hard to ask why a lawyer wants a sidebar without requiring him to reveal that which he wants to keep secret.

In any event, Mr. Hartnet did not have a case on the list, and with his right hand he was inviting the assistant district attorney up to the side of the bench with him, so a sidebar seemed harmless. I waved them up, saying nothing on the record.

Mr. Hartnet and Mr. Jonas, a smart young assistant DA and a pleasant guy, both came to the shelf at the right-hand side of the bench. I moved the microphone closer so the discussion could be recorded and leaned over the edge of the bench myself.

Mr. Hartnet began, "Judge, I want to apologize for my client last week."

I said, "I don't think I remember your client last week."

"Judge, he was the guy who was in the paper yesterday. He was arrested on Newbury Street. He was charged with stealing fifty thousand dollars' worth of clothes. I told you he'd go to Hope House, but he didn't, and he was back at it again."

"Mr. Hartnet, I haven't read the paper, but I vaguely remember your client from last week. He was fond of Newbury Street, wasn't he? He stole some clothing?"

"Yes, Judge, that's the guy," said Mr. Hartnet sheepishly. "I'm sorry, Judge. I promised he would go into treatment, but he didn't, and I really feel terrible. I feel responsible. I don't know what to say. I just wanted to tell you that I feel very badly."

"Mr. Hartnet, you don't have to apologize. There's nothing to apologize for. You're not the person who committed the crime. I know enough about substance abuse to know that nobody can be responsible for the addict or the alcoholic, and I'm certainly not going to hold you responsible. You do a very good job, and I appreciate the work you do. So you needn't feel bad on my account."

"Thank you, Judge, but I told you he was going to go the halfway house, and he didn't, Judge."

"I don't hold you responsible, Mr. Hartnet," I said again and stood up to leave. It had been a long morning. Mr. Hartnet was becoming tedious, and I wanted to get back to the lobby, or at least to a bathroom. I walked through the courtroom and went out the front door with Franny Cooney, the court officer.

I said, "That Hartnet is a good kid, isn't he? He came in to apologize because his client didn't go into the halfway house."

"Oh," he said, "that guy, young Hartnet's client. He's in the first session. He had fifty thousand dollars of stuff. He got so greedy he took the clothes off the mannequins. His car was so full of crap he couldn't see to get it out of the parking space, and that's how he got caught. He banged the car behind as well as hitting the hydrant he was parked in front of. He's got no respect. Young Hartnet needn't apologize. These things are almost destined for failure, but it's a good thing you keep taking chances on these guys."

Now I had a better memory of Mr. Hartnet's client.

Kevin Murphy had been in jail for three months awaiting trial on a probation revocation. He was being surrendered by his probation officer on a sentence of one year in the House of Correction suspended for two years that he had received a year before for having stolen $28,000 worth of suits from Il Finnochio men's store on Newbury Street, as well as $3,000 worth of sweats from another store on Newbury Street while on bail. By bringing the surrender case, the probation officer was, in effect, saying, "I can't handle this guy, Judge. I give up. He won't obey the rules of his probation. He's done it again. Send him to jail."

The crime that triggered the surrender by the probation officer was an attempt to break down the front door of Saks Fifth Avenue with a sledgehammer at four-thirty in the morning. Kevin Murphy was seen by a security guard who chased him down to Huntington Avenue, across Harcourt Street, and into the South End, where he ran into an alley between West Newton and Pembroke streets.

En route, the security guard called the Boston police, and the police chased Mr. Murphy into the alley. When Kevin Murphy saw them, he jumped like a cat burglar up onto the fire escape of a building on Pembroke Street. At one point he went into an apartment, came out, and tried to hide on the roof. The police ran up the front stairs of the building and chased him across the roof. He was caught when he got to the end of the row of houses—and to the end of the roofs. He fought the police officers, resulting in a charge of resisting arrest and two charges of assault and battery on a police officer. He was held on high bail and had been held for the past three months, until I released him for drug-addiction treatment.

At the end of the week before, Mr. Hartnet had appeared at the first call of the list and said, "Judge, my client wishes to tender a plea. The district attorney and I disagree, but I would ask for your consideration. My client has enrolled in the Salvation Army program."

I said, "Which Salvation Army program, the North Shore or the South End?"

He said, "The South End."

I said, "That's a little close to Newbury Street for me. I'm not so sure about that program for your client. He's had previous burglaries on Newbury Street besides this case from Saks Fifth Avenue, which is also close to the South End. He seems very fond of that area. I don't know whether it would be putting him in harm's way to house him in the South End only a few blocks from his favorite haunts."

The real reason I was reluctant to put him in the Salvation Army program was that I had often passed by its building and seen its residents gathered together on the street in front of Franklin Square, which was a famous drug-dealing location. I had never heard anything bad about the Salvation Army program in the South End, but I had never heard anything wonderful about it either.

Mr. Hartnet said, "Well, he got himself into this program."

I said, "Mr. Hartnet, frankly I think it's *your* duty to get him into a program. This is the twenty-first century and eighty-five to ninety percent of the cases we see here involve drugs and/or alcohol. I think *you* ought to find out about programs that would be helpful to your client and that would give the court enough security to send him to a program."

"Well, Judge, what program would you recommend?"

"It's not my place to recommend programs. I can't be shilling for one program or another; some are better than others. If you think you have a proposal, I'll listen to you."

"I think I do, Judge."

I turned to the court officers and said, "Would you please bring Mr. Murphy down."

About ten minutes later, Mr. Murphy arrived, cuffed and shackled as are all defendants when they are at the court. It looks barbaric, but when prisoners were not shackled there were escapes as well as crimes in the holding area, including rape and robbery.

Mr. Hartnet began. "Judge, I've known this man since I was six years old. We went through grammar school together. We made our First Communion together. He dated my sister. He's not going to go to the Salvation Army program. He got himself admitted to the Hope House. However, that might not be to your liking because you didn't want him anywhere near Newbury Street. Hope House is also in the South End."

"I know where Hope House is, Mr. Hartnet. It enjoys a very good reputation. I'll listen to your proposal." I didn't tell him that some of my best friends are alumni of Hope House.

"Judge, on the new case I ask that you put him on a suspended sentence—the House of Correction for two years suspended on and after the first suspended sentence, with four years probation—and that you let him go to Hope House and put other conditions on him as well. His problem is heroin, and it's been his problem for a long time. He's been detoxed while he's been in jail, and I think he's now ready to do something about his addiction. I also ask that, rather than imposing the suspended sentence he already has, that you continue the probation on the old case. He'll be looking at four years in the House if he screws up during the next four years."

"I've known him and his family for most of my life," Mr. Hartnet continued, "and he comes from a very good family. His father works for the Edison Company, and his mother works as well. They've tried very hard to raise this family. He has a brother who is a priest and a younger brother who just got a scholarship to Boston College, and his sister's a nurse. Judge, I would ask you to allow him to go into treatment."

Lawyers almost always talk about addicts' virtuous families as if the families had any power over the addicts' addictions. Usually, I interrupt and say something like, "Attorney, it is not the mother, father, or brother who is before me today." But I resisted that today because Mr. Hartnet was trying so hard.

"Has your client ever been in treatment before, Mr. Hartnet?"

"No, he's never been offered—he's never been in treatment before."

Mr. Hartnet probably switched direction mid-sentence because he had earlier heard me jump all over a lawyer who talked about his client never having been "offered" drug treatment when "all he has to do is walk into a church basement in any part of Boston and attend Alcoholics Anonymous or Narcotics Anonymous meetings. They are the most effective and cheapest alcohol and drug treatments. Most people who remain clean and sober go to AA or NA or both. People shouldn't have to be *offered* drug treatment. That's the victim game all over again. People can find some treatment very easily if they look. If they looked for treatment with half the effort they looked for drugs, they'd all be clean." Blah, blah, blah. That's my usual sermon, and most of the lawyers had heard it. So it was good that Mr. Hartnet had changed his trajectory. He wouldn't have to hear that, and neither would I.

The assistant district attorney said, "Judge, Mr. Murphy has a terrible record. You're quite right. He does seem fond of pulling these high-ticket burglaries on Newbury Street. This last attempt was more brazen than the others, and his behavior while being pursued was more heinous."

I said, "Addiction is a terrible thing. I think I'm willing to take the risk and accept Mr. Hartnet's recommendation. How long is the Hope House program, Mr. Hartnet?"

"At least six months, Your Honor."

Throughout this exchange, Mr. Murphy was quite unexpressive and unemotional. During the colloquy with Mr. Murphy that I was required to conduct to make sure he understood what he was agreeing to, Mr. Murphy said "yes" and "no," not "yes, sir" and "no, sir," just "yes" or "no." The absence of "sir" didn't bother me. It may have indicated a less than formal upbringing, or it may be that he thought he did not have to give a thing, even respect. Sometimes defendants are super deferential and other times they are antagonistic. I do not know if either is an indicator of future success or failure, but Mr. Murphy revealed nothing. He struck me as a blank, but a blank with a friend, Mr. Hartnet.

After Mr. Hartnet's apology on the Monday after the previous week's sentence, I asked Franny Cooney, the court officer, whether he would get me a copy of the police report in the latest case. He said that he would. I still had not seen the Sunday newspaper account of Kevin Murphy's most recent caper.

Later in the day, no police report was forthcoming. A discussion with a colleague who had been in the arraignment session yielded the comment, "Oh yeah, that guy was in the paper yesterday. I think it was the first case in the first session. Were you the guy who let him out? The paper said that it was Judge Early."

"No, it was me. I'd gotten a strong pitch from young Hartnet."

My colleague told me that he had set bail at $200,000 for the new offense.

I spent the rest of the afternoon reading the next day's cases, of which there were many, about twenty-four. At the end of the workday, I went down to the back door to wait for some old co-workers to go to a wake for an employee we'd all liked. As I was waiting, leaning against the radiator for the heat, Franny Cooney came by and said, "Good evening, Judge. By the way, I didn't forget your request.

It's just that Kevin Murphy made comments that were in the police report. I think the clerk's office would have thought that I was just going in to get a copy for the comments, so I didn't go in to ask."

I said, "What kind of comments? What did he say?"

"After he was arrested, he said, 'I'm not going to worry about this. I'll just get my lawyer, Matty Hartnet, and we'll go in front of Judge Let-'Em-Go-Early, and I'll be out in a day.'"

Franny paused, then added, "Kevin Murphy is not only an addict, a thief, and a liar, but also he's an ingrate. I would've thought he was cooler than that; it's not very professional of him." Franny had read my mind. "For sure, he's going to go away now, having agreed to the suspended sentence. He has to serve it if he violated the probation, and this stunt certainly looks like a violation." Franny enjoyed thinking like a judge.

I said to Franny, "What's he attacking poor Judge Early for? I'm the one who let him out."

"I knew that, but I wasn't going to tell anybody," said Franny, and he laughed.

I must admit I was a little grateful that Mr. Murphy hadn't mentioned my name and that the lazy newspaper hadn't checked to discover that it was me, not Judge Early who had released him. Although I wasn't happy that I had let him out—that I'd been conned—I did not want to let him destroy my hope that I could impose recovery from drug addiction on other people. I was not going to let him do that. I felt bad for poor Judge Early, who is a good man.

I finally did get a copy of the police report. One was left on my desk. There was no note and no indication who it came from. It was like a message from the Whiteboys, Irish Fenian rebels who would leave anonymous warning notes for their oppressors about to be victims. I read and reread the police report, then showed it to my best pal colleague.

She said, "You know, perhaps the police don't like Judge Early. Maybe they inserted this little quotation. It's an unlikely thing for a defendant to say. It's not the usual thing to have a quotation from a defendant in a police report unless it's a confession or an admission of some sort."

She was right. That thought had never occurred to me. I hadn't realized that I could be that naïve.

Attached to the police report mysteriously left on my desk was the booking sheet. There was Kevin Murphy with his head back a little, squinting, and the slightest smile on his face for the frontal shot. In the side shot he didn't look quite so tough.

The statistics on the booking sheet indicated that he was six feet, 190 pounds, had hazel eyes and dark brown hair, and was "white, non-Hispanic." He had a rose tattoo on his right shoulder. I wondered how they found that out.

The police report said that the car Kevin used, outside of which the police found two ten-dollar bills, belonged to his girlfriend. Also, when notified early in the morning on New Year's Day what had been done with her car, the girlfriend said that Kevin Murphy wasn't allowed to use her car. Nor was she happy about the dent in the front, which occurred when Kevin drove it into the hydrant. Finally she called him "a no-good junkie bastard."

EMERGENCY DUTY

Not just another Friday night for the on-call judge

§ § §

About once a year, all Massachusetts trial court judges are required to be on duty twenty-four hours a day for a week. The program is called Emergency Judicial Response.

The assignment goes from Thursday to Thursday. During my assigned week on Friday night, I was at home around eight o'clock, about to go out to eat. There had not been a lot of calls, so I thought that I was safe. All of a sudden the phone rang. It was Helena Romanoff. I knew Helena. I hadn't seen her since shortly after my swearing in, and before that I hadn't seen her for seven or eight years. On the phone she called me by my title, which meant that she was calling on hospital business. As the hospital's general counsel, she wanted to inform me that they had a problem.

A woman had been diagnosed as having had two strokes. She was now in the hospital, but she was declining treatment. The hospital wanted to hold a hearing to see if she should be required to have treatment. Why they hadn't acted earlier when the Probate and Family Court, which had jurisdiction over these cases and expertise in this area, was in session I was not told.

I had never before presided over a commitment hearing to protect somebody's *physical* health and wasn't too sure how it should be done. Fortunately, I had been given a very helpful book covering every situation that could come up during Emergency Judicial Response, and I consulted it. I quickly realized that I was going to have to round up two lawyers, one to represent the woman and one to be what is called a guardian ad litem for her should treatment be required. Truth be known, I wasn't so sure about the need for a guardian ad litem, but I wanted to have somebody there if I did need one. I assumed the lawyers would fill me in.

I went through a list of attorneys who had volunteered to serve and who were accredited to do so. Unfortunately, the list was three or four years old. I called a number of well-meaning lawyers just beginning dinner or cocktails or on their way out. Some of them did not do commitments anymore and were surprised by my call. Finally I found Alice McCarthy, with whom, fortunately, I had some experience. She had represented people on civil commitments to mental institutions, and she was a very good lawyer.

Another of the lawyers I called, who had had three glasses of wine and was about to dine, mentioned a lawyer who had previously been a nurse. I was able to track him down to become the possible guardian ad litem.

Calls were placed back and forth to the hospital, but by 8:45 PM it was clear that the case was not going to be resolved. Within another half hour we were all assembled in the hospital unit's waiting room. Fortunately, Helena Romanoff, the lawyer for the hospital, was accommodating and professional.

I had asked that a room for the hearing be set up as a courtroom and that a tape recorder be provided. I believed the statute required us to have flags in the room, but I was not going to push that. I was introduced to the young psychiatrist, who was hovering and who made faces the more legalistic I became. The fact is that I did not know how to do this informally. I suspected there was no way to do it informally, so I was going to do it by the letter.

I received two or three other emergency-response calls while waiting to begin and had to go out the door and around the corner to handle those. They were the usual—preliminary restraining orders, loved ones beating each other up. They did not require too much time or deliberation because only the victim was talking to me. The perpetrator was in jail or still drunk at home. The restraining orders I issued were good until 9 AM the next court day.

The case at hand, however, was more difficult. Alice McCarthy's client was Beulah Robinson, the patient who was refusing treatment. The lawyer who might serve as guardian ad litem was Jason Guiliani. Ms. Romanoff had never participated in one of these cases, nor had Mr. Guiliani. However, Ms. McCarthy and I had some analogous notion of how we should proceed because of our previous work together on civil commitments for people with mental health issues.

Ms. McCarthy asked for and was given an opportunity to talk to her client, and she did. They returned to the room after twenty minutes. Ms. Robinson, wearing a white robe, looked quite rational and presentable. I did not know until the hearing was over that she had been tied down to her bed since the early afternoon, when she had announced that she was going to walk out of the hospital.

Ms. Romanoff called the first witness. He was a young redheaded Irish doctor, the chief resident in neurology, William Staunton. To begin with, he had a thick brogue that I had a problem understanding. *Probably from County Kerry*, I thought. Second, he was very efficient. Third, he was very busy. And fourth, he thought we should conform to his busyness. He was constantly being paged. After he was paged the fifth time, I said, "I think you're going to have to shut that thing off. You can either be here or be there, but we need you here now, and you called for us."

Young Dr. Staunton gave us a medical history of Beulah Robinson. She had appeared in the emergency room some five days before with pains in her head. The emergency-room doctors thought that she might have had a stroke. When they said that she should be hospitalized, she left. She came back three days later and agreed to be tested. It was determined that she in fact had had at least one, if not two, strokes. It was thought that there was some blockage in the carotid artery going up her neck. The procedure for resolving these strokes was to clean out the carotid artery. Before that could be done, however, her blood had to be tested and brought to the right level of something that I did not understand. She balked at the blood sampling and said it hurt her. She finally refused any more samplings. It mystified the young Dr. Staunton that she would refuse the treatment. He failed to realize that it hurts to have blood drawn. He was so white that it looked like he didn't have any blood to be drawn.

Dr. Staunton testified that he called his supervisor, the neurologist in charge, who decided that a psychiatrist should be called—the woman who had been hovering outside as I was making the arrangements. She was very young, probably still in her twenties, early thirties at best. She was dressed chicly, gossamer white slacks and blouse, a costume that seemed to me to be more appropriate for a cocktail party at the beach. The beach may have been where she had been when we interrupted her evening. She wore an enormous diamond engagement ring.

The psychiatrist reported that Ms. Robinson was sixty-eight years old, had lived in Cambridge all her life, and had perhaps even worked in the hospital at one time. She had no immediate family, but had cousins with whom she was friendly and was very active in her church in Cambridge. She appeared competent, but objected strongly to the blood sampling and really wanted it to stop. When informed that she might die if her carotid artery were not cleaned, she had said, "Everybody has to die sometime, and this may just be my time." The psychiatrist was baffled by this response, but it made sense to me.

The wonderful Alice McCarthy inquired whether there had been any attempt to contact the cousins or Ms. Robinson's pastor. The psychiatrist reacted as if that were an extraordinary question, then replied that perhaps the social worker could be called upon to do that. Why a social worker had not "been called upon" to call already was never explained. Why it was beneath the psychiatrist or resident neurologist or someone at their direction to make the call was never explained either. It seemed to me that somebody at the hospital should have made the call long before I was called.

After two hours, the hearing ended. Alice McCarthy argued that her client was a reasonable and competent woman, but that she had been ill-treated in the hospital and did not want to continue being badly treated. Ms. McCarthy argued further that Ms. Robinson herself was capable of making this decision, which might affect her life.

Helen Romanoff fortunately offered an alternative. She sensed where I was going: I was going to let Ms. Robinson out. I had had it with the callous inefficiency of the hospital buck-passing and the arrogance of the doctors. *If this is what they're like when they are young, God help us when they get older*, I thought. The law is strongly on the side of liberty in these cases. That much I knew. And the doctors' attitudes made it easier for me to conform my decision to the law's inclination. Helen Romanoff said that the hospital could arrange for a second opinion, that they were now affiliated with another hospital and would contact a neurologist there to see whether there might not be another way to resolve Ms. Robinson's problem. She also said that there would be an immediate attempt to contact both the pastor and the cousins.

After leaning over to consult with Ms. Robinson, Alice McCarthy offered that her client would stay overnight and into the next day if the hospital would do all that Attorney Romanoff had said.

I agreed with this resolution of the case and did not order the treatment. Immediately after everybody left the improvised courtroom, I wrote a draft of my findings, taking potshots at the hospital.

By morning I had of course rethought the matter, and I removed the sarcasm before the opinion was typed on Monday. "Restraint of pen and tongue" is good advice for a judge. My findings did not need my asides to do what they had to do. I submitted the revised findings to the Probate and Family Court, which does this work regularly in the daytime.

Contrary to my usual habits, I avoided the obituaries, the "Irish sports pages," for the next month. I did not want to know if Beulah Robinson had died. I did not want to be responsible for her death just because I had upheld the principle of personal freedom, as noble as that notion may be.

Two months later I ran into Alice McCarthy outside of court, at the movies. She told me that, as far as she knew, "Beulah Robinson had not died, but she did walk out of the hospital the next morning at seven o'clock—without a second opinion."

RESTRAINT

Some situations law school cannot prepare you for

§ § §

It was a beautiful summer morning. I had just walked over the drawbridge across the Charles River and past the lagoons by the new condominiums and the shopping center. It wasn't a bad life, I thought, even though I was in exile over here at the Chelsea Court, which itself was in exile in Cambridge owing to health-and-safety code violations in its own decrepit courthouse in Chelsea. This courthouse in Cambridge had been renovated for a television series, and the courtrooms were a set designer's idea of a courtroom: lots of brass and mahogany, but no patina. It certainly was more comfortable, although less congenial, than my usual digs.

I was the second judge, which meant that I received cases from the first criminal session and heard other business, like requests for restraining orders, which take priority.

The practice there was to hear requests for restraining orders at sidebar so that domestic dirty linen was not hung out in front of the regular audience of criminal defendants, witnesses, and police officers. By hearing the requests at sidebar, yet in a public courtroom, we satisfied the constitutional requirement of open and public hearings, and we were able to make a recording with the microphone at the bench. The problem was that the sidebar conference put the opposing parties dangerously close to each other and to the judge.

The clerk called the case *Delacruz v. Delacruz*, and two men and a woman came up to the side of the bench. The woman was carrying a child in her arms, and another was at her side. On the tape later, I heard children laughing and shouting and remembered that they had played tag in the courtroom. The littler one, who was four, climbed around the jury box and hid behind the partition or the policemen sitting there. His brother, who was seven, searched for him on the other side. The little one was sandy-haired, whereas his brother was dark-haired like his mother. Their mother kept looking around for them as if they were disturbing us and as if she could stop them. They were laughing as they played. I also remembered that the court officer had tried to quiet them and that I had told him to let them play. It seemed to be the least we could do in such unhappy circumstances. The man with the woman was her brother. The other man was her estranged husband.

Lizzie Delacruz was dark-haired and petite, with sad eyes. Her brother was bigger, also dark-haired, and a little cocky. However, it's not often that we get a brother or other male family member appearing with a woman seeking a restraining order. If anyone accompanies a petitioning woman, it is usually another woman and usually a friend not a family member. Both brother and sister were dressed neatly, maybe jeans and T-shirts.

The husband, Juan Delacruz, was blond like his younger son, and about the same height as his wife's brother, five foot nine, although not as husky. He was handsome. I remember him wearing a red shirt, although this may be a detail my mind added after the fact. I asked him to stand to the right, trying to keep some space between him and his wife. I sat behind the bench, and he stood on the first step up to the bench, which put his head a little above mine.

By that time, the court officer was either on the phone or out of the room. He ran a vegetable business in the Haymarket, and during the court day when the room was momentarily silent, one could hear from his direction "twenty pounds of tomatoes" or "What do you mean, there's no celery?" You had to work around him. I thought, *Thank God for the clerk*, who was very bright, reasonably young, and healthy; he could break up a fight if the need arose. Additionally, a couple of policemen were in the room, waiting for their cases to be called.

A temporary restraining order had been granted over the weekend by the emergency-response judge, who was on duty twenty-four hours a day. That order commanded the defendant, Juan Delacruz, not to abuse Lizzie Delacruz or contact her, and to stay at least one hundred yards away from her. It also gave her custody of the two boys playing near us.

She had been required to write an affidavit earlier that morning, which she did herself. Her affidavit read:

> Juan Delacruz punched me several times. We do not live together. We've been separated a long time now. He walked out on me when I was pregnant with my last child. I went out with some friends on Friday and he tried calling me and I wasn't home. He called the next morning at 7 AM and said that he was coming over to get the kids. The kids were not home. I left the kids with my sister who lives in the next town (Revere). He came over and was yelling and screaming because I went out last night. Remind you that we do not live together. He has another woman living with him and he has a child with her also. He kept questioning me about where I went the night before and I told him it was none of his business. He said "It's none of my business huh," and then he started punching me on my back and arms. I tried fighting him but I couldn't, he pinned me down and continued to hit me. I fear for my life and for my children. He's threatened me before several times. He threatened to shoot me. I have witnesses that he said that several times.

At the sidebar more was revealed. Lizzie Delacruz repeated the facts of her affidavit, pointing out that Juan Delacruz had left her before the four-year-old was born. She gestured toward the younger child, who was crawling under a seat in the jury box.

Juan Delacruz said, "There's no reason I should be restrained on my kids."

I said that I was not prepared to decide the custody issue. I had no investigator to help me with that decision, so it would have to be resolved by the Probate and Family Court, three stops inbound on the streetcar, at Government Center. The emergency order had granted custody to Lizzie Delacruz. I repeated that I could not decide visitation but the Family Court could begin to hear the matter that day.

Juan Delacruz said, “I’d do that as long as I can see my kids.” He kept on repeating, as if in a daze, “I won’t ever see my kids” and “if I can’t see my kids.” And I kept on telling him the issue could be worked out in the Probate and Family Court.

Juan Delacruz said that Lizzie’s brother, Horatio Sanchez, “wanted me to fight him inside my kid’s house.” He wanted a restraining order against Sanchez and had written in his petition:

> Order her family to stop ~~surwhere~~ swering and talking bad about me in front of my kids 1 is 4yr, 2 is 7yrs.

I informed Mr. Delacruz that this is America, that speech is protected under the First Amendment, and that I could not stop the family from saying anything. Horatio Sanchez, Lizzie’s brother, laughed at this remark, and I realized immediately that it had not been helpful. I regretted the remark, but it appeared to me that there were not going to be any boundaries to this dispute, especially after Juan Delacruz said he had “gotten a police report” against Lizzie’s father. He did not say why. I thought he might have been referring to some kind of assault.

There is no legal process known as “getting a police report”; the police are required to write reports about everything that comes to their attention. Apparently, to Juan Delacruz and on the street “getting a police report” on somebody is a weapon in the arsenal called “using the system.” The next most powerful weapon is the restraining order, the next the criminal complaint. Maybe civil injunctions intervene. It’s hard enough keeping up with the law, never mind the street’s ranking of its mandates.

Juan Delacruz added that there had been ten years of problems and that the brother had once hit him on the chest. He finished by saying, “I’d like to press charges at the police station.”

I granted the restraining order against the brother, ordering him not to abuse Juan Delacruz. The brother replied, "I agree to it."

I again told Juan Delacruz to take the Green Line to Government Center to the Probate and Family Court.

He again said, as if in a daze, "So I can't see my kids."

"They'll make that determination," I repeated. I wonder now if he wanted me to keep him from his kids, if he had some prescience about his own madness.

Lizzie Delacruz's temporary order was formalized and extended for a year.

Juan Delacruz did go to the Probate and Family Court, where he was appointed a lawyer. By agreement with his wife, he was given visitation with his children each Wednesday from 5:30 PM to 7 PM for dinner, and on weekends from Friday at 5:30 PM to Sunday at 7 PM.

§ § §

About six weeks after they had all appeared in front of me, on a Saturday, Juan Delacruz killed both boys. He slashed the throat of the younger boy, Roberto, and repeatedly stabbed the older boy, Miguel. He had called his wife, Lizzie, at 7 PM and said, "If you don't go back with me, say goodbye to your kids because you're never going to see them again."

At 9:30 PM, Juan called his girlfriend, and the mother of his daughter. She was pregnant with another child of his. He told her, "It isn't worth killing my wife and going to jail for it. I'd like to go to heaven and be with my children."

The story in the *Boston Globe* read, "At 1:45 Sunday, police in Gilford, New Hampshire, found Juan Delacruz bleeding from knife wounds to his arms, legs, and neck, atop a highway overpass, apparently ready to throw himself to his death on busy Route 11." In the accompanying photos of the boys, Roberto, the younger boy, looks up imploringly, like one of Raphael's angels.

{ iv }

DO YOU KNOW WHAT I DO FOR A LIVING?

Although it's the biggest city in New England, Boston is still a small town. It's hard to hide here. They say that if you wait long enough outside the Park Street subway station in downtown Boston, you'll see everyone you've ever known.

After he was made a judge, my father, who lived in the smaller city of Worcester, became a recluse. I have not done the same. I live and work in Boston. Some of my gadabouting is necessary. I do not own a car, and I no longer ride my bicycle in town. I take public transportation. Most of all, it's not my nature to stay home. I like to be out. I like knowing a lot of people and being gregarious—up to a point.

The court I serve on is the court of first impression for every crime that happens in downtown Boston. If you get in trouble in Boston, you will go there. Outside of the courtroom, I inadvertently see defendants, plaintiffs, witnesses, lawyers, and court staff, as well as former jurors. I do not go looking for them, but I live in the world too.

THE RUSSIAN STEAM-ROOM INVADER

The judge can't even go to the gym without work following

§ § §

Igor first appeared in front of me about three years ago. He was short, pale, and obsequious. He had been caught for the third time in the steam room at the Four Seasons Hotel "without having any right to be there," according to the complaint submitted by the Four Seasons. He was not a guest, and he was not a day member. When confronted he did not leave, and when thrown out he would not stay away. He said that he liked steam rooms, and he smiled a little too complicitly at me when he said that, or so I thought. One of my colleagues had sentenced him to one year straight probation for trespass after his unauthorized visit to the health club on the top floor of the Ritz-Carlton.

The issue in the matter before me was whether to revoke the probation and send him to jail. I could send him away for up to six months, the maximum penalty for trespass.

I did not. I renewed the probation after extending it for a year.

When I checked Igor's record, it appeared that we were not the only court he had seen; he had been arrested all over the state for much the same thing. Most recently, he had been convicted for trespass because he had camped out, without invitation or payment, in a cabin at a roadside cottage colony in Newburyport in the off-season. The judge there sentenced Igor to six months, one month to serve in the Essex County House of Correction, the other five months suspended for one year during which time he would be on probation.

Igor was a Russian refugee, but apparently still a communist when it came to steam and shelter. He was out to liberate the natatoriums.

Some time after renewing Igor's probation, I saw him walking briskly down Charles Street and in Copley Place, a big shopping mall in the toney part of Boston. Each time he gave me a big smile, a wave that was almost a salute, and said cheerily, "Hello, Judge!" I said "hello" back, even though the first time I did not realize who he was. The second time I recognized him and found his brass amusing.

During Igor's case, the police presented a packet of hotel key cards, much like a deck of cards that he had had on him when he was arrested. Igor leaned over and told his court-appointed lawyer to tell me that they were useless because the locks changed after each room rental. He also wanted the lawyer to ask me to give them back after I released him. I didn't. He had smiled just a little too proudly as the policeman introduced them into evidence as an exhibit.

One night when I went to the gym connected to the apartment building where I live, I was surprised to see Igor emerge from the glass-enclosed swimming pool, still wearing his goggles, hunched over against the cold in a Speedo. Igor is a little guy, maybe five foot four, kind of pixielike and even endearing—at least for a few minutes. I was not absolutely sure that it was he. I headed to the locker room, and he followed, keeping the goggles on long after they ceased to be necessary. As a matter of fact, the goggles could have been dangerous. It is a bit of a hike to the locker room, and the big boys in the free weight room, which we had to pass through, are not tidy. They usually leave their weights lying around on the floor on the path to the lockers, proof of their heavy efforts, no doubt.

Because I am old and because the hot water loosens my limbs, I usually take a shower and a little steam before I begin to work out. That night I hesitated to go into the steam room for fear Igor would follow and again say, "Hello, Judge," but I decided that I wasn't going to let him disrupt my routine. It was hard enough to get me to the gym in the first place. I wasn't going to let Igor trouble my nights as well as my days.

On the left side of the shower room are four separate shower stalls with stationary shower fixtures; on the right is one stall with a hand-held detachable showerhead, presumably for the disabled. In the disabled shower, wearing clogs and scraping himself with a long wooden-handled brush, was Igor. He had taken off the goggles, but I noticed that he now wore earplugs.

He kept his bathing suit on, but left the shower curtain open, which seemed a curious modesty until I realized that it was not modesty at all but part of the game he was playing. He crouched in such a way that I could not see his face even though I was only five feet from him. However, I knew it was he. I went into the steam room and sat near the door so I could escape quickly if he came in. He didn't.

When I left the steam room, Igor was at the sink but quickly turned his head away from my view of him in the mirror. I returned to my locker, put on my gym clothes, and talked to Eriberto, the towel man who was wandering around the locker room. In Spanish I told him that we had a thief in our presence. *Hay un ladron aqui*. I didn't know how to say "steam-room invader" in Spanish, and Igor had been a thief in some instances. Eriberto, who never seemed much surprised by anything, shrugged his little shoulders and told me that Mike was in charge.

I went in search of Mike. I found him riding a stationary bike next to a very pretty young blonde woman on the bike next to him.

"Hi, Mike," I said. "I think there's a problem here." I paused, uncertain how to begin. "Do you know what I do for a living?"

"Yes, I do," he said, after his own pause.

"Well, I think you've got a problem here. There is a man in the locker room who has appeared in front of me and some of my colleagues in court. He has a bad habit of sneaking into health clubs and locker rooms, and I believe that he sometimes steals things." (I didn't want to be accused of slander, thus the qualification "I believe.")

"I saw that guy come out of the pool!" Mike said. "I'd never seen him before and wondered what he was doing here. I thought maybe he was a day-tripper. I don't know what's up; I'll keep my eye on him." After a pause, he added, "I'll go do that now," and dismounted, nodding to the blonde and heading toward the locker room. I went to the treadmill for my evening constitutional.

About ten minutes later, Mike came over and told me that he had approached our man. "I said to the guy, 'Gee, how did you get in here? I don't think I remember you; I don't find a membership for you, and I don't have any day people here today.' "

Igor said to Mike, pointing to the earplugs, "I can't hear you. These are prescription. The doctor ordered them."

Mike lingered, folding towels while Igor got dressed and then headed toward the back emergency door. As he reached it, Mike tried to grab him.

Igor snapped, "Don't touch me. I'll sue."

"The bastard bolted before the security guards could come," said Mike.

Igor had just been released from the Essex County House of Correction after serving one month of his suspended sentence. A new arrest could have sent him back for five months. In our House of Correction the showers are not so congenial, and they don't have a steam room.

LOOKING FOR LOVE IN ALL THE WRONG PLACES

Will we ever learn?

§ § §

It was my last night out with Raul. He had been staying with me since New Year's, about five weeks.

I didn't know then that it would be the last night. At Raul's suggestion, we went to a Brazilian restaurant in Cambridge called the MidWest Cafe, so named, I guess, because it was on the same street as the East Coast Grill. The restaurant specialized in meat: big slabs of red beef and skewers of pork and lamb. Raul knew that on doctor's orders I was supposed to watch my cholesterol. So it was not a good night from the get-go, but I was tired and could not think of an alternative. *I could always eat a salad*, I thought. They didn't serve salads.

About mid-meal (chicken for me), I noticed a woman across the room who looked familiar but for her blonde hair. I stared, trying to place her. She caught me staring. She smiled, stood up, and started to walk toward us.

Oh, damn, I thought. *Who is she?*

"Hello," she said, "I'm Leah. How are you?"

"Oh, yes, how are you?" I replied, unconvincingly. I still did not know how I knew her. My impression, however, was that I had liked her when last we met.

"I'm a friend of Michael and Alice's, and I've met you at their house a number of times."

"Leah, this is Raul," I said, placing her at last. I did not say, "Leah, this is my partner, Raul," or even, "This is my friend, Raul," as I usually did. I was not granting either of those appellations to Raul that night. He was not being either a friend or a partner. He was being a brat.

"How are Michael and Alice? How is Michael?" I asked. Michael had had a stroke. He had not been easy before the stroke. He was an only child, blond, rich, very handsome, and spoiled. He had become more difficult since the stroke. He had no restraint. If he thought something, he said it. He was also frustrated about the way the stroke affected his mobility and vision, and the medication did not always calm him.

Leah said, "The one I worry about is Alice. She's the principal caretaker and has to deal with Michael all the time. In the beginning, as often happens in these situations, Michael was getting a lot of attention from everyone, but that was short-lived. Now Alice has to take care of him day in and day out. Alice is the one who needs the support."

"You're right. I hadn't thought of it that way. I'll call her. Her office is downtown. We can have lunch," I said.

"I'm sure that she would like that. You probably didn't recognize me as a blonde; I used to have darker hair."

"That's it. I recognized the smile, but the hair threw me off."

"Well, maybe I'll have more fun now," Leah said.

"Is it that easy? What about me as a blond?" I teasingly asked Raul, who hadn't looked up, or missed a bite, during my exchange with Leah.

"Forget it," he muttered, not lifting his head.

The night went downhill from there, but I won't go into it except to say that the next day I heard, and not from Raul, that he was leaving Massachusetts to go back to California.

About three weeks later while sitting in my office between cases, it seemed like a good time to call Alice. We arranged to have lunch.

Contrary to my expectations, Alice, who is in her early fifties and older than Michael, looked wonderful. She looked rested and energetic and sounded enthusiastic. She was always very well dressed, never in that imitation-male dress-for-success look that some woman lawyers affect. She wore those colors only redheads can get away with—ice blue, orange, the infinity of browns, and every shade of green. Today she wore a green silk dress, which looked great.

She did not seem particularly beleaguered. After I told her of my meeting and conversation with Leah, she said, "Yes, it has been difficult. Michael has never been easy, as you may know." Then she laughed. She told me about their planned trip to Java, parties they had been to, and people they had seen. She said that she was going to retire in two years. I was envious.

I could understand that she would feel it necessary to put up a good front with me and that even her brief acknowledgment to me of difficulty was a concession to her, who made great efforts to live a perfect life. Our friendship was long rather than deep. We were loyal to each other but not intimate. I had known Michael before I knew Alice, but not very well. She and I had met ten years before on a Bar Association committee regarding the provision of legal services to people with AIDS. I really liked her. She was smart and no-nonsense but witty and clever at the same time. I had come to know them both as generous and hospitable.

Alice came to my father's funeral, and Michael would have but for the stroke. After the stroke, I visited Michael often in the hospital. As for Alice and me, it may have been a kind of professional distance that we kept. It was not our practice to talk about how we felt about intimate matters—about my father's death, for example—because it was either so obvious or it was unseemly to do so. Now she seemed almost irritated that I had mentioned Leah's concern. She brushed it off.

As a result, I felt a bit the fool for raising the issue. That she did not want to talk about how hard it had been was clear. Perhaps it was easier for her to talk with another woman, like Leah. Or maybe Leah had made it all up. Maybe Leah was projecting. I had heard that Leah's relationship was breaking up. (Alice may have given me that tidbit that day at lunch.) The long and short of it was that after the uncomfortable preliminaries regarding the purpose of my call, lunch was light and pleasant, and we both agreed that we should do it again.

You can imagine my surprise when I picked up my phone about 1 PM the next day and heard, "This is Alice."

"Alice, we cannot have lunch again today. People will talk," I joked.

"No, no, I'm not calling for lunch. I've got a legal problem," she said.

Now that was comic because Alice is a senior partner in one of Boston's largest law firms. She works in some area foreign to me, like trusts. I thought that she was joking, so I replied lightly. I said, "Alice, you know I can't give legal advice."

Alice plowed on, "Michael just called me from the Transit Authority police station. He's under arrest. He's going to be arraigned at the BMC [Boston Municipal Court] this afternoon. That's your court, isn't it? I think he was arrested at the Back Bay Station."

"Oh dear!" I said.

She did not need to say any more. We both knew what the offense was.

"He should get a lawyer," I said without hesitation

"A lawyer? Would we need a lawyer? Who should we get?"

Everyone in the gay male community knew that for years men had been getting arrested for having sex at the Back Bay Station. Four or five arrests came into the arraignment session each week. It was a local gay joke. "Where did you find *him*? In the Back Bay Station men's room?" Someone must have mentioned to Michael how patrolled that place was. I wanted to say, "We? Alice, *you* weren't arrested in the men's room at the Back Bay Station with your pants down."

This situation was very sad.

Alice knew that Michael was gay when she married him, as did most everyone else. They kept a house in Provincetown. They really loved each other and were very good to each other. They were not trying to pass. She adopted his life and friends. Alice had three kids from an earlier marriage, and Michael was great with them right from the start, when the youngest girl was in high school and the oldest was a senior in college. I admired him for that. He was much more exciting than their dullard father who drank too much and did nothing but live off his inheritance.

Michael had lost a lover to AIDS early on in the epidemic, in the mid-eighties. That's why Alice had joined the Bar Association AIDS Services Committee. After her divorce, she had been a neighbor of Michael and his sick lover in the Back Bay.

Michael was devastated by this death, but Alice took care of him and revived him. They were good for each other. They bought the Cape house together, and they did it over to the nines. He sold his apartment. They bought and moved into an apartment in the South End.

So why did Michael have to screw it up?

I gave her the names of good criminal defense lawyers, including some she knew socially. I think she was too embarrassed to hire any one of them, because she did not respond to my suggestions. I then realized that some of the young lawyers in her firm were doing criminal defense work in my court, in a program that was a sort of noblesse oblige endeavor on the part of the firm. It was a mutually beneficial arrangement. The firm looked good for sending the lawyers prepaid, and the lawyers earned combat badges in the courtroom.

I gave Alice the name of a lawyer at her own firm, a Mr. Grealey. Alice did not know him, but she looked him up in the firm directory as we spoke. He was just a baby, a second-year associate, but he was at her firm, and he could say "not guilty" at an arraignment as well as a lawyer charging $5,000. It did not seem that Michael would be held without bail or that bail would be set at all. Michael was not a risk of flight. I expected that Alice would hire a more experienced lawyer if the case went to trial.

I knew that I could not hear any part of this case, nor could I mention it to any of my colleagues. I also could not talk to either Michael or Alice for a while. All that bothered me. I felt even more restricted than I knew I already was. In the past I had seen Michael and Alice more in the summer at the Cape than in the winter in Boston, but now I knew I wouldn't be able to accept their hospitality. I would have to keep my distance.

So why did Michael screw it up? I felt like my feminist colleagues who had said of the former president, "Why couldn't he just keep it in his pants?"

Thank God, I was not the judge assigned to arraignments that week. I knew that the woman who was would be kind. Of course, I could say nothing to her. I couldn't even inquire about the case. Fortunately, the docket entries (the calendar of past and scheduled events) were on the computer, and I could find out what event was scheduled when and act accordingly—that is, I could make sure that I not touch the case. This prohibition did not stop me from hoping that everything would work out and that Michael's caper would not destroy the marriage.

I felt disloyal for being unable to support them separately or together. However, I remembered that my best pal colleague had told me when I first became a judge, "It's a lonely job, and you only realize how lonely it is until after you've done it for a while." I also felt disloyal for thinking that Michael was stupid to look for sex in such a dangerous place. One of Michael's old friends had appeared in front of me for a similar offense in an alley in the South End. I had never told Michael about that but thought the old friend might have. I was not going to tell anyone about this incident. I'm not interested in hurting anyone, particularly someone who has been good to me.

Fortunately, the incident occurred in Boston, and these things do not get the publicity they do in other places. In Worcester, where I grew up, criminal arraignments are published in the daily newspaper. When I was in high school, the father of a classmate was brought in for "bastardy" (which is no longer a crime) for fathering a child by one of his employees at the department store where he worked and which his wife owned. The court notices had been published opposite the funnies so every kid read them.

Similarly, the mayor of Boston once wanted to have the local cable station film the court appearances of men arrested in stings for soliciting undercover policewomen in tiger-skin spandex. He went so far as to send out a press release saying the city cable station was going to videotape the proceedings. However, he forgot to ask the court's permission to put cameras in the courtrooms. The men all covered their faces anyway, just like real criminals.

Everything we do is part of the public record, as some of us have found out to our detriment after losing our patience in the courtroom. The defendants in these cases lost confidentiality when the policemen arrested them. Everything became public information.

Michael was charged with open and gross lewdness, the most serious of the three offenses with which he could have been charged.

As usually happens, the charge was reduced to lewd and lascivious conduct, which does not sound any better but is, believe it or not. You do not have to register for twenty years as a sex offender if convicted of lewd and lascivious conduct. Nor do you have to give a blood sample for the DNA registry to be used to match your DNA with that found after a heinous sex crime. This was a significant comfort, although Michael and Alice might not have realized it immediately.

Eventually, the case was "continued without a finding" for six months, a disposition that does not exactly speak the truth. The fact that it was "continued without a finding" is itself a finding and is noted on the computerized probation record, even though the case is dismissed after six months if nothing else terrible happens during that time. Even the dismissal appears on the record. The computers are unforgiving.

Of course, the disposition was not the most important thing; Alice and Michael's relationship was. Alice has stayed with Michael, but they are selling the Provincetown house and moving out of the South End to Newton. They do not give so many parties. They are off some of the charity fundraising committees, even the AIDS organizations.

I recently saw Alice on Tremont Street as I was coming out of the

Parker House. She was on the other side of the street. She smiled, waved, and walked on.

Although I knew better, I felt a little hurt; I hadn't done anything. I guess that it's the shame of my knowing or she could be trying to protect me.

It can be a lonely job.

THE ARMANI SCAM

Everybody goes to Harvard Square at one time or another

§ § §

"I'm no scamster, Judge."

These were the first words the defendant said to me. He was nervously energetic like Ratso Rizzo in *Midnight Cowboy*, but smaller and younger. He didn't look real good. In fact, he looked like a junkie—a little gray-complexioned, in an old nylon jacket with pants that were too big for him and distinctly non-designer sneakers.

"Judge, I've been in detox, and I'm going to meetings every day. I'm staying out of the North End. That North End is a killer, Judge, Your Honor, Sir."

"And where do you go to meetings, Mr. Scamboni?"

"I go to the START program every day, Judge. I've got a counselor there, Judge. His name is Joey Z., Judge. And I go to NA meetings in Medford, East Boston, everywhere." He meant Narcotics Anonymous.

"And where is the START program, Mr. Scamboni?"

"In the North End, Judge."

"I thought you were staying out of the North End."

"Ah, Judge!?" he said, lifting both hands to shoulder level in a gesture older than Michelangelo as if to say, So you got me, Perry Mason! What are you going to do? Kill me?

What he actually said was, "I only go there for meetings, Judge, Your Honor, Sir."

"Where was Mr. Scamboni picked up?" I asked the probation officer.

"In the North End, Judge."

I paused. "I am appointing Ms. Sack to be your lawyer."

"I don't need no lawyer, Judge. I'll come back. They think I scammed them, but I didn't do nothing. I worked at Armani's. I really did."

My curiosity was so piqued by what he had said that I looked at the police report in the file. It read:

> The suspect, Rico Scamboni, told the five victims named above that he could get them $1,000 Armani suits for $300 per suit. The victims each gave him $600 except for Gennaro Angelini, the suspect's brother-in-law, who gave him $1,200. The suspect had had a job in the stockroom of the Armani store but was fired after five weeks for excessive absences. The job would have entitled him to a 15 percent discount after nine months.

Rico Scamboni was charged with five counts of larceny over $250. His lawyer, Ms. Sack, asked for time to review the papers. I asked the assistant district attorney what he recommended for bail.

With a little smirk he said, "Thirty-six hundred dollars, Your Honor," which not so coincidentally was the amount Mr. Scamboni was alleged to have stolen.

"My client is unable to post any bail," Ms. Sack said. "He had a serious drug problem for which he is now in treatment at the START program in the North End. In addition, he goes to AA and NA meetings in Revere, East Boston, and Medford. He has been clean for four weeks and assures me that he will return."

"Where does he live, Ms. Sack?"

"For reasons that are apparent in the police report, the defendant is alienated from his family. He now lives with a friend in Revere."

"Can your client post any bail?" I asked.

"He tells me that he has an Armani suit, Your Honor, but no money," she said, smiling.

Not in my size, a 46 long, I was willing to bet.

The record showed three arrests for possession of heroin, two for cocaine, and one for marijuana. He also had two outstanding restraining orders. The most recent had been granted five months before—sadly to Mr. Scamboni's own mother, Giovanna Scamboni.

"The defendant will be released on his own recognizance," I said, "with the conditions that he abstain from all drugs including alcohol, that he attend at least five AA or NA meetings per week, and that he stay out of the North End except to go to the START program. When can you be ready for trial, counselors?"

The lawyers agreed on a date two months away.

"Thank you, Judge. I'll be back. I swear on my mother's grave," said Mr. Scamboni.

"Your mother is dead?" I asked. "When did she die?"

"A year ago," he said.

Six weeks later, I was in Harvard Square at the newsstand reading the latest *L'uomo Vogue*. It was a beautiful evening, and there were a lot of people wandering around. Suddenly, someone was in front of me, circling me, saying loudly, "I know you! I know you! Who are you?"

The setting sun was in my eyes, so I couldn't see the speaker. It can be nerve-racking to be recognized, but there is also something comic about it. I never know how I'm going to respond. Sometimes I just say, "A judge? That's my brother. He's a prick."

"I know you. You're the judge who let me out! He's the judge who let me out," the man announced loudly to a passerby and a portly man he had been talking to. By this time I could see him. I said, "How are you doing, Mr. Scamboni? Are you going to meetings?"

"I went today in . . . uh . . . Medford."

"Great. Keep it up."

"What are you doing here?" he asked, as if Harvard Square were foreign territory—his territory, not mine.

I paused, then said, "Actually, I'm meeting a friend who's going to a meeting."

"What?"

"I'm meeting a friend who is going to a twelve-step meeting."

"Where?"

"In that church over there," I said, pointing to the Unitarian Church across the street.

"I know that I'm not as important as you guys," he said. "But can I go to that meeting?"

"Sure you can, but you may not feel too comfortable."

"Yeah, I know, I know. It's only for you big shots. Say, can you be my sponsor?"

"No, I don't think that would be appropriate, Mr. Scamboni. And that's not it. It's not about big shots. It's a gay meeting. Most of the people there are gay." They all were, but I didn't want to scare him completely.

With that, I walked across the street to the Harvard Coop to wait for my friend. Mr. Scamboni kept looking at me, even pointing occasionally, as he continued his conversation with the portly man, no doubt recounting his triumphant release from custody six weeks earlier. They then walked down JFK Street toward the Charles River. I cracked open a copy of the *Boston Herald*.

Five minutes later, Mr. Scamboni appeared on my side of the street. He walked up to a phone seven feet from me and dialed. It didn't matter that there were fifteen pay phones in Harvard Square and that most of them were on the side of the street he had just left.

He said into the phone, watching me all the time, "Hey, asshole, where were you? I got to get to a meeting. Yeah, yeah, yeah. I went at noontime to the meeting in . . . uh . . . Revere, but I'm going again tonight. You know I go twice, three times a day. Yeah, the judge says I got to go. I do what they tell me. Hey, I'm no scamster."

As he was saying this, he looked at me and winked.

{ V }

DON'T HURT WHEN YOU CAN HELP

This aphorism is easier said than done. First of all there has to be a willing defendant. Sometimes I try to make the defendant willing. However, I am not always dealing with a rational decision maker, and even when it appears that the spirit is willing, the flesh is weak.

As an example, it is very difficult to recover from addiction. Yet it can be done and is done all the time. When confronted with addiction, I can only hope that this time recovery will catch. That outcome involves a confluence of motivation, the depth of "the bottom," the severity of the consequences, and hope and grace. That recovery did not happen before, or that it did not last, should not deter me from trying again—unless the risk to the public is so great that another attempt would be dangerous and foolhardy.

The other difficulty is finding the resource to fit the problem. Many social programs do not want to deal with our clientele. There is not, in the end, a screw for every nut. It is difficult to keep up with the good programs. We have to rely on information from a number of sources both in and out of court to find out what works.

Finally, opportunities for alternative sentences diminish as the crimes become more serious.

NUDE DESCENDING

After the rum, he couldn't keep his clothes on

§ § §

Rodney Dell, known as R.D., cannot drink. He takes his clothes off when he drinks and flashes at women who happen to pass by. He is in denial about all that. He also has his poor mother buffaloed about his predilections. I suspect he thinks that because he has her conned, we all should believe him, too.

I came in on the travails of R.D. for a probation surrender after he had already been convicted of open and gross lewdness. He had worked out a deal on three cases before another judge. In exchange for pleading guilty, he took the short-term gain of a suspended sentence and probation, keeping him out of jail.

When he appeared in front of me, he was with his mother. They were like birds: he had all the plumage; she was drab and gray.

R.D. was twenty-three, well-built, and well-dressed in a fashionable Italian sports jacket and a handsome tie. He looked like a muscle-bound George Clooney. At the time of his arrests, he lived on Anderson Street on the back of Beacon Hill and had a good job as a techie for a financial house downtown, hired straight from college.

R.D.'s first case involved a nurse from Mass General who was walking home early one morning up the back side of Beacon Hill after finishing her shift. When she first saw R.D., he was dressed in a pair of red running shorts. When she saw him again a little farther up the hill, the red shorts were in one hand and his erect penis was in the other. He was on the opposite side of the street and was moaning.

"Kiss me, just kiss me," he was saying.

The second incident occurred at the Park Street T Station. R.D.

exited from his sweatpants on a spring afternoon in front of a Harvard coed waiting for the train to Harvard Square. She had walked down the platform to the last bench to read Byron. She noticed R.D. passing by a few times, wearing less clothing each time until he was down to the sweats. She hadn't worried until his shirt came off. Then he slipped behind a pillar and came out in all his glory, ready to leap into the Bosporus, I assume. Lady Caroline Lamb screamed frantically. The only way out for R.D. was up the stairway, but first he stopped to put on his sweatpants, giving the police time to block his exit.

The third occurrence was observed by a state trooper, who brought a lesser charge of indecent exposure. The police report said R.D. was observed in red shorts, running on Phillips Street heading toward the Charles. He was naked on the return, with the shorts around his neck, and was arrested as he turned onto Anderson Street. This was at three in the afternoon in late October, a bit chilly unless you're working up a sweat.

These offenses were packaged together. R.D. admitted to all three charges and received the nine-month sentence, to be suspended for two years. If he violated the terms of his probation during the two years, he would go to jail for nine months. Each of the police reports said R.D. smelled of alcohol at the time of his arrests. After entering his guilty plea, he told his probation officer that he often sat in his apartment drinking rum all day and that he had blackouts. He did not remember any of these incidents.

It seemed to me that if he took his clothes off in public only when drunk, R.D. needed to learn how not to drink. A good lawyer would have put him in treatment for alcoholism and exhibitionism right away and would have asked for straight probation during which the treatment could occur. That way if there was a violation of probation, the screw could be tightened a bit with more treatment, but not with nine months in the House of Correction. What the first lawyer had failed to do I was trying to achieve now. R.D. was before me for failing to report to his probation officer. His excuse was that he'd moved to Plymouth and wasn't able to get up to Boston because he was so busy working. As time went on, it became increasingly clear that he did not appreciate the gravity of his situation.

I appointed Mr. Hayle, a passive, docile lawyer, to represent R.D. because he was the only lawyer in the courtroom when the case arrived before me. Theoretically, Mr. Hayle was qualified because the Committee for Public Counsel Services said he was. I told Mr. Hayle that R.D. should get treatment for his alcoholism and consult a specialist in exhibitionism. We live in Boston: there's a specialist for every aberration. Then I scheduled another hearing five weeks out in the hope that they would find the recommended treatment.

Five weeks later, R.D. appeared again with his mother. I'd seen them in the corridor. This time he was wearing a polo shirt with the name of the computer company he was working for embroidered on it. Although she was a young woman, his mother looked dowdy and long-suffering and was this time overdressed for the weather.

"My client has found a therapist, Your Honor," said Defense Attorney Hayle.

"And what qualifies the therapist to deal with your client regarding these problems of exhibitionism and alcoholism?" I asked.

"My client assures me that he's a good therapist. He's a psychiatrist."

"Do you have his curriculum vitae?" I asked, using the Latin to sound more serious. *This lawyer is being led by the nose by his client*, I thought. R.D. was going to end up in the slammer as somebody's boyfriend.

"Yes, Your Honor. The doctor went to Harvard." He handed the CV up to me with a cover letter on Harvard Medical School stationery. That did not impress me. Almost every other doctor in Boston is an adjunct or associate professor at Harvard Medical School. In spite of my skepticism, however, this one looked like he knew what he was talking about.

There was some bad news from the probation officer, however. R.D. had done it again.

Late at night in Brighton, a woman had left an Irish bar by the back door to get to her car in the parking lot. Thinking she heard someone in the lot, she stopped to adjust her eyes. She saw a figure run from one side of the lot to the other; then she saw R.D. begin to run in circles around her, grabbing himself while repeating "just a kiss, one kiss."

As fate would have it, a police car pulled into the lot. Two young officers got out and chased the defendant. They found his clothes behind a stack of empty beer bottles and later found his Jeep in the lot. They found him under a van—in his socks.

"What happened to the Brighton case?" I asked.

"The defendant received a probationary term, two years," the probation officer said.

"Were there any conditions?"

"They required him to get treatment," said Mr. Hayle, as if all treatment were equal.

In this case, effective treatment was my goal. Nine months at the South Bay House of Correction was not going to stop R.D. from getting drunk and taking off his clothes. Prison might give him a different audience, and maybe even a more receptive one, but it wasn't going to solve the problem. I wasn't sure that anything would, but I was hopeful.

"Mrs. Dell," I asked, "does your son have an alcohol problem?"

"Sometimes, not often, he drinks too much. His father was an alcoholic, but R.D. is not that bad."

"Do you think he has a problem?"

"He just acts up every once in a while. That's all."

"Has he gone to AA since the Brighton case?"

"Yes, he's gone."

"How often?"

"I'm not sure. Two or three times maybe. He works a lot since he moved back in with me in Plymouth."

All of a sudden it occurred to me that R.D. probably was the sole support in the family. I would have asked, but there is something so unseemly about having a mother testify against her child. I just wanted this inquiry to be over.

All through his mother's testimony, R.D. continued to look up at me impassively. It was uncanny. Could it be that because he blacked out during these episodes in his mind they had never happened? He certainly didn't seem to realize how close he was to going to jail.

The case was continued again to see if R.D. would comply with the treatment program—one-on-one alcohol counseling at a substance-abuse treatment facility near his home; no drugs, including alcohol; AA or some equivalent at least five times per week; and therapy with the doctor who specialized in sexual issues and exhibitionism.

A few weeks later, I inquired of his probation officer about R.D.

"Oh, him? He went to Rhode Island and got arrested again for flashing. He's in default. No one knows where he is and that includes his mother, but I suspect she's lying. He stopped seeing the doctor after a couple of months and never went to AA. He always said he could do it on his own."

He can't.

BABYSITTING

There was plenty of fault to go around in this mess

§ § §

"Don't worry about jury trials! What's to worry about? You don't have to make the decision. The jury does the work. You just have to sit there and look judicial," my chief justice said the first time he assigned me to the jury session.

His words were small comfort because there's a whole ritual that has to be gone through in a jury case. The pitfalls begin with the impaneling of the jurors and continue through the Commonwealth's opening and every stage of the trial thereafter. Besides, as the chief justice pointed out, there is the performance aspect; you have to act like a judge—no yawns or indiscreet scratching, no little asides, no criticism of lawyers on the loose in front of the jury. After all, this is the moment that they went to law school for: they're anxious to perform.

In my first jury trial as a judge, the defendant, Tom Dexter, was charged with indecent assault and battery on a child under the age of fourteen. He was an inspector on the Massachusetts Bay Transportation Authority, the T, and had been suspended from his job pending the result of this case.

The victim was an eleven-year-old girl, the daughter of a policeman and a salesperson for a national company. They were divorced, and the mother had custody.

The undisputed facts of the incident were as follows. The mother had to go on a business trip, so she left the child with a woman named Sally Tipton, who was the girlfriend of Tom Dexter. Sally Tipton was taking care of her sister's three-year-old boy that weekend as well. Ms. Tipton and Mr. Dexter lived in a two-bedroom apartment, but one of the bedrooms was used as Tom Dexter's den. There was a couch in the living room and a waterbed in the bedroom. Tom Dexter had gone to work early in the morning and returned in the early evening. Around midnight, Sally Tipton's sister arrived and persuaded Ms. Tipton to go out nightclubbing in Brockton, at least an hour away. Arianna Brown, the victim, went to the conjugal king-sized waterbed to sleep. The three-year-old boy was already sleeping there. Tom Dexter removed Arianna's jeans while she was on the waterbed. He touched her again when he got into the bed. Arianna took a pillow and ran to the kitchen and stayed there until Sally Tipton and her sister returned. Tom Dexter left the house.

Arianna Brown said that Tom Dexter rubbed her bum (her word) and her upper leg. Tom Dexter said that he might have grabbed her waist to move her over as he tried to make room for himself in the bed.

The jury was selected fairly easily, five women and three men, which gave us two extra in case any of the six regular jurors become incapacitated. There had been four challenges, nothing unusual. Amongst the jurors selected were a school principal, a school administrator, the spouse of a law-office administrator, a registered nurse, a self-described student/housewife, a father of four, and an administrative assistant who was the mother of two. Such a mix of blue- and white-collar people was typical of juries in Boston. Two of the jurors were also African Americans, one man was Asian, and one woman Latina. Two were single, and only three had no children. Considering his defense theory, Tom Dexter's lawyer may have been wise to let so many parents serve.

In his opening, Tom Dexter's lawyer said that he was going to introduce evidence that Arianna Brown, now seated next to her parents in the first row of the audience, alert and well behaved, had made everything up and that she had earlier said variously that Tom Dexter put his penis in her vagina or on her bum, or fondled her breasts. The assistant district attorney said in the Commonwealth's opening little more than the above facts except that Tom Dexter had removed

Arianna Brown's jeans, that the touching was to her buttocks (his words) and legs, and that it frightened Arianna Brown.

At the beginning of most jury trials, a spirit of civic camaraderie exists amongst everyone—the jury, the judge, the lawyers on each side, the clerk, and the court officers. This spirit contains a certain innocence. The jury is searching for cues from whatever source. For a little while the common feeling is that we are all in this together and what we are doing is a good thing. That feeling of unity splinters when the jury realizes it has to decide for one side or the other, guilty or not guilty. The jury can't please everyone. And the jury may get mad at the judge as well.

In this case, it seemed to me that the defense attorney shattered the unity all too soon by being so graphic in his opening and by positioning himself (and, thus, his client) at the opposite end of the spectrum from Arianna Brown.

Arianna Brown had a beautiful and calm presence and was very well spoken. She walked to the witness stand as if she were about to give a piano recital. She was dressed like the schoolgirl she was, in dark slacks, a clean white blouse, and a sweater. She still had some baby fat, but otherwise was almost a young woman.

Because of her age, I had to examine Arianna before the trial to see if she was "competent" to testify, to determine if she knew the difference between the truth and a lie, as well as the consequences of not telling the truth.

She was a very effective witness while responding to my questions, and she was neither rattled nor moved on direct examination or cross-examination later. She was upset that Tom Dexter's lawyer had called her a liar, however.

Her mother, who was in her early thirties and obviously very upset, testified too. She was angry, and she was not hiding it. But the amount of blame going around was also palpable during her testimony. It was apparent that the mother blamed herself after she blamed Sally Tipton and Tom Dexter. Her anger may well have been compensation for her guilt at having left her daughter in such bad hands; however, she could only testify to the facts up to the delivery of her daughter to Ms. Tipton because she was not present the rest of the night.

The mother testified that she did not know Sally Tipton very well: Ms. Tipton had cared for Arianna once before, but not overnight. The mother also said that Arianna had reported that Tom Dexter had been drinking that night.

Arianna's father was a policeman. He appeared very detached as he testified. "I was called early Sunday morning. My daughter began to cry when she saw me, and she told me that Tom Dexter took her pants off and then touched her on her rear and her leg." His testimony was very powerful because of both the weight of his office and his role as the father of the victim. In addition, he was a big and distinguished-looking man, and his integrity was apparent. There was something in his presentation that seemed to say, "I have my troubles. I have to make sure that my daughter gets through all this. So you just do your job, judge and jury. I have my daughter to worry about, which is more important than whatever game you are playing with all your formalities."

I suspect that he had no illusions about the cathartic result of a trial, although he had turned the case over to us. His wife thought it was her duty to convince us of the defendant's guilt, perhaps to relieve herself of her own guilt. If we found Tom Dexter guilty, she was off the hook—a bit.

The defense attorney did not dare get too close to the father, figuratively or physically, except to ask, "Did she ever tell you anything different?"

"No," said Arianna's father, succinctly ending that line of questioning.

The Commonwealth rested its case after the father's testimony.

Sally Tipton was the first witness for the defense. She was clearly nervous, although she probably would have looked nervous in any situation. She was very thin, almost anorectic, and had dark angular features like a Native American. She was dressed more formally than everyone else, in church clothes perhaps; only a hat was missing. She took us through her day with Arianna, which included a trip to the Public Gardens where they rode on a swan boat. From there they walked over to the Charles River. Arianna helped her with the three-year-old nephew. Ms. Tipton offered no explanation for the late-night trip to Brockton, which mystified me, and no explanation was sought by either lawyer.

Sally Tipton said that when she returned from Brockton Arianna was in the kitchen crying. Ms. Tipton asked Arianna what was wrong. Initially, there was no reply. Tom Dexter told her, "I don't know what's wrong with her."

"No, it did not appear that Tom Dexter had been drinking," Ms. Tipton testified. "Yes, I did suggest that Tom Dexter leave the house. It calmed the waters."

According to Ms. Tipton, Arianna Brown gave three different accounts of the case after Mr. Dexter left the house: one that Tom Dexter tried to put his penis in her vagina, another that he put his penis on her behind, and finally, that he touched her breasts.

Arianna Brown sat between her parents during this testimony, closer to but not quite leaning against her father. She watched intently as she had all through the trial. Tom Dexter, on the other hand, looked terrified. He had already been suspended from his job at the Massachusetts Bay Transit Authority, and the potential maximum penalty that I could give was two-and-a-half years in the Deer Island House of Correction, which was on an island in Boston Harbor and was then about 150 years old.

Mr. Dexter testified that on the day in question he had worked all day, come home, played computer games with the kids after his girlfriend went out, put Arianna to bed, removed her jeans at her request, fell asleep at a chair in front of the computer, and then went to bed himself at about two-thirty or three in the morning, moving Arianna over by placing one hand under her knee and the other under her waist to make room for himself. There were no other beds in the house. At that point he had on a red bathrobe and underwear and maybe thermal underwear. Water rocked in the bed, and Arianna woke up "disturbed, frightened, and upset," and she went to the kitchen where she said, "Just leave me alone."

"No," Tom Dexter said when asked if he'd been drinking. "I hadn't had anything to drink."

"No, I didn't touch her except to move her. Maybe my hand grazed across her rear, but I doubt it," he added.

Arianna's mother, who had been steaming during Sally Tipton's and Tom Dexter's testimony was called to testify in rebuttal. She said that the very next day Sally Tipton had told her that Tom Dexter had been drinking and that Ms. Tipton had found a bottle in the trash. She, the mother, had made notes of this call.

On cross-examination, the mother emphatically said that she had been on a business trip, not a social trip with a boyfriend as the defense attorney intimated.

Contrary to television and in accord with real life, there was no intense or brilliant cross-examination, and no one broke down and recanted. After the openings, the case assumed a quiet, deliberate tone—no drama, just facts.

The closing arguments were predictable. The defense attorney asked the jury, "Did your kid ever lie to you?" The assistant district attorney said, "you heard her demeanor" and "when the cat's away, the mice will play," both of which statements seemed to me to minimize the facts he was trying to prove. I would have referred to "hawks and sparrows" in my prosecutorial days.

I instructed the jury on the law. They began deliberating about quarter to three. They were unable to reach a verdict that day and returned the next morning to continue. Around noon they returned with a verdict. I was summoned from the judges' lobby upstairs, and the parties and lawyers were rounded up.

"Guilty," said the foreman.

The jury was discharged.

I thought about letting the jurors stay for the sentencing, but it was not the custom to do that at the BMC. When I was prosecuting cases in the sixties in another county, we did it all the time in the belief that juries wanted to know what happened to the people they found guilty. Perhaps since then there had been a case that came down from one of the appellate courts that frowned on the practice. I did not know, so it seemed to me to be better to follow custom. *When in doubt, don't* is a very good maxim for a trial judge.

After the jurors left, as permitted by law, the victim's father made what is called a victim impact statement: "My wife and I are very shaken by these events but pleased by the guilty verdict. We are grateful for the courtesy and consideration of the Court. The defendant has serious problems regarding minor children. My daughter may need psychiatric assistance in the future; she has gone to counseling already. We want the defendant to get help with his life in the future. I am a black man as well as a policeman, and I have seen too many black men in jail. Jail is not the solution to this man's problems."

The defendant had no prior record of any kind. The assistant district attorney recommended one year in the House of Correction, sixty days committed, the balance suspended for two years. Defendant Tom Dexter should participate in court-ordered psychological treatment, the nature of which the assistant district attorney did not specify.

The defense attorney argued that commitment was "inappropriate" and that Tom Dexter should be put on probation with psychiatric therapy. He was already suspended from his job and would not be reinstated after the guilty finding. Again, no particular kind of psychiatric therapy was suggested. I ordered a court-clinic pre-sentencing report with particular attention to child sexual abuse and substance abuse, and I continued the case for sentencing for four weeks.

It was at this point that my problems began. (The chief justice had been right up to this point.) At the follow-up hearing four weeks later, it seemed that the defense lawyer could not accept that his client had been convicted or that the jury had believed Tom Dexter had molested Arianna Brown. Mr. Dexter was a solid citizen, the lawyer kept saying, and he again suggested nonspecific therapy.

I insisted that he find an expert on child sexual molestation to treat his client, or I would have no choice but to accept the recommendation of the Commonwealth. The defense lawyer either failed to get it, or he hoped to wear me down. I continued the date for sentencing.

There were two more hearings and reports. One report revealed that Tom Dexter had been fired as a police recruit when he tested positive for cocaine and marijuana.

Arianna's father's victim statement allowed me some room. It seemed to me that if Tom Dexter was a child molester, and the jury had determined that he had assaulted this victim, what I should try to prevent was a return to that behavior whether or not he served sixty days. He needed treatment that was appropriate to his problems.

Mr. Dexter's lawyer had a good reputation, and I knew that the lawyer knew what I was looking for in spite of his initial thick-headedness. I knew that such treatment existed in Boston and that the attorney could find it if he got serious. I think his obstinacy had more to do with his ego: he had bet that Tom Dexter's respectability would win the jury, and that argument had lost. Now I had to remind him what the jury's verdict meant. A lawyer's duty to his client does not end with the verdict, if the verdict is guilty. In this case, it just began. We, both lawyers and judges, protest that we are not social workers. Of course we are. Maybe we are a primitive and untrained form of social worker, but everything we do has "social" implications.

Finally, after a number of hearings, Tom Dexter's lawyer realized that I would not budge. He found a psychiatrist who dealt with sexual dysfunction and pedophilia and who also knew about substance abuse. He gave me the doctor's curriculum vitae and a treatment plan.

My sentence for Tom Dexter was one year in the House of Correction, suspended for three years, treatment with the psychiatrist already named who specialized in sexual abuse or with another counselor approved by the probation department. In addition, Tom Dexter was to contribute $5,000 to a fund to be set up within three years for counseling of the victim up to age twenty-one. This provision was suggested to me by someone who herself had been the victim of childhood sexual abuse and had spent a lot of time in therapy getting over it.

In my opinion, the jury could have gone either way, and I would not have been surprised, but it was my first jury trial as a judge so I did not put too much stock in my opinion. Proof beyond a reasonable doubt is a very high standard. In later trials I often believed that someone had committed the crime even when the jury returned a not-guilty verdict.

On the other hand, after the verdict in Tom Dexter's case, Franny Cooney, the court officer, said as he walked me back to the lobby, "It was all over for him when he climbed into the water bed with the kid."

MEGAMAN

"It was the vitamins, Your Honor"

§ § §

Room 371 is a beautiful old courtroom between two airshafts so it gets light and air from both sides. The room is painted a wonderful blue, like a palace in Saint Petersburg in Russia or a house in the Caribbean—a blue beyond pastel with a touch of green. There are four tall, arched windows on either side. The room is more or less square and has old, dark oak wainscoting about seven feet high. There is matching oak furniture, which one of my colleagues has added to from the diaspora of original furniture scattered around these buildings. There are also funny antique lamps sticking out in unlikely but curiously helpful places, like behind the judge's chair to the upper right. This particular lamp casts a nice light on the papers on the bench and creates a back light on the judge. The lights were gas lamps that have been converted to electricity. Behind the bench are tall oak bookcases with glass doors. There are jury boxes to both the right and the left of the bench, as well as a solid-oak movable witness stand on the right. The room looks like the scene of the Lindbergh baby trial except that there are shiny modern chrome microphones sticking up here and there like cranes in a marsh.

The only portrait left in the room is above the bench, a five-foot-by-four-foot modern painting of our first African American chief justice. Although portraits of Daniel Webster and an early Supreme Judicial Court justice used to hang on the back wall, only their dusty shadows now remained.

The case of Fernando Paniagua had been called a number of times during my two-month assignment to that room. The first time he did not show up, and he was defaulted. Later that day, his lawyer, the attentive Genevieve Riordan, reported that he was at McLean Hospital, a prestigious and expensive psychiatric hospital in a Boston suburb. The default (the failure to appear) was removed from the docket of the case, and he was given another date. He was still hospitalized on that second date, so a third date was selected.

Ms. Riordan, who had been appointed his lawyer at arraignment, is a private attorney paid by the state on an hourly basis to represent indigent defendants, that is, people charged with crimes who cannot afford to pay for a lawyer. She looked particularly splendid on the third trial date. She was in her upper sixties, at least, and wore a magnificent Dolly Parton-like wig. Ms. Riordan went to law school later in life. She lived an hour away, and took the bus into town every day. Her clothes were very good, Chanel suits and other designer clothes. This day, a hot Thursday in August, she had on three strands of real pearls, a lace dress, hand-stitched by Belgian nuns no doubt, a lavender chenille sweater, three pins of good gold, one with two diamonds. She wore silver flats, and her fingernails were painted with blue metallic polish. Incongruously, she had a white plastic clip firmly planted in the back of her hair—to indicate that she meant business, I guess.

Ms. Riordan talked very fast, and when she really wanted to make a point, she leaned on the rail of the bench on one elbow and said something like this: “I'll be candid with you, Judge. I told him he never should have done it.” She had been known to win rulings yet keep on arguing, causing the judge to remind her that she had already won the point. She would then apologize and smile victoriously. In spite of her quirks, she always worked hard for her clients, and her efforts in this case were no exception.

On this, the third date the case was called for trial, Ms. Riordan reported at the first call that Mr. Paniagua was on his way from his home in East Boston with his wife and that he would be present momentarily. I had been waiting to see him. I was curious. He appeared about twelve-thirty.

According to the complaint, and my eye agreed, Mr. Paniagua was five foot six and weighed 225 pounds. He wore black pants and a black shirt, as well as a black-and-white cowhide belt with a fancy western buckle. He stood with his head down during the entire proceeding. Alicia Cruz-Alvarez, one of the beautiful and aristocratic Cruz-Alvarez sisters from Seville, was interpreting, dressed like a matador's assistant in red and black with bright red lipstick setting off her jet-black hair. Mr. Paniagua's wife was in the courtroom, sitting in the back row. She was about the same size as her husband and wore black tights and a T-shirt.

The assistant district attorney representing the Commonwealth, Ellen Horan, a plain young woman—all the plainer next to Ms. Riordan and Srta. Cruz-Alvarez—appeared to have had little experience at anything other than school. She expressed concern about Mr. Paniagua's present competency to stand trial and requested an examination by the court clinic.

Similarly, Ms. Riordan, for the defense, wanted the court clinic to comment on Mr. Paniagua's criminal responsibility at the time of the incident. He had been arrested for open and gross lewdness, a five-year felony over which the court had jurisdiction. Conviction for open and gross (in the shorthand we use for this charge) could result in Mr. Paniagua being deported to El Salvador, would require him to register as a sex offender for the next twenty years, and would require him to give a DNA sample to the probation department to be used for God knows what. We all knew these consequences. Presumably Ms. Riordan had told Mr. Paniagua about them. He had reasons to worry—not the least of which was his wife sitting in the back row under the dusty rectangle that Daniel Webster's portrait had once covered. If, on the other hand, Mr. Paniagua was not criminally responsible at the time of the incident, he would have to be found not guilty.

As a result of the concerns about Mr. Paniagua's mental status, I sent the defendant to the court clinic, a psychiatric office at the court run by the Department of Mental Health, to be examined by a psychologist to determine whether there was cause for concern.

Depending on who does the examination at the court clinic, this can be a risky business. It became riskier after the Department of Mental Health contracted out its court clinics to private businesses. You never knew who would be doing the examination, and just when you found a person whose judgment you trusted, she was transferred.

This time we got Dr. Flipante, a psychologist. He was a loose cannon who felt free to say whatever he wanted about a case and about the person he examined instead of offering what should have been limited opinions about competency to stand trial or criminal responsibility at the time of the alleged crime. Dr. Flipante did not disappoint in this case. First, he gave his conclusion, which was that Mr. Paniagua was competent and could be held criminally responsible at the time of the incident. He then added gratuitously that Mr. Paniagua was overmedicated today, although still competent. This aside caused problems for me. If Mr. Paniagua was overmedicated, how could I let him plead to this offense or some lesser version of it, should he be so inclined?

Dr. Flipante then proceeded to recite Mr. Paniagua's version of the events surrounding his arrest, even though no one had asked for it and even though it was outside of the testimony required of a psychologist in these circumstances. However, no one stopped the doctor, including me. I probably was curious.

"Mr. Paniagua worked for a cleaning company," Dr. Flipante began. "Some other employees were spreading rumors that he was having an affair with the head of the company. He became so upset at this slander that he increased his dose of Megaman vitamins, which increase potency, from one pill a day to ten pills on the day of the arrest. When the vitamins kicked in, he was forced to rush to the Back Bay Station men's room to ejaculate, which he did in the last stall. Whereupon he was arrested by the Transit policeman."

Mr. Paniagua's wife appeared to understand English and nodded approvingly throughout this explanation. No wonder! It left out the other man who was arrested with Mr. Paniagua, and it gave testament to her husband's virility, albeit super-vitamin-induced. The

Transit policeman, who was standing to the right in the jury box, could hardly contain his surprise at these remarks.

The policeman was a frequent witness in cases arising out of this men's room. He was a young bodybuilder with arms as big as most men's thighs bursting out of his uniform. He had a different story. His police report indicated that the Transit police had received a call from a Mr. Olmeida of Taunton complaining of men having sex in the men's room of the Back Bay Station. When he went into the men's room, he saw Mr. Paniagua in a stall masturbating while facing another man similarly occupied at the urinal.

Mrs. Paniagua, who had nodded approvingly at everything Dr. Flipante said, scrunched her face and shook her head negatively as the officer's report was being read by Ms. Horan, who held it at a distance as if it smelt.

Mr. Paniagua had no record. It was obvious that a conviction of this charge would have grave consequences for him, his wife, and their two children. I wanted to know if there was any way to resolve the case short of trial, so I asked if there had been any attempt at resolution.

"Well, Your Honor," said Ms. Riordan, "I have asked them to reduce the charge to lewd and lascivious or indecent exposure, but I've received no response."

These charges are misdemeanors and do not require registration as a sex offender or the providing of a DNA sample. Substantively, the only differences between the misdemeanors and the felony charge of open and gross lewdness are that the felony requires that someone be alarmed or shocked by whatever conduct occurred and proof that the defendant intended public exposure. The Transit police always charge open and gross, and the District Attorney's Office always approves it. Then, if prompted by the defense attorney, the assistant district attorney will request that the court reduce the charge. If the unfortunate defendant does not have a lawyer who knows enough to request a reduction, then woe to the defendant.

In this case, Ms. Horan replied to Ms. Riordan's request with,

"We are reluctant to request a reduction of the charge unless there is going to be a guilty plea."

Ms. Riordan said, "My client is not going to plead guilty to a charge with such serious consequences for him and his family." Then looking at me, she added, "I am happy to hear that they will reduce the charge, but the prosecution has not told me anything until now regarding reducing the charge under any circumstance."

"Well, it's the court that reduces the charge, Ms. Riordan," I said, "but it does so on the motion of the Commonwealth. I can't reduce it if they don't agree. If the charge should be reduced, it should be reduced because the facts do not prove the original charge," I added pedantically.

I then asked, "Are you prepared to prove the more serious charge, open and gross lewdness, Ms. Horan? Do you have the person from Taunton who was 'alarmed and shocked,' Mr. Olmeida, I believe his name is? Is he here to testify?" I peered through the papers then looked around the courtroom, which was empty except for Mrs. Paniagua and the Transit police officer.

"The Commonwealth moves to reduce the charge to lewd and lascivious conduct," Ms. Horan rushed to say.

"Why not indecent exposure?" asked Ms. Riordan.

I looked over my glasses at Ms. Horan. She did not have a response. She shrugged affirmation.

I announced, "The charge will be reduced to indecent exposure. Now what are we going to do about it?"

"We would agree to a guilty finding on the condition that the defendant go to Project AIDS for AIDS education and pay five hundred dollars' costs," said Ms. Horan.

I wanted to ask Ms. Horan if she knew of any cases of transmission of AIDS by separate but mutual masturbation. However, I bit my tongue lest I be reported to the Judicial Conduct Commission or the Court Gender Bias Committee for sexual harassment.

"My client cannot plead guilty," said Ms. Riordan. "He will be deported. His wife has a little job, but my client is the main support of his family—his wife and two kids, three and five. We will not agree to the reduction and would waive a jury trial. They cannot prove their case. There is no 'Mr. Olmeida,' and if there is," she said, dramatically craning to look around the courtroom still empty except for the Transit police officer standing to my right and Mrs. Paniagua weeping into her hands in the back row, "he is not here today to testify."

I looked inquisitively over my glasses at Ms. Horan and said, "What about a six-month pre-trial probation on the charge of indecent exposure, with the condition that Mr. Paniagua continue his psychiatric treatment and stay out of the men's room at the Back Bay Station?"

"We'll go for that," said Ms. Riordan. The case would be dismissed after the six months if Mr. Paniagua behaved.

"The Commonwealth agrees," said Ms. Horan reluctantly, after a long pause.

Mrs. Paniagua raised her head and smiled.

RECOVERY

She has HIV and a new pal with a heart of gold

§ § §

Missy Mortimer appeared again in the second criminal session. At the time, we judges still rotated among the sessions and courtrooms in the old and new buildings that made up the Suffolk County Courthouse. I hadn't seen Missy there in a while. The women's holding cell is adjacent to the second session courtroom, which is why all women are arraigned in that room. Hanging over the bench is a portrait of an old, long-dead judge who the prostitutes greatly feared. Supposedly the women would come in the courtroom door, see him on the bench, and flee, not to return until his weekly duty in that session ended.

The holding cell adjacent to the second session is a stark place with shiny yellow-tiled walls, small barred windows, and wooden benches along the sides. At one time a place on that bench could have had Missy's name on it. She used to be a regular here, often wearing a ladies-to-lunch navy blue suit with detachable white collar. And usually she was preceded or followed by another good-looking blonde, similarly attired, the two them like alumnae of a finishing school. Missy did not look so chic today. She was in jeans and a T-shirt, and her skin color was the off gray of an addict's.

There used to be four of them, Missy, two other blondes, and a brunette, and they worked together, not as a team but all on the street at the same time, flagging down cars. Usually they were "hotel girls," I was told, but they liked excitement and would sometimes work the street just for the thrill of it. They often got arrested, usually near the Don Bosco School and the Eliot Norton Park by Sergeant Detective Dunkirk. All of them were attractive and good-humored. They would flirt with the judges while in the dock, even with the women judges.

Missy was born in Winchester, a toney Northwest suburb, and she claimed that she now lived with her grandmother in Wakefield, also a quiet suburb, although I suspected that was not true. She was such a con that she would have said she lived in a convent if she could get away with it.

Missy had often been arrested for what was known as a "BMC disorderly" or a "Dunkirk disorderly," named after the rumpled detective who made so many of the arrests and brought the defendants to our court.

The evidence in a Dunkirk disorderly was always presented in a staccato fashion and sounded like this: "Sergeant Detective Dunkirk, Your Honor. The defendant was standing on Tremont Street; Wang Center; Zebra spandex; flagging down cars with male occupants; traffic backing up all the way up the street; cars beeping their horns; people shouting; 4 AM, Your Honor, sir."

This kind of arrest was so predictable that Sgt. Dunkirk made up a mimeographed form for the application for the complaint; he only had to fill in the blanks for the outfit, the date, and the time. I think that the signature swearing to the truth of the above facts was mimeographed as well.

The charge itself was the remainder of an ancient statute, first enacted in 1699, which rings with Puritanism and most of which has since been declared unconstitutional. This is what remains.

MGLC272 SEC. 53

COMMON NIGHT WALKERS, COMMON STREET WALKERS, BOTH MALE AND FEMALE, COMMON RAILERS AND BRAWLERS, PERSONS WHO WITH OFFENSIVE AND DISORDERLY ACTS OR LANGUAGE ACCOST OR ANNOY PERSONS OF THE OPPOSITE SEX, LEWD, WANTON AND LASCIVIOUS PERSONS IN SPEECH OR BEHAVIOR, IDLE AND DISORDERLY PERSONS, DISTURBERS

> OF THE PEACE, KEEPERS OF NOISY AND DISORDERLY HOUSES, AND PERSONS GUILTY OF INDECENT EXPOSURE MAY BE PUNISHED BY IMPRISONMENT IN A JAIL OR HOUSE OF CORRECTION FOR NOT MORE THAN SIX MONTHS, OR BY A FINE OF NOT MORE THAN TWO HUNDRED DOLLARS OR BY BOTH SUCH FINE AND IMPRISONMENT.

The Dunkirk disorderly suffered a fatal wound as the result of a case decided by the state's highest court, the Supreme Judicial Court, in April of 1989. It took a while for the reasoning in this case to filter down to us, but eventually Missy's lawyer added it to his repertoire of defenses. I bought the argument, and not just because I was tired of Detective Dunkirk's canned complaints. There was no variety to them for one thing. They had become boring.

The case that toppled the Dunkirk disorderly is called *Commonwealth v. Feigenbaum*. It held that in order to find someone to have been "disorderly," the State has to prove as part of its prosecution that the person was acting "with no legitimate purpose." And even in these cases that is not an easy thing to do, short shorts and halter tops notwithstanding. (In the flesh business, life imitates art—or at least the movies. Hookers look like hookers, and pimps look like pimps; so do their cars.) The fact that Feigenbaum was a political protester at an Air Force base and not a prostitute is of no matter. It is the principle that counts, and the principle is that you cannot be convicted of disorderly conduct unless the state has first proven that you acted "with no legitimate purpose." As we all know, criminal defendants do not have to offer any defense. They don't have to say anything. The Commonwealth has to prove that there was "no legitimate purpose."

In any case, Missy Mortimer had been the recipient of charges for violations of this statute and other euphemisms for the same activity thirty-two times since April 9, 1986. Charges for the possession of Class A drugs, heroin, began on April 4, 1989, and there were about twenty arrests for that. There were many charges for possession of a hypodermic needle as well.

The day before I saw her, Ms. Mortimer had been picked up on her way out of City Hospital, where she had had a tooth pulled, according to her appointed lawyer. She had been in default for a couple of years on a number of charges.

For all her troubles, Missy Mortimer still looked pretty good. Of course, when she was picked up she had not had the opportunity to put on her going-to-court suit, but she could still have fit into it.

Fortunately for Ms. Mortimer, sitting in the courtroom that day was Ms. Harriet Golden, the representative of a wonderful organization called Social Justice for Women. Ms. Golden's name describes her heart. She looks like she has seen it all, has come out the other side, and still has hope even when her clients do not.

During a recess so Ms. Golden could talk to Ms. Mortimer, Ms. Golden determined that Ms. Mortimer was on methadone, which she had not had that day, and that she was also on the "cocktail," a combination of protease inhibitors for the AIDS virus. Ms. Golden added that the Nashua Street Jail would not continue her on the protease inhibitors if she had to go there because I set bail that she could not meet, which was just about any bail at all.

In addition, Ms. Mortimer, who was petulant and angry through this proceeding, tossed out that she had just "terminated a pregnancy two days ago." Was that what her lawyer had called having a tooth removed? She paced the dock, a space about six feet by eight feet, restlessly, sometimes turning her back on all of us, particularly when her past was being discussed.

Of course, the young assistant district attorney wanted me to set high bail and, of course, Ms. Mortimer had no money and could not raise it. Ms. Mortimer was not being helpful; she was being junkie-bitchy as a matter of fact, absolutely negative about everything. There was no flirting with the judge today.

Missy Mortimer said, "The cops usually take me to BCH [Boston City Hospital] so I can get my methadone, but not these guys. I don't want to go anywhere for anything. Just let me out of here. Everything is cleared up in Roxbury and the thing in Lynn is a big mistake. It's a technical default."

I advised her frequently that Ms. Golden was trying to help her, and she would calm down for a few moments only to raise another obstacle. I knew that one cannot interrupt the taking of protease inhibitors and that to do so is to risk death. Ms. Mortimer had not been working the streets for over a year; at least she had not been arrested in that time. I don't think her absence was due to a conversion as much as to being worn out. But that is a reformation, isn't it? If she returned to the streets again, she would soon be caught. Maybe Ms. Golden could save her. You have to have hope, and experience shows that hoping that addicts can and will be rehabilitated is not always misplaced.

So I let Missy Mortimer go with Ms. Golden, who agreed to take her to other courts to clear up other defaults and to make sure that she took her medicines. Ms. Golden was going to do all this in spite of the fact that her program does not endorse the use of methadone.

As I passed the clerk's office on the way back to the judge's lobby, I saw Missy Mortimer and Ms. Golden requesting the paper that recalls default warrants.

Missy Mortimer turned toward me and mouthed silently, "Thank you."

{ vi }

ALTERNATIVES TO WAR

Family disputes appear in a variety of cases. Discovering the source of a particular family's dysfunction is not our job. The Law holds all people to standards of permissible behavior—even if they are related. Civility is the minimum behavior required in the courtroom, and often the behavior most lacking outside of it.

The title of this section is a variant of a statement my father, also a judge, made after a bomb exploded in his courthouse in the late sixties. His court officers carved out the inside of a law book to make a box they put a pistol in. After carrying the book and pistol to and from court for a few days he said, "I can't do this; I'm supposed to be an alternative to violence."

Courts are an alternative to the domestic wars in these stories. The parties in these cases have developed ways of dealing with each other that are overbearing, impolite, often nasty, and sometimes dangerous. The formality of the courtroom tries to level the playing field. It is in cases like these that I feel most stuffy. I think that I ought to be wearing a wig to add to my gravitas—in order to get people to behave decently to each other, at least while they are in court.

FAMILY BOUNDARIES

The computer shatters the family

§ § §

Norman and Michael Young are the brothers of Wendy Hassler, who is the mother of four-year-old Harry Hassler. The mother and grandmother of them all is Sophie Young. Michael Young lives with his wife and children across the street from Wendy Hassler in Braintree, a suburb south of Boston. Norman Young lives elsewhere in Braintree with his wife and children, and with the mother, Sophie.

Wendy Hassler came to court to obtain a restraining order against her brothers, Norman and Michael, to prevent them visiting Harry, who was a patient in the Massachusetts General Hospital with a potentially fatal kidney disease. Harry's father never appeared in court, and his name was never revealed. According to the brothers and the mother, the husband had been cuckolded by the computer.

The first time the case was called in front of me, only Ms. Hassler and her brother Michael were present. Wendy was short, slovenly, a little overweight with an old hairdo, a mullet, short on the top and long in the back. She wore jeans and a pink sweatshirt with bluebirds on it.

A very young lawyer, who introduced herself as Trixie McPhee Salerno, came forward and asked for a continuance. She said, "My boss, Attorney John Francis X. Walsh, the real lawyer in this case, is not able to be present today; he is in the Federal Court."

"Which Federal Court?" I asked.

She looked puzzled and added unresponsively, "Neither Norman Young nor Sophie Young are able to be present today either, and Sophie would be an essential witness."

There were two respondents in the case, so I asked Ms. McPhee

Salerno, "Who are you appearing for?" She seemed puzzled by the question and responded tentatively, "Mr. Walsh?"

I said, "I have just read the affidavit, and I do not think that Mr. Walsh is a party to this case. Which party do you represent?"

After a while, she replied, "The family."

I asked, "Which family?"

She looked puzzled again and said, "The Young family."

This was not much more helpful because, as Wendy Hassler's affidavit indicated, they were all members of the Young family, and they were in court because they were fighting amongst themselves.

I asked Wendy Hassler what her position was regarding the proposed continuance.

"They're just trying to wear me down," she said. "They've known of this date for two weeks. I don't know where Norman is, but I bet he's at work. I know my mother's at home; I talked to her twenty minutes ago. They probably haven't paid this guy Walsh and that's why he's not here. I could be with my son right now in the hospital. I've had it. Why can't we go forward without Norman? He had notice and he's not here. Mr. Walsh is Michael's lawyer. He doesn't represent Norman."

"Ms. McPhee Salerno, do you or Mr. Walsh represent Norman Young?" I asked.

She looked confused, then looked at Michael and said, "No."

Michael did not disagree.

"Then we'll have a hearing regarding the request for a restraining order against Norman Young, who, without excuse, has failed to appear. And, Ms. McPhee Salerno, at your request, I'll continue the case against Michael Young until a week from today. Tell Attorney Walsh that he should be here or to send someone who can handle the case. Ms. Hassler, please take the witness stand, and I will hear you regarding your request for a restraining order against Norman Young."

Wendy Hassler testified that her four-year-old son, Harry, had been admitted to the hospital at the end of May with severe kidney disease and that her brother Norman agreed to spend the night with him on various occasions. Her family did not appreciate that she did not spend twenty-four hours a day at the hospital. One time her brother Norman tried to pull her son away from the nurse at the hospital. Norman had been barred from the hospital. The hospital allowed Wendy Hassler to decide who could visit and who could not. She had both her brothers barred.

Two days after being barred, Norman came to the hospital and burst into the room saying, "No one is going to stop me from visiting my nephew."

This testimony was more or less in conformity with Wendy's affidavit, which accompanied the original request for the restraining order. Because Norman had not appeared after having received notice and had presented no excuse for not appearing, I granted the restraining order against him.

A week later I heard the case against Michael Young. Again Mr. Walsh was not there, although both Young brothers were. There was a new lawyer, a plain middle-aged man whose name and face I did not recognize. It was hard to distinguish between the two brothers. They were both tall, thin, and balding with a rim of dark hair. Norman wore glasses, and Michael didn't. They were very fidgety. Obviously this case was a matter of great concern to them. They sat with their mother on the left-hand side of the spectator's section. They wore jackets and ties, and their mother was appropriately dressed as well, in a dark suit.

Wendy, who had assumed her place at the plaintiff's table in front of me before I came out on the bench, again wore jeans and a sweatshirt. This one had cats on it. She was slouched in her chair as if she were watching a television set—or a computer screen. She did not seem discomfited by the legal process. As a matter of fact, it seemed like this was the day she had been waiting for.

These cases are always difficult, and their issues usually go back further than we are being told. In this case, I suspect the problem went back to the playpen. Wendy was younger than her brothers. She was thirty-seven; they were in their forties. She was the only girl in the family. I had the sense early on that her bringing this proceeding was a declaration of independence, if not the opening salvo in a revolutionary war. I was sure there had been skirmishes before, and I was not wrong.

As mentioned, they all lived in the same town, and Michael and Wendy lived across the street from each other. It turned out that Wendy's missing husband had been a friend of the brothers. Why he was missing from this proceeding was never explained, but it turned out that he was still on the hospital's list of permissible visitors. With absolutely no evidence, I surmised that he probably wanted to stay there, so he knew better than to mix in this fight. Because he had no part in these proceedings, I could surmise whatever I wanted about him.

Again Wendy testified first because she was the petitioner, the person seeking the relief, as we quaintly but aptly say.

She said, "My son Harry is very sick. He's in the hospital now; he's been there for five weeks. He's only four years old. I took care of him at home; he'd been sick for a long time, before this kidney problem was detected. My brothers don't think I spend enough time at the hospital. They want me to be there twenty-four hours a day. Sometimes I just can't do that. I have to get away. He's at the Mass General, the best hospital in the world. He has very good care. He's not alert. He doesn't even know that I'm there sometimes. Even though he doesn't appear to know that I'm there, I talk to him and comfort him. I'm a good mother."

She began to weep.

"My brothers are mad because I separated from my husband," she continued. "He was their friend. They took his side. They've always pushed me around. They've always bossed me. They think they can run my life." There was a long pause, and then she added, "Well, they can't."

She went from tears to triumph.

"When they come to the hospital, they argue with my friends. Michael got into a big fight with Joe Garvey, a friend of mine who's been a big help to me. They don't like him because he wears leather jackets and rides a motorcycle. I don't understand them. They've never understood me. They don't want to understand me. They treat me like a baby—a dumb baby. I just want them to leave me alone and to stay away from the hospital and stop disrupting my life and my son's life."

The brothers were leaning forward on either side of the mother in the back of the room. The mother had her hands to her face and was shaking her head from left to right. I felt very bad for her, not so bad for the brothers, and was somewhat sympathetic to Wendy.

The law under which Wendy was proceeding, Massachusetts General Laws, Chapter 209A, was originally created to prevent husbands from beating their wives. It has not been entirely successful in that regard, but probably more successful than it is given credit for. Of course, there are a number of men who continue to beat their wives or girlfriends, 209A restraining order or not. The law has been expanded to include people in all kinds of live-in relationships and other relatives. The drafters of the law probably did not anticipate the present situation, but according to present definitions, Wendy and her relationship with her brothers fit. However, implementation of the law in this case, if that's what I decided, would require some jerry-building.

The next witness was Michael. He said, "I love my sister. I've always loved my sister, but I'm not going to stand by and watch my nephew die." Becoming more emotional as he went on, he pounded on the little shelf on the front of the witness stand. "I swear on my father's grave I will not let my sister destroy these children." Apparently, Wendy also had two other children who were a lot older than poor Harry.

I told Michael, "I appreciate that this is an emotional matter for you and your family, but pounding on the witness stand is not going to help convince me that you should not be restrained from taking out your anger on your sister either here or outside this courtroom.

These outbursts only help convince me of the merits of your sister's case."

That advice was a little stronger than I usually give, but it seemed that somebody, like me, had to tone the situation down. It was obviously a war, and if we, the courts, were about anything, we were about being alternatives to these kinds of wars. In addition, although such drama may have worked in other forums, probably the mother's living room, it was not going to work here. I thought that Michael ought to know that.

Michael's lawyer came over to talk to Michael. Up to that point the lawyer had been a cipher, but if he could calm Michael down, I'd be grateful. Michael's brother, Norman, also came over. I tried not to eavesdrop even though I was only four or five feet away. I finally got up and walked to the other side of the bench.

More quietly, Michael continued: "All I want is the best for my nephew and the best for my sister, but she has been neglecting her family. Wendy has become addicted to the Internet sex chat rooms. After she got her husband out of the house, the way her kids have been taken care of has gone downhill. She spends three hundred dollars a month on long-distance phone calls. The kids don't go to school. We're going to have to call DSS [the Department of Social Services].

"What she calls a threat by us was 'please focus on your children.' Her kids' teachers also told my mother that the kids were being neglected long before Harry went to the hospital. This is what I want to talk to her about. That is what this is about. Wendy switched Harry from the local hospital to Mass General. She just sits there and plays with her laptop and giggles while the baby lies there sick or dying.

"Yes, I had a confrontation with her friend. I don't know where he came from. She found him on some computer chat room, a sex chat room. That's right, I'm the villain. She barred my mother, myself, my brother, and tried to bar the baby's father from the Mass General. My mother said 'I'd love to smash the computer.' We're trying to get her to focus on the children. That's it. That's all.

"I had a fight with her friend, Joe Garvey, or whatever his name is. He said to me, 'What's your fucking problem?' Pardon my language, but that's what he said. I gave him a piece of my mind. We were both upset. My brother and I have never physically or mentally abused my sister. I was going to buy a house with my sister."

The next witness was the mother, Sophie Young, who said, "Wendy was an excellent mother until she got hooked on the computer. Then her husband was no good. She got angry at me. All her husband asked her to do was to stop clicking all day and night. The husband had to get the children ready for school; he had to wash their hair; he had to dress them. One day when Harry got sicker, when he was peeing blood, Wendy called me at my sister's house and said she wanted me at the hospital. So I went at 10:45 PM. When I got there, I wasn't even on the [visitation] list. I couldn't get in. The next day at twelve o'clock noon she called me again and said, 'If you want to see Harry alive, you have to go to the hospital.' I took a cab from Quincy to Boston. Michael went as well. Some big guy came flying out of the room and just about knocked me over. Wendy said, 'Harry, look who's here! Grandma's here. Now you'll get well.'

"All of a sudden Wendy went flying out of the room. Then the nurse came flying into the room. The nurse is her friend. The nurse said, 'You must be Sophie Young.'

"'Yes, I'm the terror,' I said. I was joking. It was no threat. Meanwhile, my oldest son, Norman, stayed at the hospital while Wendy went home to click on the damn computer. I've given her thousands of dollars. She's thirty-seven years old, she should know better."

I glanced over at Wendy during her mother's testimony. She had a little half smile. At last they were listening to her. At last they had to pay attention to her. She had to come to court to get them to listen to her.

The child was Wendy's. The child was not her brothers'. She was not trying to keep her mother away.

I granted the restraining order, preventing the brothers from visiting the child in the hospital and keeping Norman a hundred yards from Wendy. Michael, who lived across the street from his sister, Wendy, certainly had to be allowed to enter and exit his own home. He, however, was to have no contact with his sister. The mother and brothers were visibly upset. Wendy appeared happy.

Just before I got off the bench, after the brothers and mother left, a tall blond man in black jeans and a leather jacket with a Harley Davidson emblem on the back came into the courtroom. He leaned over and put his arms around Wendy.

This must be Joe Garvey, the computer courtier, I said to myself.

CULTURE CLASH

A surprise witness clinches the case

§ § §

The issue was whether or not Hormosz Pahlevi had violated a restraining order put upon him by the Family Court at the request of his estranged wife during their much-contested divorce. If he had violated the order, his probation on an earlier case could be revoked, and he could go to jail.

The Commonwealth's evidence, which was provided by the divorce attorney for the ex-wife, Hillary O'Neill, was that after yet another custody battle in the Family Court a call was received at the house of Hillary's mother and that the mother had recognized the caller to be Hormosz Pahlevi.

If the call had indeed been made by Mr. Pahlevi, it was in violation of the restraining order that prohibited him from contacting Hillary directly or indirectly.

The consequence of a finding that Hormosz Pahlevi had made the call could be that he serve a sentence of one year in the House of Correction. This sentence had been suspended after he pled guilty some nine months earlier to a charge of assault against Hillary O'Neill. In that case, his ex-wife claimed that she and Hormosz had an argument during a period of reconciliation and that he went into a rage and began tearing the apartment apart. She claimed that at one point he ripped the phone from the wall and threw it at her. When the police came, they found the phone detached from the wall and behind the sofa. Hormosz Pahlevi was arrested, held over the long Fourth of July weekend in the Nashua Street Jail, and prosecuted. He had no money, so a lawyer had to be appointed for him. Unfortunately, that appointed lawyer was not very good, and she allowed and maybe even encouraged him to plead guilty and to accept the one-year suspended sentence and two years' probation.

Hormosz Pahlevi's new lawyer, Lisa Good, was one of the best in the stable of private lawyers who do bar advocate work. I was happy to see her because I knew that the case would be well tried from the defense side.

The father of the bride was an announcer on one of the most popular television shows in Boston. His name was Bradford O'Neill. That wasn't his real name, but rather the name he assumed upon coming to Boston. He had hoped that the name would evoke the best of two worlds: the Yankee Bradfords (the first governor of the Plymouth Colony and the fifty-seventh governor of Massachusetts were named Bradford) and the Irish O'Neills (the O'Neills were the first kings of all Ireland, and recently, of course, there had been Tip.)

Bradford O'Neill had been in the city for about twenty years, long enough for some people to forget that he came from Indianapolis and that his birth name was something else. Lucky for him that he looked Irish—or Yankee. He could pass. That is why he lived in the Back Bay.

He was kind of a "hoper" in the New World. Hopers were poor Catholic people in Ireland who went to bed hoping that they would wake up something else, like rich Protestants. If they actually became Protestants, they were called "soupers" or "ricers," which meant that they had taken the soup or the rice that the Protestants held out to them during the Famine in exchange for their conversion. It was hard to know if Bradford O'Neill had converted to anything: nobody knew what he had started out as.

Mr. O'Neill had the good sense not to appear at the trial of Hormosz Pahlevi, his ex-son-in-law. The starved-for-a-story media would have swarmed to the courthouse. A year before, they had all come to see a sportscaster in the dock charged with beating his girlfriend. Mr. O'Neill's wife, Cynthia, on the other hand, was present, and she had a lot to say. As a matter of fact, she was the key witness. It was she who claimed that Hormosz Pahlevi had made the incriminating call after the Family Court hearing. In the alleged phone call, the caller didn't say more than five words, but Mrs. O'Neill was sure that it was Hormosz Pahlevi who said them.

"Let me talk to her" were the words spoken, according to Mrs. O'Neill. If Mr. Pahlevi proved to be the speaker, he could go to jail for a year. That's seventy-three days per word.

Mrs. O'Neill testified that Hormosz Pahlevi had originally been extremely caring during his courtship of their daughter, but that later he did not seem to know how to be her partner rather than her master. He had been born and raised in Iran and had come to this country by way of Canada six years earlier. Most of his family was in either Canada or Iran.

"I can say honestly that my husband and I took this young man in," said Mrs. O'Neill, "but his behavior was mercurial and erratic. We were not dealing with a person who appreciated what we were doing."

Mrs. O'Neill's daughter and Mr. Pahlevi had married two years before. They had a baby girl, Eliza, who was now eighteen months old. The marriage began to have problems shortly after Eliza's birth, and the couple separated. Divorce proceedings were under way. There had been ongoing problems and many trips to court. Mrs. O'Neill said, "Hormosz Pahlevi has not behaved at all well during this entire matter. My daughter has been very loving and very eager to work at it throughout."

On the day of the phone call, Hillary O'Neill was scheduled to be in Family Court with her lawyer to try to resolve custody and visitation issues. Hormosz Pahlevi had petitioned for more visitation time with his daughter. Before Hillary O'Neill arrived home from court that day, Mrs. O'Neill had received two or three hang-up phone calls. At 5:30 PM came the caller who said, "Let me talk to her." Cynthia O'Neill remembered the time because she looked at the clock knowing that she would have to remember it in order to report it.

Mrs. O'Neill continued, "I replied, 'Who is this? What do you want?' and the caller hung up. It was very upsetting. I know that it was Hormosz Pahlevi. I had heard his voice a number of times. He has a high voice for a man his size, as well as an accent. I know it was him."

On cross-examination, Mrs. O'Neill revealed that she had a device on the phone that permitted her to retrieve the numbers of callers but that she did not use it on that day. She also indicated that she and her husband were paying for their daughter's divorce and that the divorce lawyer, Henry T. Gilles III, Esq., was called right after the call in question, before her daughter returned from court. Mr. Gilles III recommended that the police be notified. When Hillary arrived home shortly thereafter, she and Mrs. O'Neill discussed the events of the day at the Family Court, and Mrs. O'Neill learned that Hormosz Pahlevi had received greater visitation.

"No, I was not happy about that," said Mrs. O'Neill in response to Lisa Good's question.

Her daughter and granddaughter were on public assistance. They lived with her and her husband in their house in the Back Bay. Hillary had a part-time job at a television station.

"Yes, it is true that I did not want my daughter to marry Hormosz Pahlevi," Mrs. O'Neill replied after much prompting by Ms. Good and over the prosecutor's frequent objections. The question was admissible to show bias. It was apparent that Mrs. O'Neill was the closest thing to a percipient witness in this case. It was her observation that would sink Hormosz Pahlevi, if anything would, and if that observation was colored by her dislike of him, then the bias should be revealed.

The next witness for the prosecution was the divorce lawyer, Henry T. Gilles III, Esq. It is very unusual for a lawyer to testify in any court proceeding, and prohibitions exist against lawyers testifying in certain circumstances. Based on what I had heard thus far, I could not imagine what he would add, but as this was not a case in front of a jury, little harm could come of his testimony. Besides, the defense attorney, Ms. Good, did not object. And if it proved to be unethical for Henry T. Gilles III, Esq., to testify, he would pay the consequences determined by the Board of Bar Overseers, the ethical committee that oversees lawyers.

Another factor in my decision to allow the attorney to testify was that I share the sentiment that there should be open and full disclosure in matters heard by a judge without a jury. The rationale for this sentiment is that the judge can cull out what is irrelevant and that it is important for parties to feel that they have had their say. This sentiment is insulting to the *Rules of Evidence*, particularly those about relevance and materiality, but the law is full of paradoxes, just like life. Frankly, I do not think that losing parties take consolation from anything if they are convinced that they are right.

Be all that as it may be, Henry T. Gilles III, Esq., testified. It would have been better for his side if he hadn't, and I guess that Ms. Good had taken his measure and knew that that would be so. Lisa Good let him go on and on, and as he did he became more and more pompous—almost as pompous as he looked in his three-piece English suit, two-toned shirt, watch fob from the lapel, and foulard bow tie. He talked about Mr. Pahlevi's behavior at hearings that cross-examination revealed Mr. Gilles had not attended; he had sent his "very able assistant." On cross-examination, he revealed that it was his suggestion to contact the probation office to bring this revocation hearing, that he was being paid $400 per hour to represent Hillary O'Neill, and, most damning, that he was billing for his attendance and testimony at this hearing.

His interesting news was that Hormosz Pahlevi was obsessed with the O'Neill family and that he had leafleted their Back Bay neighborhood with "dozens, no, hundreds of flyers accusing Bradford O'Neill of all kinds of dreadful things, including trying to keep Hormosz Pahlevi away from his daughter." Curiously, Mr. Gilles did not have even one of these flyers, even though he had gone to court "on behalf of the family" to enjoin this behavior.

Even though the hearing may have been more open and complete as a result of Attorney Gilles III's testimony, the testimony was by and large irrelevant to the issue at hand and expensive for the O'Neills in more ways than money.

However, Mr. Gilles III's testifying was relevant in a way that I am sure he had not intended. It appeared to me that he was using this procedure, with its possible outcome of Mr. Pahlevi's year-long imprisonment, to gain leverage and bolster his client's (or her mother's) position in the divorce proceeding. I had heard that some divorce lawyers constantly harassed opposing parties with Family Court appearances for trivial reasons. I had also heard about their abuse of restraining orders.

The next witness was the supposed real party in interest, Hillary O'Neill. Except that she had dark rather than gray hair, she looked like her mother—about five foot six, solid, plain in an intellectual way, in a full-flowered skirt and a black jacket, no makeup.

There was a reluctance about her. She hesitated to say anything bad about Hormosz Pahlevi. She said that during the entire time that she had known him his only physical act of abuse was the throwing of the telephone, which had resulted in the assault conviction, but she expressed uncertainty that it had been thrown at her.

Oh, great! I thought. *This guy may be going to go to jail, and now you're saying that you are not even sure that you were assaulted, that the phone was aimed at you? Where were you when he needed you, at the time of the plea to a one-year suspended sentence? Are you taking a dive for this guy now? What is the reason for this less-than-passionate testimony?* Maybe she now realized that he was being railroaded by her parents and this bogus duke in the three-piece suit. Maybe she still loved the guy! She certainly was not as prosecutorial as her mother.

Hillary O'Neill had gone to a private country day school in the Boston suburbs and then to Brown; she had traveled in Europe for a while and then worked in New York for a film-production company. She was now twenty-five years old and had been back in Boston for a little more than two years. She met Hormosz Pahlevi at a bookstore in Cambridge, and they went out a few times. When she realized that she was pregnant, she wanted to have the baby whether he married her or not.

Hormosz Pahlevi had said he wanted to marry her, and she was willing for the baby's sake, although she was not optimistic about the marriage. The cultural differences were too great. He thought that he owned her once they were married, and he expected more help from her father than was forthcoming. Her father had been very helpful, renting a house for them in Somerville and lending Mr. Pahlevi $10,000 for his plumbing business. When the business failed, Hormosz Pahlevi blamed her and her father for not supporting him enough.

Mr. Pahlevi had abided by the terms of visitation laid down by the Family Court, which included a supervised drop-off of the baby, Eliza. He appeared to love Eliza, and she appeared to love him.

"My family dislikes Hormosz Pahlevi because of the leafleting," Hillary said. "They don't want our dirty linen hanging out all over the Back Bay."

Although Hillary was "not in fear of Hormosz"—she said "his whole mode of argument was threats, for example, 'If you don't do this, I'm going to spit on you' "—she seemed wearied by his Middle Eastern drama.

As for his courtroom behavior this day, Hormosz Pahlevi had been well instructed by his lawyer. He did not move an inch during Hillary's testimony. I don't think that he even blinked. As a matter of fact, he was very well-behaved during the entire proceeding, in marked contrast to the way his adversaries were testifying he had behaved in the Family Court. Mr. Gilles III had testified that the Family Court judge had called in extra security because of Mr. Pahlevi, and Hillary O'Neill had reported that he constantly interrupted everyone, including the judge.

Now there may have been any number of reasons for the difference in his behavior. Here he was represented by counsel. He may have thought lawyers behaved differently in the Family Court and presented himself in kind. He may have realized that his liberty was at stake in my court. The difference may have been sexist: the Family Court judge was a woman. Perhaps he was recreating the way trials were conducted in Iran. The trial of the mayor of Teheran seemed to have been a donnybrook. Or, like so many other parties who represent themselves, he may have thought the way cases were tried on TV was the proper way to proceed. Whatever the reason for his prior bad behavior, I was glad that Lisa Good kept him under control.

Hillary O'Neill acknowledged the over-influence of her family and called it that. On the other hand, Hormosz Pahlevi also leaned on her father, who tried to resolve their disputes. It was clear that she resented Mr. Pahlevi's appeal to male solidarity and her father's apparent acquiescence in it. "It was as if he said to my father, 'Here's what your daughter is doing; you correct it; we're the men here,'" she said.

And then on a third hand, just as I was thinking I knew where Hillary O'Neill was coming from, she said, "I don't like having my family threatened."

She was understandably dealing with a lot of mixed feelings, and she was more credible as a result. I knew what Hillary's mother wanted and that Mr. Gilles III wanted to gild his divorce case and its fee, but Hillary O'Neill was a more difficult read, even to herself. Of course, the only issue for me to determine was whether Hormosz Pahlevi had breached the term of probation that forbade contact with Hillary O'Neill.

I thought that the case was going to end at the conclusion of Hillary O'Neill's testimony, and it was close to time for lunch. However, when the Commonwealth rested, Attorney Lisa Good surprised us all by announcing, "The defense calls Ms. Janine McMurray."

A plump, blonde woman, who had been sitting unobtrusively in the back row throughout the trial stood up and came forward to the witness stand. The prosecutor and Mr. Gilles III looked at each other quizzically.

Ms. McMurray was thirty-seven years old. She had been a social worker with the Massachusetts Department of Social Services for fourteen years after receiving her master's degree in social work from Tufts University. She specialized in domestic-abuse cases and had been the head of the regional section of the department for Middlesex County for five years. From the qualifying questions and answers, I thought that she was going to be testifying as some kind of expert witness. I was wrong.

"I met Hormosz Pahlevi in September six years ago," she said, "when he came to repair my sink. We began going out a few months after we met, and we lived together up until the time that he married Ms. O'Neill. We live together again, since his separation.

"I was with him the day of the last hearing, the day of this alleged call. I picked him up at the courthouse, and we returned to my house. I was with him all the time after that case. He never made a phone call. As a matter of fact, at 5:30 PM we were in my car on the way to a restaurant in Cambridge. He was very happy that he had received more visitation time; he was happy with the hearing that day. We were going out to celebrate. He loves his daughter. All that he wants is to be able to spend more time with her. He is afraid that the O'Neills will make his daughter forget that he exists and that they are trying to get him deported. That is his worst fear."

I declined to surrender the defendant and continued the probation to the original date.

MOTHER AND SON

Drunk driving and maternal devotion don't mix

§ § §

I was in the men's room on the Provincetown-to-Boston boat. I sensed somebody to my right, a couple of urinals down on the starboard side, but I was not going to look. Men can get arrested for that kind of behavior. Besides it was my blind side, and it was hard enough for me to tend to the business at hand on the rocking boat. I could, however, sense that he was looking at me. He finished before I did. He was at the drying machine drying his hands when I got to the sink.

He said, "I know you. Uh, huh, Judge, do you remember me? I bet you don't recognize me."

I looked a little more closely with my one good eye and said, "But I do."

He was about five foot ten, good-looking in a soft, slightly sad way, kind of like an Italian movie actress, almost pretty. He was dressed in designer blue jeans and an expensive sweatshirt. He had a good tan, although he was dark to begin with.

One afternoon, two or three years before, I had been called back into the second session in the late afternoon, and there he'd been, in the dock, drunk—Joey Iaconi. The daily duty bar advocate had already talked to him. At arraignment, my task was to inform Mr. Iaconi of the charge against him, determine if he could afford his own lawyer, appoint the bar advocate if he could not afford his own lawyer, set bail or other terms of release, and arrange dates for further proceedings.

Joey's mother was in the audience. She was also tall, probably about fifty-five and handsome in a suburban way—frosted hair, tortoise-shell sunglasses, and a brown tweed suit. Joey had been arrested the night before for his fourth violation of driving under the influence of intoxicating liquor and was certain to go to prison if convicted. There was no getting around it. It was a mandatory sentence. His mother wanted him to be released on bail and to go back to her.

I recognized Joey that day in court too. I had seen him before in the South End. He was a friend of someone I knew, but I could not think of who. To the extent that I had thought about him the first time he was in my company, I had thought that he was silly. My first instinct in court that day was to withdraw, known in legal terms as recusal, but then I realized that I did not really know this guy at all. At most I had been introduced to him once. What I did know was not going to influence me, so I rethought recusal. What if I were the judge in Nantucket where everybody knows everybody else, where almost everybody is related? I gave myself the Massachusetts test for recusal: *Could I be impartial?* Yes. *Could my impartiality reasonably be questioned?* No.

It is extraordinary how well-behaved most criminal defendants are in court. By and large, they are respectful. They don't speak out, don't interrupt, and appear to respect the process even when it is going to result in incarceration for long terms. Temper tantrums and outbursts are rare.

Drunks are different, as are entitled suburbanites. Joey Iaconi was both. Somewhere in the court papers was a court-clinic psychologist's examination that gave short shrift to Joey's alcoholism but had a great time speculating about his dysfunctional relationship with his mother. Hints of "emotional incest" abounded. I flipped through it while I decided whether or not he should be released on bail.

I also read the police report, which indicated that Joey Iaconi's truck had been seen weaving down Boylston Street at 5:30 AM. Ten minutes later, Joey was found standing across the street from it, urinating on the Kahlil Gibran memorial in Copley Square. Nobody could put Joey behind the wheel, however. The prosecution was going to have a problem proving that Joey was the operator, and "operation"—doing anything that would get the vehicle moving—was an essential element of the crime. The case could not even go to a jury if there was not some evidence on this point, and inferences alone were not sufficient to prove operation.

Although the probation department's intake report indicated that Joey could afford to pay for his own lawyer, he was in no condition to call one, so I appointed the daily duty lawyer who had talked to him to represent him for arraignment only. The issue at hand was whether or not I should set bail and in what amount. His appointed defense lawyer's first words were, "His mother is here and would like to speak." I said, "I don't really think it is necessary that the mother speak. You are Mr. Iaconi's lawyer today, and you can tell me what his mother has to say if it is relevant to this proceeding."

As I was saying this, the mother came charging through the bar and approached close to the bench. She remained far enough back that she could keep an eye on her son in the dock to her left.

"I'm Joey's mother," she started in, "and I do have something to say. He was a wonderful boy until he went to high school and began to drink, but he's not really an alcoholic. I know he's been arrested for this and that, but he's not an alcoholic. He's a wonderful boy, and he's just troubled."

At this point, the bedraggled Joey in last night's disco outfit started screaming at his mother: "You've never understood me! You've never accepted the fact that I'm gay. You want to run my life. You won't leave me alone. Get out! I don't want to see you! I don't want to have anything to do with you. Get out! You never accepted me."

The mother moved toward him in the dock but was gently guided back by the court officer. She said, "Joey, I accept you. I've always accepted you the way you are—whatever way you are. Don't say that! You know that I have, Joey. I don't care if you're gay. It doesn't matter to me that you're gay. Just stop all this and come home with me. I know your brothers have been mean to you, but you know I love you however you are, whatever way you are, so please stop this and come home with me."

As his mother approached, Joey moved back even though he was confined in a space no larger than eight feet by six feet. He screamed, "I'm not going anywhere with you! I'd rather spend two years in jail than be with you! Judge, tell her to get out of here! Tell her to get out of my life!" He looked up at me. "Do what you can, just get her out."

Realizing that this was a duet that had been sung before in just about every key, I finally said, "This is enough. You both have to be quiet. I'll hear from the lawyers. Mrs. Iaconi, please return to your seat." Unbelievably, both Joey and his mother became quiet.

The assistant district attorney, an earnest young woman in an imitation man's suit with a skirt, said, "Judge, this is his fifth driving-under-the-influence case. He's facing suspended sentences in two other courts. It's clear that he's drunk now. He was caught in a truck full of old furniture."

Again from the dock, Joey stumbled toward the rail, "It's only the fourth! And it isn't old furniture. Those are antiques. They were commodes and shutters and Sheraton chairs."

"Just be quiet now. I'm going to let your lawyer speak," I said as authoritatively as I could under the circumstances.

"Judge, it isn't old furniture," Joey said getting the last word, with a drunken grin. He was the center of attention now, and he was not going to let go of it. The mother had returned to her seat where she sat with that ancient Italian maternal gesture, biting her hand.

"Ms. Defense Attorney," I asked, "What do you say?"

"Judge, he hasn't been convicted of this operating-under-the-influence case, whether it's his fourth or his fifth. There is a presumption of innocence. His condition may not be so terrific today, but we don't know whether he was the driver of the truck when it was weaving down the street. Even if he was, we don't know if he got into this condition before he got in the truck or after he got out of it at Copley Square. Judge, you can see that the Commonwealth is going to have a hard time proving 'operation.' We don't know whether his condition influenced his ability to operate the motor vehicle. I don't think you can draw the inference. I think you have to give him the benefit of the doubt. My client is a reputable antiques dealer in Wellesley. He has lived in this area all his life; his mother lives here; his family lives here. He is not a risk of flight."

"All right, thank you very much."

I filled out the bail form, checking off previous convictions, previous defaults (of which there were many), and drug dependency (where I wrote in "alcohol" in case the Superior Court judge to whom this bail decision was appealed did not know that alcohol is also a drug). I noted that Joey was also being surrendered on his probation for a previous similar charge, and I set bail at $5,000. The clerk read out, "Bail is set at five thousand dollars. Please pick dates for motions and trial."

From the dock Joey yelled, "Ma, get that money out of my account! Get that money out of my account and call that bastard lawyer who cheated me out of twenty thousand dollars. He said he'd keep me out of jail the last time. He owes me. Get the money out of my account! Ma, get it out!"

"Ma" still had her hand in her mouth. I got up, left the bench, and went back to my lobby hoping that Ma wouldn't rush to the bank.

MOTHER AND DAUGHTER

"My daughter is a drug addict. Let me out of here."

§ § §

One afternoon while I was hearing a civil case in Room 377, the main civil-trial courtroom, the chief court officer for civil business slipped in, came to the side of the bench, and waited for me to acknowledge him and slide my chair over. He quietly asked if I would hear a restraining order. I think I made a face. I was in the middle of an interesting trial, it was not my assignment to deal with restraining orders while I was sitting in that room, and I was not the judge who had issued the preliminary restraining order. I agreed to the request, however. Having been told that all the other judges assigned to civil cases were busy, I trusted that the chief court officer had exhausted the alternatives. He was a master diplomat at dealing with us judges, who sometimes could be difficult. Furthermore, restraining orders take precedence over other civil matters. There is an urgency about restraining orders. All of which left me with little choice but to interrupt the trial I was hearing.

The original restraining order had been issued the previous Friday night by an emergency-response judge not on my court. I understood this would be the second hearing to extend the order for a year if the person who was the object of the order was present or had received notice of its terms.

An attractive blonde woman in her late sixties came into the courtroom accompanied by a younger woman. The clerk informed me that rather than have the second hearing to continue the order, he had been told (by whom I do not know) that the older woman wanted to vacate the restraining order against her daughter. I presumed that the young woman with her, who was plainly dressed in a serious modern-yet-fashionable way, was the daughter.

I asked the older woman, the petitioner, what it was that she wanted. She looked toward the younger woman, and the younger woman started to talk. "Mrs. Gritti wants to vacate the restraining order," she said.

"Wait a minute," I said. "Aren't you the respondent, the daughter, in this case?"

"No, I'm not. I'm Mr. Wiley's law student."

"Excuse me?" I asked.

"Yes, I'm the law student working with Mr. Wiley."

"And who is Mr. Wiley?"

"Mr. Wiley represents the daughter, Monica Gritti, who is being held in the women's dock in the second session on a charge of assault and battery with a dangerous weapon."

"On whom?" I said, surrendering to the tyrannical "whom," but only so I could hang on the *m* for emphasis, as one does with "Ommmm."

"On her mother, Mrs. Gritti," said the young woman.

"Let me get this straight. You work for the criminal defense lawyer who is representing the daughter, the respondent, the person against whom this restraining order was sought?"

"Yes, and Mr. Wiley suggested that I escort the mother down here to vacate the restraining order."

"Well, she can't just vacate the restraining order," I said haughtily. "Only the court can vacate the restraining order. It is an order of the court."

The law student looked at me, mystified, wondering why I was obfuscating and obstructing this process, which had been so clearly explained to her by Mr. Wiley.

"Mrs. Gritti," I asked, "what do you want?"

She shrugged her shoulders in resignation, like the great Italian film actress Anna Magnani, indicating that she was only doing what she was told. The world, and especially this world of lawyers, judges, and drug-addicted daughters, was too much for her.

"Look, Judge," she said, "I'm going to Florida tomorrow. Saturday night I asked my daughter to come over and get some of her stuff. I've had a lot of problems with my daughter, but I wanted her to be able to take her stuff out of my house before I moved. She came over. She was high again. We got in a fight. She started hitting me with a lamp. I called the police. She got arrested, and I got another restraining order. I'd gotten two of them before because I just can't have her around. She steals everything and that's why I'm moving to Florida. But she's in jail now, and her lawyers say this will help her if I get rid of the restraining order."

"Well," I said, "Mrs. Gritti, I'm sympathetic to your position, but I don't think I'm going to do that, and Ms.—what's your name?"

"Holmstrom," said the aspiring lawyer.

"Ms. Holmstrom, as for Mr. Wiley, you tell him that I believe that his conduct is unethical, that the *Canons of Ethics and Disciplinary Rules Regulating the Practice of Law* prohibit him from talking to this woman and giving her advice as to what she should do about this restraining order. Tell Mr. Wiley to look at those rules, particularly Rules 7-104(A)(1), and (A)(2)."

That was before lunch. In the middle of the afternoon, when I had returned to the interrupted civil trial, Mrs. Gritti, the mother, appeared and sat in the back of the courtroom. Shortly thereafter, Mr. Wiley, a man in his early forties, skinny, slovenly, and rude, appeared through the back door of the courtroom, walked up to the clerk seated in front of me, and began to talk to him loudly. I quietly told him to sit down and pointed out that we were in the middle of other business. He sulked, left the room, but reappeared shortly and sat right in the middle of the chairs lined up in front of the bar. At some point I took a recess from the matter I was hearing and left the bench for as long as it took me to visit the facilities in the judges' lobby.

The clerk announced as I returned to the bench, "Mr. Wiley seeks a rehearing on the motion to vacate the restraining order of Mrs. Gritti against her daughter, Monica." Although the temptation was to say "denied!" right away, I resisted and told the clerk that we would do so at the end of the testimony of the witness in the case I was in the process of hearing.

Mr. Wiley began, "Judge, I demand a rehearing on the motion to vacate the restraining order sought by Mrs. Gritti against her daughter, Monica."

"And who do you represent?"

"I represent Monica Gritti and, in addition, I resent your implication that my conduct is unethical in talking to her mother."

"It wasn't an implication and resent it you might, but it's a violation of the disciplinary rules for you to represent a party on one side of a civil matter and to advise a party on the other side of the same civil matter, especially when the advice you give is not in her interest. Look at the disciplinary rules."

"But, Judge, in order to mount a good criminal defense, I have to talk to the mother . . ."

"That's not what I'm talking about, Mr. Wiley, and you know that. What are you doing talking to this woman who has to leave town because her daughter's been stealing from her for so long that she can't stay in her own house? I think you're taking advantage of the weakness of the mother, and I'm not inclined to vacate the restraining order."

I should note that the daughter had been brought in during the recess as well. She was sitting in handcuffs near the court officer at a table next to Mr. Wiley. She was probably in her late twenties, and she had a head of long golden curly hair like a Sienese painting of an angel—but her face looked whipped by drugs. She was dressed neatly in jeans and a white shirt, but she could not sit still. She was probably still detoxing. She never looked at her mother, although the mother sometimes sneaked a peek at her.

"This is the third restraining order Mrs. Gritti has taken out against her daughter. Obviously the other two didn't work because she had to come back and get another one. I'm not inclined to grant your request."

"But, Judge, Mrs. Gritti wants it. The mother told me she wants it. I'm here to tell you that."

"Mr. Wiley, you do not represent the mother." Then leaning to the mother, I asked again, "Mrs. Gritti, what is it that you want?"

"They told me to come back here and ask you again," she said with resignation and dismay, and she looked at Mr. Wiley and his student. "They told me it would be better for my daughter if I did that. I can't live with her. I can't have her around. I just want to get out of town. I'm supposed to leave tomorrow or the next day. They told me that she'd probably get out of jail if I came here and got rid of the restraining order. That it would look better for her if I—what do you call it?—vacated it. She's my daughter, I don't want her to stay in jail, but I can't live with her. I can't have her around. She abuses me. She steals from me and makes my life miserable. I just want to go to Florida."

Mrs. Gritti had just given me all the reasons for extending the order.

I said to Mr. Wiley, "In order for a restraining order to be vacated, a judge has to approve a request to vacate, am I correct?"

"Yes, you are."

"So, if the judge can approve, the judge can also disapprove?"

"No, he can't. He or she can't, ever," said Mr. Wiley, ever gender correct even though he was going to take advantage of this poor old woman for the sake of his abusive client.

"If I have no choice in the matter, why am I given a choice?"

"You're not given a choice."

"Then you don't need me to do anything? Why are you here? Why did the Legislature require that a judge vacate these orders?"

Finally there was no response. So, after the pause, I said, "The motion to vacate is denied."

SLANDER

A case is expensively solved for short money

§ § §

The members of the Kyrenia Club of Boston were former residents of a town on the north coast of Cyprus, many of whom had been driven out by the Turkish occupation in 1974. They bought a row of buildings deep in a part of the city where nobody else lived, where there were only warehouses, parking lots, and body shops. They had a clubhouse in the middle of the row with its name printed on the arch above the door in Greek uncial letters. I had often passed by their buildings on my way to somewhere else and recalled having read an article in the home section of the *Boston Globe* about the buildings' conversion. I admired the club members' industry.

The facts of this case were not in dispute. Four years before the trial there had been a national meeting of the Kyrenia clubs of North America in Boston. While the plaintiff, Nicholas Patakis, was speaking, evoking the members' common heritage in front of delegates from each of the other forty Kyrenia clubs in the United States and Canada, the defendant, Harry Vafiades, shouted out in Greek, "Don't believe that guy; he's a crook. He's a crook! He stole fifty thousand dollars from the club, and he spent it! Nick Patakis stole fifty thousand dollars from the club."

The defense lawyer was willing to stipulate that the statement had been made by his client. I tried to figure out why, and at first speculated that he may have wanted to avoid the sting of its repetition by the plaintiff and his cohorts with their displays of the appropriate emotions of shame, rage, and hurt. In addition, the answer to the complaint did not deny that Mr. Vafiades had made the statement.

Rather, the defense was going to be that the statement was true! Truth is a defense to slander, unless the slander is malicious.

The plaintiff, Nick Patakis was represented by his nephew, John Patakis. The nephew, who was second-generation American, was taller than everyone else. It must've been the milk. He was also bald, but compensated with a Van Dyke beard and mustache and a big chest. He wore a double-breasted, blue Italian suit and a beautiful tie on a winged collar shirt. His uncle was not so sartorially accomplished; he wore an old gray-tweed jacket and a two-toned brown tie loose at the collar. He was probably in his sixties and had wiry gray hair.

The defendant, Harry Vafiades, who looked like Nick Patakis two sizes larger, except that he had suspiciously black hair, wore a brown cardigan sweater. He was represented by the sixty-seven-year-old Alan Masson, a workhorse in our court and a very good civil-trial lawyer, usually in contract cases. Mr. Masson often frustrated judges because he would not give an inch. He once told me regarding his opponents, "If they bring me to the courthouse, I am going to try the case. I settle before the trial date or not at all."

It was not going to be an easy day.

The parties and their respective retinues sat in back on either side of the spectator section of the courtroom. On the left, Nick Patakis, the plaintiff, was sitting with a stocky, blondish woman about his age and three other middle-aged-to-elderly men. Harry Vafiades, the defendant, was on the right, flanked by two young men who were his sons. One of them appeared to be interpreting for him. There was another man, thin and ascetic-looking, right behind them.

Nick Patakis was the first witness. Over Mr. Masson's objections, he told us that he had come to America as a fourteen-year-old kid and got his first job in a shop belonging to "an Italian guy" cobbling shoes. He eventually bought the shop but lived in a room in back for five years. He moved to an apartment so that he could send back to Kyrenia for a wife. After she arrived, he brought his brothers and sisters over, and he eventually bought a house in Roslindale. He and his wife had no children.

His wife, he said, "God rest her soul, God rest her soul, had died three years before this incident. Thank God, she didn't live to be embarrassed by this humiliation." Mr. Patakis testified that he had spent the past four years "trying to restore his reputation in the local club and nationally because of this outrageous slander which was spread across the country by that Vafiades," and he glared at Mr. Vafiades.

I was very impressed, but my first impression was about to be slightly diminished. Plaintiffs present their case, and then the defendants present theirs. Because plaintiffs may not get another chance to speak, they and their lawyers often feel obliged to respond in advance to what they expect the defense to be. In this case the defense was that the statement was more or less true, meaning that Nick Patakis felt he had to tell me why it wasn't true, and that involved a complicated story that removed some of the gilt on his lily.

In 1992 and 1993, the treasurer of the Kyrenia Club was Mr. Patakis's nephew—not the nephew trying this case but another nephew named Demetrios. Demetrios had "borrowed" some money from the club, not the $50,000 mentioned by Mr. Vafiades but $14,000 to pay off some of the debts for his gas station, as well as for part of a down payment on a two-family house in Roslindale.

Nick Patakis was not happy about Demetrios's "loan to himself" from the club, but the matter had been resolved, and everybody in the club knew what had happened.

"Was there full disclosure, Mr. Patakis?" asked the lawyer nephew.

"What?"

"Was there full disclosure, Mr. Patakis?" repeated the nephew.

"What's that?" said Nick Patakis.

"Did you tell everybody in the club about your nephew and about his borrowing fourteen thousand dollars?" asked John Patakis again, with heavy emphasis on "borrowing."

"I did, and he did. We had a meeting of the membership, the entire membership. It was announced on the radio, and my nephew—I made my nephew stand up and tell everybody what he'd done, and I helped him out to repay the money. And that guy," he said, pointing to Mr. Vafiades, "was there as was his son, the one on the right. They all heard my nephew say what happened, and they all were there."

There is nothing like a good display of righteous indignation. Nick Patakis choked up as he spoke. I did too as a matter of fact, but I had to duck down and pretend that I had dropped something. I am not supposed to show my emotional response to the evidence of one side or the other. Mr. Masson jumped up, objecting. I overruled the objections.

Although the case was being heard four years after the incident, time had not dissipated the bad feelings. They had become more intense. In a slander case it is essential that the plaintiff prove that somebody else heard the slanderous statement. Just as someone must see the tree falling in the forest, the slanderous statement must be made to someone else—"published" is the legal jargon, but in this context it does not mean printed. The more people who hear the statement, the greater the disgrace but the better for the plaintiff in terms of damages to be recovered.

Therefore, the blondish woman who had been sitting to the right of Nick Patakis was called to testify. Her name was Anna Athanopolous. I was a little worried about her. During the defense attorney's opening, she had practically hissed from her seat in the back. She kept nudging the plaintiff and pointing at Mr. Masson, as well as looking darts at the defendant on the other side of the room. At one point I had to ask her to please compose herself. When she didn't, I called the lawyers to the sidebar to inform the plaintiff's lawyer, the nephew, that she was doing his side no good with such dramatics. Because he was facing me he could not see her. I told him that no jury was there to see her grimaces and gestures and that I was impervious to them, which is probably not true. I find such antics irritating.

Attorney John Patakis walked over and had a brief conversation with her. Thereafter, she sat up straight and buttoned her lips, for my benefit, no doubt. If she were that loose a cannon off the stand, what would she be like while testifying?

Like Mr. Patakis, Anna Athanopolous was in her sixties. But unlike Mr. Patakis, she had been born in Boston, and she had gone to Boston public schools, Girls' Latin, and then to Simmons College. What was astonishing to me was her accent and formal grammatical construction. She spoke like one of the nuns who taught me in grammar school, broad *a*'s and all. Where other people would have said "I will," Ms. Athanopolous said "I shall."

From her age, I could tell that she would have gone to school in the days when most of Boston's teachers were Irish American spinsters. (A friend who is a former Boston city councilor is an expert on the various Boston accents. If he had heard her, he could have picked the parish of her teachers.) She was maybe five foot two, shorter than all the men concerned, who were about five foot six and built like hydrants. The blonde was by her own hand, but not recently, and was mixed with steely gray. She wore a gray suit, a blouse up to her neck, and low, sensible shoes.

In response to Attorney John Patakis's questions, Ms. Athanopolous said that she had been the secretary of the Kyrenia Club for almost twenty years and that she was present on that fateful day in May of 1994 when Harry Vafiades had defamed Nick Patakis. If we wanted her opinion (which I didn't and which wasn't admissible), it was "nothing but a power play and an attempt to take over the club by Vafiades's friends."

Mr. Masson again got to his feet to object. She glared at him.

I sustained his objection. She glared at me.

At this point I was inclined to agree with Anna Athanopolous, but I could not permit her to decide whether these remarks were slander, as much as she was determined to do so. Therefore, I constrained her to answer the questions and to keep her opinions to herself. She apologized contritely, if not sincerely.

Ms. Athanopolous added most emphatically that the event had been a very important meeting of the national organization. She repeated again how terrible it was for Mr. Vafiades to have slandered Mr. Patakis in this fashion. She said that Harry Vafiades was jealous of Nick Patakis's success; that he, Harry Vafiades, had never amounted to anything because he wasn't as hard-working as Mr. Patakis. In addition, Harry Vafiades had had a little too much wine that night, which was not unusual, by the way. She pointed out that the statement was not an isolated attempt to remove Nick Patakis or his friends as organization president and officers. Three years prior, there had been an attempt to run an opposition slate. "Someone had even run against me," she said.

She was very articulate, very appropriately angry, and not to be reined in by me or any of the lawyers. She also had a sense of humor and invoked false humility: "I don't know what I'm supposed to say or not say. Just tell me when to be quiet. They say I talk too much, but I'm too old to change."

Anna Athanopolous praised the plaintiff as being single-handedly responsible for the well-being of the Kyrenia community in Boston. Most recently he had donated $2,000 for the young people's dancing troupe so that they could buy or make new costumes. He had been one of the three founders of the local organization, which itself had been one of the first Kyrenia clubs in North America. The other two founders were dead.

The only other witness was the treasurer of the organization, Costa Kavafis. He was the poetic-looking man sitting behind Harry Vafiades and his sons. He was very sensitive to the whole situation. He may have initially sided with the insurgents, the defendant's camp, in the power struggle, but he certainly didn't sanction the remarks that the defendant had made that night.

Called as a witness by the plaintiff, even though he had come to court with the defense, Mr. Kavafis discussed the plaintiff's nephew's loan and the secrecy that surrounded that affair. When pressed by Attorney John Patakis, he acknowledged that Harry Vafiades had said that Nick Patakis, not Demetrios Patakis, had stolen $40,000. The defense made much of the discrepancy between $40,000 and $50,000, which was the amount alleged in the complaint, but the amount was irrelevant. The relevant part was that Harry Vafiades had called Nick Patakis a thief at all.

The treasurer corroborated Nick Patakis's generosity to the local Kyrenia community, but he also indicated that Nick Patakis had become a tyrant and that younger members of the organization, probably meaning himself, and newer members of the organization, meaning more recent immigrants, wanted to have some say in the way the club was run. This did not seem unreasonable to him.

By this time in the trial, it was apparent that not only was I hearing a lawsuit but I was moderating, maybe not the dialogues of Plato, but a gripe session involving equally weighty issues like Tyranny, Honor, and Truth. I realized that it was important to let everyone have his or her say, to the greatest extent that the *Rules of Evidence* would allow. I do not usually believe that trials should be therapy, but this one seemed to offer a valid civic catharsis, with historic precedent. I fantasized that we were on the Plaka outside of the Parthenon.

The problem was the lawyers. They wanted to do their tap dance. Each objected to most everything the other side attempted to introduce. Gradually, they realized that they were going to be overruled, that I was going to let almost everything into evidence because this was not a jury trial, and they objected less frequently.

After Mr. Kavafis testified, we addressed a problem that at the outset had threatened to prevent the trial from occurring at all: nobody had hired an interpreter for the defendant.

In criminal cases the court provides the interpreter, and the state pays for the service, but in civil cases that's not so. Making things more difficult, interpreters can't be just anyone off the street who claims to speak the language. The interpreter has to be certified by the Administrative Office of the Trial Court (the AOTC). (In my young lawyer days there had been a notorious case in which a judge unknowingly allowed the actual culprit to interpret for the accused in a serious criminal case. Of course, the accused was convicted because the culprit confessed on his behalf in open court.) For the less common languages, like Greek these days, the Certified Court Interpreter Services Bureau of the AOTC would have needed at least a couple of weeks to round somebody up. And this trial had been delayed long enough.

Now Harry Vafiades didn't want to testify. That was one reason why his lawyer, Mr. Masson, had conceded that his client had made the statement—to keep him off the stand. Nick Patakis and his nephew wanted Harry Vafiades to testify, probably for dramatic effect and probably so the nephew could squeeze out revenge for the uncle. I ruled that if the plaintiff, Nick Patakis, wanted to call Harry Vafiades as a witness, he, Nick Patakis, would have to provide a certified court interpreter for him.

I suspected that John Patakis was representing his uncle without a fee for the honor of the family, and that neither John nor Nick wanted to put out money, even to gain the possible humiliation they could inflict on Harry Vafiades and the insurgents. Therefore, after Mr. Kavafis, the treasurer, there were no more witnesses, and the evidence part of the trial was over.

Each attorney was allowed to make final arguments. The defense, Mr. Masson, went first, and his argument was brief. He argued that there was merit to Harry Vafiades's accusations. Nick Patakis' nephew Demetrios's taking of the money was not borrowing but stealing, and the only reason the money was returned was because Demetrios got caught. Mr. Masson made no mention of the fact that his client had publicly accused Nick Patakis, not Demetrios Patakis, of stealing.

Nick Patakis's lawyer, the good nephew, John Patakis, Esq., began strong. He became more excited as he went on. All his client wanted, he said, was justice and the restoration of his good name.

"He's not interested in the money. Harry Vafiades has no money; he's never had money. The defendant is a waiter in a restaurant and is sixty-eight years old. Although he has his own house, it's unlikely that he has much money. Nick Patakis is not out to ruin the defendant but he does want justice. He wants a finding in his favor—even if the judgment is for one dollar."

I do not know if Attorney Patakis meant to go that far or if he just got so wound up that his own momentum delivered him there. But Mr. Masson jumped up in dismay and disgust nonetheless. He shouted, "If I knew we could settle this for a dollar, we would have done that two years ago. I have never heard such nonsense. These cases are supposed to be about real money, not one dollar. Judge, why has the plaintiff been wasting our and your time?" As he was saying this, Mr. Masson began ostentatiously searching in his pocket, presumably for the dollar.

I left the bench and decided to write my opinion right away, but as is my custom and as I had been advised when I first became a judge, I kept it overnight before filing it.

I found for Nick Patakis for $1.

Nobody appealed.

{ vii }

YOU GET WHAT YOU DESERVE

Trials were originally endurance contests—knights on horses trying to knock each other to the ground. Although the terms of the contests have changed, the term "trial" has survived, and with reason. Trials still are extremely stressful for all concerned. One measure of a judge's worth is how well he or she can control the proceedings.

Most people, including some judges, try to avoid trials. As a result, most cases, civil and criminal, are resolved without one, hopefully to the satisfaction of both sides. Nevertheless, as one of the following stories involving a plea disposition without a trial demonstrates, even these cases can present challenges.

In the event of a trial, the *Rules of Evidence* and *Rules of Procedure* help control the trial. Even so, trials can easily go off on tangents. The following stories present people who deservedly won at trial: people who lost may have received what they deserved as well.

SHAMROCKS AND CHAMPERTY

The old "boyos" fight it out

§ § §

Liam Harrahy sued three people. The first was Mrs. Kate McCarthy, the mother of an infant who died while in the care of certain doctors and nurses at a suburban hospital. The second was Attorney Harry Kelly, Mrs. McCarthy's first lawyer in a medical-malpractice suit against the hospital, its doctors, and nurses. The third was Mrs. McCarthy's next lawyer in the same case, Attorney Victor Brill. Attorney Brill took over Mrs. McCarthy's claim from Attorney Kelly.

Attorney Brill settled Mrs. McCarthy's claim for $600,000 before trial. Mr. Harrahy claimed that he was entitled to 10 percent of the $600,000 recovery, or $60,000.

Attorneys Rownan, Riorden, and Roche, the lawyers for the three defendants, came into the lobby for a pre-trial conference with Liam Harrahy's lawyer, who also had an Irish surname, Duffy. The three defense lawyers were all about the same height and age, five foot nine and early sixties. Mr. Rownan was portly and bald with a Friar Tuck tonsure of black hair; Mr. Riorden had gray hair and was stocky; Mr. Roche had a full head of brown hair, courtesy of Grecian Formula, and was built like the boxer he had once been. He seemed to be always ready to jump back into the ring.

As we were walking to a back conference room, Mr. Rownan turned to me and whispered loudly, "Judge, I told the others that we should've worn purple ties today, Your Honor."

"Why's that?" I said, thinking the familiarity unusual but curious nonetheless.

"Holy Cross, Judge; Holy Cross."

"What's Holy Cross got to do with anything?"

"You're from Worcester, Your Honor, and purple is Holy Cross's color," he said, smiling proudly.

"I didn't go to Holy Cross, Mr. Rownan."

"Oh, I thought you did. I used to try cases in front of your father up in Worcester, and he went to Holy Cross."

"He didn't go to Holy Cross either, Mr. Rownan," I replied, and we all sat down.

"Now about this case, is there any chance of a settlement?" I asked.

"No," the three defense lawyers—speak no evil, hear no evil, and see no evil—spoke in unison. The plaintiff's lawyer, Mr. Duffy, agreed.

So off we went on the long, labyrinthine route to Room 396, the furthermost courtroom in the Old Courthouse in Boston. This room had a nonworking fireplace, a portrait of our stone-faced first chief justice from the nineteenth century, lots of uncomfortable oak furniture, and a brass light with a large, green, glass shade bolted to the bench, blocking the judge's view of the witness stand to the left—blind justice indeed.

Court Officer Franny Cooney accompanied me as I led the procession. He said, "Judge, do you remember that poor woman from upstairs who's always down here smoking cigarettes? She'd drink out of a sewer, Judge. She took a pledge last year on the Sacred Heart—a very fervent prayer. The next day, bingo, shit-faced. She was on the phone to me. 'It didn't work, Franny,' she said. She's gotten more breaks than an orthopedic, Judge. Her ass will get on fire, and she'll come back to the program, Judge. And who are these boys?" he added without letting up for air, looking back at the three defense lawyers. "They look like the ushers at the Holy Name Church in West Roxbury. You're going to have a good day," and he laughed to himself.

"I'm just going to drop you off, Judge. I don't think my ticker can take the excitement. I'm doing double duty with you and the courtroom next door. There's a sexual assault in there—the psychiatrist who groped the priest on the subway. She says she didn't do it, that she's a lesbian."

When we arrived at Room 396, I saw Liam Harrahy, the plaintiff. He looked like El Greco's painting of St. John the Evangelist, the beloved disciple—wan and pale, prematurely white-haired, a little pink to the cast. His clothes matched his complexion. The layout of this tiny courtroom required that he and his lawyer, Mr. Duffy, sit five feet in front of and below me. There was a distinct odor of whiskey wafting up, and it wasn't coming from Attorney Duffy.

In a case with so many lawyers, usually each one thinks that he or she has to say something, even if it has already been said. However, I was happy to see that the defense lawyers seemed to defer to the garrulous Attorney Rownan.

What follows are the bare bones of the claim: as usual, the flesh was more interesting. Liam Harrahy, the plaintiff, owned a corporation that consisted of him. He called it Medical Research for Lawyers, Inc. In 1977, Mr. Harrahy met Attorney Kelly at a conference of trial lawyers at a Boston hotel. At that time Attorney Kelly had a client, Mrs. McCarthy, whose daughter had died in the hospital shortly after being born.

Mrs. McCarthy wanted to sue the doctors, the nurses, and the hospital. However, Attorney Kelly needed some research done to get over the first hurdle, a medical malpractice tribunal, the purpose of which is to screen out unworthy medical-malpractice cases. The panel is made up of a lawyer, a doctor, and a judge.

Liam Harrahy told Attorney Kelly that he would either charge $100 per hour or collect 10 percent of the recovery for his medical-research services. Attorney Kelly and Mrs. McCarthy opted for the 10 percent, although Mr. Kelly expressed some concerns about the ethics of this arrangement. Liam Harrahy claims that he, Mr. Harrahy (a nurse), called the Board of Bar Overseers (BBO), the disciplinary agency for lawyers, and was given oral approval from some unnamed person that he could receive a contingent fee.

As coincidences often happen in Massachusetts, I had earlier worked as a prosecutor at the BBO and was among the people who answered ethical questions—for lawyers only. I knew that it was unlikely that anyone at the BBO would talk to, never mind give advice to, a non-lawyer such as Liam Harrahy. I was not sure what I could do with that personal information in this trial, however.

After Attorney Kelly and Liam Harrahy made their arrangement, they went to see Mrs. McCarthy and encouraged her to sign the contingent-fee agreement. Mr. Harrahy did do some research, and the case did get by the medical malpractice tribunal. Thereafter, Attorney Kelly stopped calling Liam Harrahy because he had turned the case over to the third defendant, Attorney Victor Brill, a medical-malpractice specialist.

Attorney Brill testified that he spotted Liam Harrahy for a faker. Mrs. McCarthy's case was eventually settled by Mr. Brill for $600,000 in 1987 without paying Liam Harrahy his 10 percent. Liam Harrahy left the country for a while, then returned, wanting that 10 percent, $60,000 plus interest.

An added complication was that Attorney Kelly wanted to make sure that he was not credited with being the author of Mr. Harrahy's written contingent-fee agreement because it was a violation of the *Canon of Ethics and Disciplinary Rules Regulating the Practice of Law* for any lawyer to draft a contingent-fee agreement to share the proceeds of a case with a non-lawyer, such as Liam Harrahy. For anyone other than a lawyer to share in the proceeds of a lawsuit with the injured person is the ancient offense called champerty. Liam Harrahy, because he was a layman, and his young lawyer, Mr. Duffy, perhaps because the offense was not taught in law school anymore, did not seem to have a clue about champerty.

The syllogism of the defense lawyers, Rownan, Riorden, and Roche, went like this:

1. Liam Harrahy's contingent fee is a champertous agreement.
2. Champertous agreements are illegal.
3. The court cannot enforce this champertous agreement.

The opening statements of the attorneys (which are summaries of the evidence the lawyers hope to present, and not the evidence itself) laid the issues out. They were predictable, albeit hyperbolic. Apparently, Liam Harrahy was incensed by them, however. While testifying, he twice burst out, "They're liars when they say . . ." and he referred to some point made in the openings that was not terribly significant to the case but was obviously very important to his ego.

Liam Harrahy's lawyer silenced him before I did at these outbursts. We had taken a break after the openings, during which Mr. Harrahy may have refreshed himself. It did not help his case to be so intemperate when he was trying to pass himself off as a professional in aid of litigation, particularly when the matters that aroused him were of such small consequence.

Otherwise, Liam Harrahy proudly said that he had been a surgical technician for fourteen years and that as part of that job he both read and wrote medical records. He had never been told of anyone's dissatisfaction with his work. He claimed that until 1981 he did research almost every day in the Countway Medical Library at Harvard Medical School and that he went to Attorney Kelly's office three or four times per week to dictate the results of his labors to Attorney Kelly, who took notes. Mr. Harrahy also claimed that he visited Attorney Kelly at his home for the same purpose. He had no notes of his own to document or bolster these assertions. He said that his former wife stole them and burnt them during an acrimonious divorce. Much to the relief of Mr. Kelly, I am sure, Mr. Harrahy was anxious to take credit for drafting the contingent-fee agreement between himself and Mrs. McCarthy.

In the afternoon, the defense attorneys asked if they could present an expert witness out of order because he, the expert, was very busy (and expensive too, they might have added. They didn't want to pay him for sitting around.)

"An expert on what?" I inquired.

I had already seen the dignitary sitting in the spectator's area of the courtroom for an hour or so before lunch. I had wondered what his interest in this case was and, more to the point, who was paying him. I knew he didn't come cheap.

Mr. Harrahy's lawyer objected, both to the use of the expert and to his testifying out of order, but I overruled the objection. I noted that there was no jury to get confused by the witness being called out of order and that the value of Liam Harrahy's services was the major issue in the case. Mr. Harrahy glared and whispered angrily to his lawyer. I expected that Mr. Harrahy would produce his own expert at some point as well, but that never happened.

The defendants' expert was a medical-malpractice specialist who had been president or chairman of just about every professional trial-lawyers' organization in the state and beyond. He testified to the reasonableness of Liam Harrahy's fee as a medical consultant. The expert said that he had a nurse in his office whose only job was to do what Liam Harrahy claimed he had done in this case. The expert valued Mr. Harrahy's work at $25 to $35 per hour for twenty-five to thirty-five hours. Liam Harrahy laughed disdainfully at this appraisal. I wondered where Mr. Harrahy had taken his lunch.

Having been offered as an expert, the worthy became "Dr. Irwin Corey, the world's leading authority." He offered to comment on Attorney Kelly's conduct in allowing his client, Mrs. McCarthy, to sign the contingent-fee agreement with Liam Harrahy for 10 percent of the recovery—biting the hand that fed him, it seemed to me. Attorney Kelly's lawyer had the good sense to ask no more questions after this threat, and after a feeble cross-examination by Mr. Harrahy's lawyer, the expert was excused.

We returned to Liam Harrahy on cross-examination by the defense lawyers. Attorney Rownan went in for the kill.

"Did you ever go to Attorney Kelly's office drunk?"

"Did you have to be escorted out of the building by the police?"

"Have you been drinking alcohol today?"

"No, to all your rotten questions. I never went to Kelly's office drunk or under the influence of drugs. I don't drink, and I had only one beer at lunch today."

It must have been in a keg, I thought, which would have been uncharitable except that it was me Liam Harrahy was breathing toward.

And no, he did not threaten to go to the defense attorneys for the hospital and the doctors in the medical-malpractice action after Attorney Brill, Mrs. McCarthy's second lawyer, told him to have no further contact with her.

If the defense lawyers were looking for a fight, Liam Harrahy was fortified to give it to them and to anyone else who crossed him, including me it seemed. I searched for the inkwell for self-defense and made burning glances at Franny Cooney in his court officer's perch. I wanted him to stay alert, should I need protection.

The most devastating revelation of the cross-examination was that Mr. Harrahy did not have the credentials he claimed to have. He had not been in the Boston University class of 1971, as he had written in his CV. He had received an advanced Red Cross certificate and a scuba-diving certificate, but never had been a certified operating-room technician. He had no graduate certificates and no training in physiology or endocrinology as he claimed.

As a matter of fact, his name was not even Liam. He had changed it to Liam from William after his recent trip to Ireland. That is why the agreement in question referred to William Harrahy.

The plaintiff rested, and the defense attorneys knocked each other over to make motions for dismissal. I exercised that wonderful tool of my trade and reserved judgment on their motions. The only more useful tool for a judge is to stand up and declare a recess when you don't know what to do; I was taught that my first day by the senior judges on my court.

After making their motions, the defendants mercifully rested. I had fears of each of them producing numerous, voluble witnesses.

Ultimately, I wrote a lengthy opinion on the law of champerty and awarded Mr. Harrahy thirty-five hours times $35, or $1,225, based on a legal theory called *quantum meruit*, roughly translated as "you get what you deserve."

THE SWINDLE

"If you're a boozer, you're a loser," unless you can stay sober for your day in court

§ § §

A very wise mentor once said to me that you should always try to say something nice about somebody, even if you do not like them. The mentor happened to be bald, so what he usually said was, "He has nice hair."

Well, the defendant in this case, Therese Daley, had nice hair—long, blonde, streaked hair in kind of a pageboy, like a debutante. It was a very expensive job, probably from a Newbury Street colorist. Otherwise, Ms. Daley was built like a short refrigerator, the kind they have in cabins by a lake. She had a tan that no Irish person should ever get. Her face was like wrinkled leather. For her appearance in court, she was dressed nautically in a blue blazer, a white skirt to the middle of her thick calves, a middy blouse with a bib, white stockings like a schoolgirl, and navy and white spectator shoes with a low heel. The blue blazer was double-breasted. It kind of had to be; she was about five foot two, both ways.

Looks would not matter except that Ms. Daley's personality went with hers. In spite of the Ralph Lauren ingenue outfit, she was what my mother's generation called hard. I suspect that she smoked Pall Malls and drank Manhattans. Ms. Daley was accompanied by her "friend" and housemate, Patrick Warner. They both were in their early sixties. Patrick Warner was also short, had thinning hair, combed wet, flat back from his brow. He wore a brown suit, a small patterned tie and highly polished oxblood cordovan shoes. He looked like the chief sexton at church, the guy to whom the other sextons brought their collection baskets right after the offertory. From his hands to the monsignor's, we hoped.

The plaintiff, Larry Dyer, looked older than his age, whatever it was. Everything about him was gray—his hair, his worn suit, his tie, his skin, and his once white shirt.

I was not too confident that he was going to make it through this trial, nor, I suspect, was he. His claim was that the defendant, Therese Daley, had cheated him out of his house in South Boston, and he was suing for the money she should have paid him. He was represented by a black lawyer with a Dutch name, Jakob Van Ostend, and a difficult accent. Mr. Van Ostend was originally from South Africa and had been admitted to the bar only a year earlier.

An irony was that the property in question was in a neighborhood that did not have the reputation of being congenial to African Americans. So here in America, an African-born attorney was asserting the right of a poor, alcoholic white man to receive fair compensation for his house in a neighborhood that the attorney probably would have had a difficult time moving into—if he even had wanted to.

Larry Dyer testified that he did not remember much about the sale of the house, except that he knew that he had sold it to Ms. Daley. It soon became apparent that he had not been prepared by his lawyer, probably because the alcoholism made it impossible. This lack of preparation in a perverse way added to Mr. Dyer's credibility, but it made the plaintiff's case awkward.

As strange as it may seem, it was not really that important that Larry Dyer testify about the sale because a sale is a paper transaction; in these circumstances, the paper speaks, if you will, louder than spoken words. This is called the parol evidence rule. When there is a written contract, like a purchase-and-sale agreement for a house, verbal explanations cannot alter the terms of that contract.

Larry Dyer's lawyer, Mr. Van Ostend, produced two purchase-and-sale agreements. The first was dated September 10, 1988, and provided for the buyer, Therese Daley, to buy and the seller, Larry Dyer, to sell the house for $9,800. That was a peculiarly low amount for a house anywhere, in any shape, in Boston at that time.

The second purchase-and-sale agreement had a sale price of $80,000 and was dated November 30, 1988, less than three months later. The second agreement provided that after payment of the outstanding electric bills, water bills, and taxes, the plaintiff's two children were each to receive $20,000, to be put in trust. Larry Dyer would receive the remainder at the time of the deed.

A deed for the house was given by Larry Dyer to Therese Daley on December 30, 1988, and recorded that day at the registry of deeds. Mr. Van Ostend provided a copy of this agreement. There was no objection by Therese Daley's lawyer to any of these documents. Larry Dyer acknowledged his signature on all, but otherwise had no memory of the events because he was "drunk a lot in those days." Not only "those days," I suspected. Given his shaking hands grasping the rail on the witness stand, he had probably been drunk the night before too.

Finally Larry Dyer testified that neither he nor his children ever received any funds and that no trust that he knows of had been established.

At the time of the sale, there were liens on the property in the amount of $19,000 from the Boston Edison Company, the Water Department, and the gas company. Some of the bills had not been paid since 1969, when Mr. Dyer inherited the house. Other documents, also introduced by Mr. Van Ostend, showed that on the day the deed was recorded Therese Daley gave a mortgage for this property to, and received a loan for $125,000 from, a local bank that was no longer in business.

Mr. Van Ostend called Ms. Daley to the stand. She testified that in 1988 she worked in a variety store—a spa, she called it (and so would most Bostonians)—that the plaintiff went to every morning to buy coffee for himself and soup for his grammar-school daughter with whom he lived in the cellar of the house in question because the upstairs had fallen apart. Ms. Daley "wouldn't say he was an alcoholic, but he did drink a lot."

Her defense, like Gaul, was in three parts. However, no one of them jibed with the others.

The first defense was that she was supposed to pay only $9,800 for the house in accord with the first purchase-and-sale agreement, and that she had done that. The second was that over time she had given Mr. Dyer a lot more money when he drunkenly demanded it. She said she also gave him a used Buick worth $700. The third defense was that the property was uninhabitable, a white elephant in Ms. Daley's words, and that she did not buy anything worthwhile for whatever amount it was that she paid or was supposed to have paid.

She was testy and appeared to be put out at having to testify at all, like this was all so apparent that it was a waste of her and my time.

The examination and cross-examination of Ms. Daley went on for quite a while, and I worried that we were going to lose Mr. Dyer if we went into the afternoon. He did not look as though he would come back after lunch or that he would even make it through lunch. I was thinking of which court officer to send to The Littlest Bar nearby to rescue him. There was no way I could rush the testimony, however.

Ms. Daley's consort, Patrick Warner, with whom she had lived in the house since 1990, did not testify, although he was acknowledged by her as her "friend." He was conspicuously visible in the almost empty courtroom, and he was with Ms. Daley at the breaks, smoking Tareytons over the canister ashtray in the hallway.

One of Ms. Daley's nieces testified out of order, in the middle of her aunt's testimony, because she was a banquet waitress and had to work late at night and sleep in the day. She was a young woman, probably in her late twenties, single, good-looking, and not credible after stating her name and address. The niece said that on at least seven occasions she drove her aunt to the bank to get money for Mr. Dyer, who had come to the house drunk, demanding it. The niece testified that she had frequently seen her aunt write checks to him.

When she returned to the witness stand, Ms. Daley also testified that after the sale Mr. Dyer often appeared at the house drunk demanding money. She would drive him to the bank, deposit him in a bar across the street, cash a check made out to "cash," and bring the cash over to Mr. Dyer at the bar. However, Ms. Daley had no record of any payments to Larry Dyer.

Her lawyer did introduce eighty-six checks made out to cash, some of which had initials in the corner. Those initials indicated people who had witnessed her payments to the plaintiff, Ms. Daley said. None were available to come into court to verify their witnessing. One of them was Ms. Daley's brother who had died, another was a sister in California, the third was another niece whose absence was not explained. As for the others, she wasn't too sure who they were. The initials of the niece who had testified to having seen some of these transactions were not on any of the checks.

To say it was difficult to believe Therese Daley is an understatement. She gave no history of herself prior to her work in the variety store in the eighties. The testifying niece said that Ms. Daley had run a dog-grooming business in Plymouth for twenty years before coming back to the city.

She must have had good credit or the property was in fact worth something, or both, considering the surprisingly favorable mortgage she obtained—$125,000 for a property she was supposed to have paid $80,000 for, if one accepted the second purchase-and-sale agreement. Ms. Daley said that she and Mr. Warner were in the business of rehabilitating property. It appeared to me that she was a woman interested in making a profit.

During examination by Mr. Van Ostend, Therese Daley managed to hang her lawyer. She testified that the $80,000 purchase-and-sale agreement was "just a piece of paper," a sham, in words other than hers, to be used to get the bank to give them a mortgage for $125,000, which represented the purported purchase price of $80,000 plus another $45,000 for repairs. When asked who drafted this agreement, she pointed to her lawyer and said, "Him, Mr. Legatt, my lawyer."

This revelation required me to report Mr. Legatt to the Board of Bar Overseers, the dreaded BBO, which in turn would probably report him to the U.S. Attorney. About this time, some distinguished people in Boston, including some lawyers, were going to jail for inflating the purchase price of property on closing documents in order to obtain mortgages.

Mr. Dyer, the plaintiff, did return in the afternoon and managed to stay the day. Neither his daughter nor his other child, the sex of whom remained a mystery, testified or even appeared.

I took the case under reservation. Sometimes I do that because I cannot make up my mind, sometimes because I need to look up the law, sometimes because I do not want to create a scene, and at other times, like this, because I do not want to publicly embarrass one side or the other.

Of course, Mr. Dyer won. God knows what he will do with the money. He may end up with the house again because I suspect that Ms. Daley and Mr. Warner don't have a lot of cash lying around to pay a judgment of $60,300—the purchase price minus the $19,000 in liens minus $700 for the Buick. Maybe his lawyer would take the house for his fee.

I am not surprised that since Ms. Daley's purchase the house has sported a fake brick front.

JOEY RYAN

"Hizonna" gets a comeuppance.
That'll teach him to get therapeutic.

§ § §

Joey Ryan stabbed a neighbor who had been one of many kids bullying him for years. Though husky, Joey spent a lot of time with his mother and sisters in their house in Brighton. Other boys would go by, taunt him by shouting, "Fag, sissy, Mary Ryan, Mary Ryan!" and bang on the door or the fence outside. They'd been doing this since Joey was twelve. He was now seventeen. One day he snapped. He came barreling out of the front door with a knife and started swinging.

At first his antagonists thought he was kidding. He ran after the biggest, Michael O'Shea, whose friends stood in disbelief as Joey Ryan stabbed Michael in the shoulder.

So here Joey was, in front of me, taking his chances on justice and compassion in the court system.

His lawyer convinced him to plead guilty to a charge of assault and battery with a dangerous weapon—the steak knife. Surprisingly, the assistant district attorney was agreeing with the defense recommendation that Joey get probation with psychiatric help. The victim, Michael O'Shea, hadn't shown up, so the Commonwealth couldn't go to trial. Neither side proposed exactly what the psychiatric help should be. I had to fill in the blank.

I decided to require Joey to attend a twenty-six-week anger-management course and receive individual psychological counseling approved by the probation department. I trusted certain people in probation to know what was good therapy and what wasn't. Joey ought to go to someone who could show him that he didn't have to stab his tormentors.

Before the reading of the sentence by the clerk, I saw Joey tugging at his lawyer's sleeve. She tried to keep him quiet. Finally, she said, "Judge, my client would like to say something."

Thinking he was going to express regret and that this might be therapeutic, I said, "All right."

Joey stood up and started. "I'm sorry about this incident. I'm sorry that it occurred and that I hurt Michael O'Shea. I'm grateful that you are doing this. I could benefit from counseling," he said. "But I want you to know those bastards have been chasing me for years, and I'm glad I got him. And if you don't like that, then fuck you!"

After a moment of awkward silence, everyone in the courtroom turned to me. I did what judges always do when they don't know what to do.

I stood up and said, "Recess."

§ § §

Now, you should understand that in Massachusetts we don't usually allow criminal defendants to address judges at the time of sentencing, except in capital cases (murder, rape, arson, and treason.) The right of the defendant to be heard not under oath at the end of a capital case is called the right of allocution.

It is very dear to the Irish. In 1848, Thomas Francis Meagher, an Irish patriot, also a lawyer, was charged with "levying war against the queen" (the British Queen, Victoria.). He reportedly told the judge before sentencing, "If you let us go this time, please be assured that we'll do a better job the next." His death sentence was commuted nevertheless, and he was transported to Australia. He later escaped to America and led the Irish Brigade in the American Civil War. Out of admiration, my great grandfather, who also fought in the Civil War, changed the spelling of our last name to conform to Thomas Francis's.

Another famous peroration, that mainstay of Catholic school declamation contests, Robert Emmet's speech from the dock, has the defendant saying to the judge, "When my country takes her place among the nations of the earth, then, and not till then, let my epitaph be written. I have done." He was then hanged.

As you can see, there is good reason for discouraging these speeches, both here and in Ireland. The judge never hears what he wants to hear. Some people, like Joey, just need attention, for themselves or their cause.

I returned to the bench and accepted Joey's guilty plea. Both sides had agreed to it, after all. The law doesn't require remorse; it is only in the confessional that you must show that. I, however, now had a lot of questions for myself. What would I have done if the plea had not been agreed? What if there had been a trial and I had to sentence Joey without agreement? Why was the assistant district attorney willing to let Joey go to counseling?

One reason was that he had no record.

Another may have been that Michael O'Shea, the victim, was not present. Perhaps he had disappeared. Maybe the shame of being stabbed by the likes of Joey was too humiliating for him. Maybe he had a long record, and not a pretty one either. These bullies often do. But I had no way of seeing Michael O'Shea's record.

My identification with Joey was strong. I had even thought about recusing myself. Instead I asked myself, *If I were a woman judge and a woman had stabbed Michael O'Shea after he taunted her as he had taunted Joey Ryan, would I be required to recuse myself?*

TRAVESTY

The Lamb warning proves to be a lion

§ § §

One of my colleagues once said a judge has been successful at a mental-health civil-commitment hearing if they let the judge out of the hospital. My colleague suggests that the judge wear an armband marked JUDGE to increase his chances of getting out. I'm not so sure that would work. The authorities might just think the person with the armband is delusional.

Instead of holding these hearings at the courthouse, we go to the hospital with a clerk and a court officer. We're supposed to be put in a room with both the Massachusetts flag and the American flag. Some of my colleagues wear their robes during these hearings. I don't. In more recent years we tape-recorded them, which is a good thing, except that the court had no reliable portable tape recorders, so we sometimes had to use somebody's old Walkman. During one of my first civil-commitment hearings, the randy old male court officer wandered off to chat up the cute female orderly, leaving the little clerk and me alone with a man who had once killed both his brother and his mother.

One of the hospitals we go to was designed by the famous architect Paul Rudolph, the former head of the Yale Architecture School. When told of Mr. Rudolph's prominence, a witty clerk said, "He must have designed it early in his career." It is an interesting and mysterious building but unsuited for a mental hospital. Among other problems, the route from the entrance to the usual hearing room is labyrinthine. The walls in the corridors are rough concrete, and the medicated patients scrape their bodies walking along them, particularly the obsessive ones who feel compelled to touch the walls at all times.

On the day in question, we arrived at the hospital to find they had changed the visitors' entrance. After we located the new entrance, we asked the receptionist how to get to the hearing room. He picked up the phone and presumably called the law department: "Hello, Law Department? I got some guys here. They want to know where the hearing is today." He then said "yes, yes, yes, yes" into the phone, turned to me with the phone still squeezed to his ear by his shoulder, and said, "Who are you anyway?"

The court officer told him, "He's the judge, and we're his staff."

The receptionist said, "You go up one flight of stairs down to the end to the elevator, around the corner and down to the third, up the first set of stairs, then take the first right and . . ." and so on. The receptionist seemed to take perverse delight in his instructions.

I interjected and asked him to please call the law department to send someone for us.

The receptionist looked surprised but placed the call. They sent Ms. Lynch, the lawyer who was going to prosecute the case, and another woman who turned out to be the psychiatrist and the principal witness for the department. Ms. Lynch looked like one of those exceedingly plain girls with whom my sister had gone to the Sisters of Notre Dame for high school, and she had a quiet nun's voice to match. She was short, thin, and very pale. There was also a peculiar detachment about her, considering the sad drama of these cases. Her manner would have been appropriate if we were talking about land titles, but it was too bloodless for these human tragedies. Yet at the same time Ms. Lynch acted as if she really believed that the hospitalization was going to do more than warehouse the patients. Ms. Lynch had been prosecuting these cases as long as I had been hearing them. She was usually very docile in her presentation. I often had to tell her to speak up.

I had hoped that the law department would send somebody not associated with the hearing, a secretary, for example. I should not have been having conversations with or be in debt, however slight, to one side or the other. Thus I was a little nervous about the *ex parte* (one-sided) association with Ms. Lynch and the testifying psychiatrist, but I saw no way around it. How else was I going to get where I was supposed to go? It was too late now.

We did go one flight up, down two, around a corner and so on until we arrived at a door through which I could mercifully see windows. The windows made me happy because I could see a building outside that I recognized. This wasn't the usual hearing room but I knew that I wasn't lost. I could jump out the window and know where I would land.

As I pushed the door open farther, imagine my surprise: standing before me was John Wright in a navy blue polka-dot dress, light makeup, long hair, and cat's-eye glasses. At first I thought that he was the patient and that I would have to withdraw. I hadn't seen John Wright in six or seven years, and although I'd been friendly with him at one time, we migrated to opposite sides when he tried to fire my good friend, his employee at one of his previous jobs. I knew that he was having trouble then and that things got worse after, but he disappeared and my friend kept his job. I didn't know the resolution of Mr. Wright's problems. Apparently this transformation into a woman was it.

Ms. Lynch, the Department of Mental Health attorney, said, "Judge, this is Attorney Johanna Wright, who will be representing the respondent."

I replied, much more coolly than I felt, "Thank you, Ms. Lynch. I know Ms. Wright. How have you been?"

"Very well, Judge. Thank you for asking." This was more personal conversation than I wanted to have, but it seemed the least I could say. Maybe it balanced the escort service to the hearing room provided by the law department and the psychiatrist.

Ms. Wright looked plausible as a woman. Rather than resenting the craziness he had visited on my friend, I was happy to see that she was functioning better.

I still wondered if I should recuse myself. The first question running through my mind was whether I would be biased because John

Wright had treated my friend badly. I didn't think so. The next question was whether I would lean the other way to compensate for that possible bias if I were to hear the case. Again I didn't think so. My head was already hurting, and I was having trouble following my own psychological twists. I then asked myself the two questions required by the *Canons of Judicial Ethics: Could I be impartial?* and *Could my impartiality reasonably be questioned?*

My answer was "yes" to the first and "no" to the second. Furthermore, I thought sophistically, I had once known a man named John Wright, but I had never had any dealings with Johanna Wright. Besides, it was a Friday afternoon in the summertime, and at this hour no other judge was available to replace me. Yet I don't deny that valor may have gotten the better part of discretion when I stayed in the case.

This ethical decision-making occurred in the ten feet and twelve seconds it took to walk from the door to the blue vinyl chair with chrome arms from which I was to preside. It sat at the head of the long, presumably Paul Rudolph–designed wooden table that echoed the oval shape of the blue and rough concrete room.

The other people sat down. Ms. Lynch and the psychiatrist sat on my left, and Ms. Johanna Wright sat on the right. Various people, it was hard to tell whether they were patients or workers, wandered past the door that I wanted to keep open for ventilation's sake at least until the respondent, the subject of this proceeding, appeared.

Before that could happen, Ms. Wright said, "I have motions in limine [literally, "at the threshold"] to exclude statements made by the respondent."

Ms. Wright moved right in, "And Judge, I would ask you to look at the record and the papers concerning the respondent's admission to this facility. You'll see that the only documentation of a 'Lamb warning' is at the beginning of the admission sheet of the respondent. We are not even certain whether it was given then because this doctor here today did not do the admission, and the note following the printed warning is silent as to my client's response."

The Lamb warning was at the top of the form in bold letters. The purpose of the warning is to advise people that the examining physician, psychiatrist, psychologist, or whoever is asking the questions is not talking to them to treat them, but rather to gather information that possibly could later be presented in court. (It is called a "Lamb" warning because the case that first required it involved someone named Lamb.) The recommended protocol is to ask the patient to repeat the warning back to the examiner and then to note that the patient agreed to continue to speak. The form that the questioner is supposed to fill out has a space in which to describe the nature of the assent, whatever it may be—words, a nod, or a wink.

Ms. Wright was right. The form failed to indicate what her client, Pierre Lamour, described as a thirty-two-year-old Haitian man who had arrived in the United States in 1992, had assented to in response to the Lamb warning. Ms. Wright leaned back in her chair after tossing this bomb.

I was impressed by her research. Some lawyers do not read anything beforehand, and others read and miss. She had read and found.

Throughout the argument, however, I could not always remember that John Wright was now Johanna Wright, and so a number of times I said, "Thank you, Mr. Wright, Ms. Wright."

Attorney Lynch presented Dr. Eleanore Beauregard Baker, the woman who had escorted us through the hallways, down the stairs, etc. These psychiatrists always seemed to have two last names. She gave her credentials: Duke University, Duke University Medical School, and Georgia State Medical School.

I had heard cases with Dr. Beauregard Baker before. She never liked the fact that a judge was able to second-guess her, and it showed. Her disdain for this process was evident in spite of the charm of her slight southern drawl. She looked intense and was. I had the feeling that she always thought that she had more important things to do. She was tall, in her late thirties or early forties, with short dark hair, tailored clothes, and a big diamond engagement ring, which seemed inappropriate both on her and in this austere setting.

Dr. Beauregard Baker said, "Doctor Wu gave him the Lamb warning. I know she did. She told me she did. And she told me that he said—"

"Objection. Hearsay," said Ms. Wright.

"Sustained."

"She told me that he said—" continued Dr. Beauregard Baker.

"Objection," Ms. Wright said again, a little more loudly.

"I've sustained that objection. You cannot respond," I said to Dr. Beauregard Baker.

"She told me that Mr. Lamour said, 'So I can't trust you,'" continued Dr. Beauregard Baker, blithely ignoring my ruling. It was going to be her way or no way, it seemed. Dr. Beauregard Baker's stubbornness seemed a useless impertinence; it gained her nothing.

Ms. Wright then said, "Additionally, there is no indication in the record that my client was given a Lamb warning on the other occasions when this doctor claimed she examined him."

On the other side of the table, Dr. Beauregard Baker pulled a little book out of her purse and listed nine different dates on which she had examined Mr. Lamour. "And I always give them Lamb warnings," she added.

I wondered how she would describe "them." It seemed to be a pretty impersonal and dehumanizing lump. I was going to ask, but instead said, partially for the Walkman making a record but also for my edification, "Dr. Beauregard Baker, you're looking at a small book, two by three inches. What is that book?"

"That is my personal diary, my personal notes."

Ms. Wright interjected, "So it's not part of the medical record? You're reading from something that's not part of the medical record?"

"Yes," spat Dr. Beauregard Baker. "It's not part of the medical record. These are my personal notes."

Ms. Wright said, "Do your personal notes indicate that *you* gave the Lamb warning on the occasions that *you* spoke to Mr. Lamour? Or, more to the point, do your personal notes indicate what you said to Mr. Lamour and what he said in response? Do they say that? Is all that recorded in your personal notes in that two-inch by three-inch book?" Ms. Wright also had to be specific in her questions because the clerk's daughter's old Sony Walkman was recording all this. If Ms. Wright's client lost the case and wanted to appeal, the record of testimony would be essential.

Because Ms. Wright was asking at least three questions at once, an objection would have been sustained if it had been made. However, Ms. Lynch was a quiet, almost soporific, lawyer, not accustomed to so much turmoil. Or she may have been as fed up with Dr. Beauregard Baker as the rest of us.

Dr. Beauregard Baker just glared and then said, "No, but it triggers my memory of what I said, and I always give them Lamb warnings." *Again the "them,"* I noted silently.

"Well then, what did Mr. Lamour say in response on May seventh, nineteen ninety-eight?" asked Ms. Wright.

Dr. Beauregard Baker glared and remained silent.

Ms. Wright said, "Judge, I would ask that you instruct the witness that she should answer the question."

"Dr. Beauregard Baker, would you answer the question."

"I can't remember."

"And what did Mr. Lamour say to you on June ninth?"

"I can't remember."

"And what did he say to you on—what was the next date that you saw Mr. Lamour?" Ms. Wright asked, ramming it in.

"June eleventh. I can't remember that either. I can't remember what he said on any of the dates, but I know he understood me because his responses were very complex."

Did that mean that we lawyers and judges would not understand the responses, and thus she should not have to reveal them?

Ms. Wright continued the question for each of the nine dates that Dr. Beauregard Baker claimed she had talked to Mr. Lamour. Finally, Dr. Beauregard Baker blurted out, unsolicited, "Judge, this is a very dangerous man. He assaulted another patient. We were at your court again yesterday getting a criminal complaint against him. You cannot release him."

Such testimony, if that's what you can call such an outburst, was out of order, improper, and irrelevant. The issues we were dealing with right then, in limine, at the doorstep of the hearing, was whether the doctors gave the Lamb warning and whether the respondent, Mr. Lamour, understood it before he talked to this or any other doctor.

We hadn't even touched the very real issue of whether the respondent, who had arrived from Haiti in 1992, understood English well enough to respond to what had been told him. And, of course, there was the larger issue that never seems to come up. How could I credit as "voluntary and knowing" the assent of someone who was suffering a major mental illness so grave that he should be hospitalized and medicated involuntarily?

"Is there anything you wish to add, Ms. Wright?" I asked.

"No, Your Honor."

To Ms. Lynch, the lawyer for the Department of Mental Health, I asked, "How do you respond to your sister's argument that in this case the Lamb warning was either not given, not understood, or not waived?"

Ms. Lynch replied, "I'm not sure I can. It appears that it was given once and that the respondent, Mr. Lamour, did talk to the doctors."

"Well, I'm afraid that I must allow Ms. Wright's motion. How do we proceed now?" I asked.

Ms. Wright jumped right in, "I move to dismiss." Dr. Beauregard Baker's eyes widened, and she looked astonished, as though she were thinking, *How can this be happening?*

Dr. Beauregard Baker leaned over to Ms. Lynch and whispered. Ms. Lynch said, "Judge, can we have a five-minute recess?"

I was inclined to deny the request but said instead, "This case has been continued twice. There doesn't seem to be much more to say."

Ms. Lynch, calm up until now, interrupted, "Judge, I just got this case this morning at nine-thirty."

That put me over the edge. "It's not my responsibility that you haven't had the time to prepare. Some lawyer had the case last week when it was continued until today; somebody else had it before then. But I will grant you a recess to see if you can come to some resolution with Ms. Wright."

Ms. Lynch and the psychiatrist left the room. Ms. Wright stayed seated at the far end of the left side of the oval table, apparently basking in her triumph.

I said, "Ms. Wright, I would appreciate having this room to myself at the moment, and I would like you to talk to the petitioners in this case. May I ask you to leave?"

"Oh, yes, Judge. I'd be happy to. I'm sorry." And out she went. I began to read the medical record that would have been admissible except for Mr. Lamour's statements.

It seems that three days before the hearing, a patient complained to an attendant that while the patient and Mr. Lamour were in the men's room Mr. Lamour called him names and threatened him. The attendant returned to the men's room with the patient, who apparently felt empowered by the attendant's presence. The patient approached Mr. Lamour and slapped him in the face, saying, "That'll teach you to call me 'faggot.'" Mr. Lamour punched the patient in the eye, causing him to be sent to the nearby Massachusetts Eye and Ear Infirmary for emergency surgery.

It became even more apparent why Dr. Beauregard Baker was anxious to keep Mr. Lamour hospitalized. Her employer, the Department of Mental Health, might have incurred liability as a result of the attendant's folly in bringing the patient and Mr. Lamour into such proximity.

Eventually, all parties returned.

Ms. Lynch said, "Judge, we are unable to resolve this matter."

"So where do you go from here?" said I, meaning, *Do you have any case without Mr. Lamour's statements?*

"Judge, I'd agree to the motion to dismiss. We will probably be bringing another petition, however," Ms. Lynch added unnecessarily.

"The motion to dismiss is allowed." The clerk, court officer, and I all got up.

Ms. Lynch and Dr. Beauregard Baker were hustling out of the room to a door off the hall when the court officer said, "Judge, I don't know how we get out of here."

I said to the fleeing Department of Mental Health team, "Excuse me, can you tell us how we get out?" Dr. Beauregard Baker was holding the door for Ms. Lynch. The doctor turned and smiled slyly—at our discomfort, I suspect. "You go through that door over there, up one flight, down two, around a corner and down the stairs." We followed her directions as best we could and eventually got out.

The armband was not necessary.

MELEE

The young "boyos" fight it out

§ § §

Giovanni Melchiorre Bosco, aka Saint John Bosco, aka Don Bosco, was born in 1815 in Becchi, Italy, in the Piedmont region. He died at Doreno in 1888 and was canonized by Pius XI in 1934.

His father died when Don Bosco was two years old, leaving the family (himself, two brothers, and his mother) poor. As a youth, he worked as a shepherd (perhaps a metaphor for his work to come.) He also performed as a magician (also perhaps a metaphor for his future work). He is the patron saint of magicians.

Don Bosco was ordained in 1841. Legend has it that in the same year, as he was getting dressed to say Mass, he heard the cries of a ragged urchin being driven out of the church by the sacristan. Don Bosco brought the urchin back into the church, and thus began his ministry to poor boys. By his kindness, Don Bosco soon attracted numerous other boys, and they met for prayer and teaching in various locations in Turin until they were able to rent the shed that became their first oratory. His clientele, ragamuffins and what today would be called juvenile delinquents, was not popular with the religious establishment of the day. Don Bosco probably would have agreed with Father Flanagan of Boys Town that "there is no such thing as a bad boy." Don Bosco did not believe in punishment as an educational or behavioral tool. He said, "Try to gain love before inspiring fear."

Don Bosco founded the Salesians in 1859, named after St. Francis de Sales, a sixteenth- and seventeenth-century saint from France who tried "to show how ordinary life 'in the world' can be made holy." The *Penguin Lives of the Saints* says that "Don Bosco was an outstanding figure in the efflorescence of heroic sanctity in North Italy in the nineteenth century. His genius with boys was partly inborn, partly the fruit of experience." By the time he died in 1888, there were 250 Salesian houses in all parts of the world, containing 130,000 children.

In Boston until recently, the Salesians had a school on the edge of what is commonly called the Combat Zone. Called the Zone for short, it was the result of an attempt to locate all of Boston's seediness in one controllable spot. The neighborhood contained strip clubs, gay and straight peep shows, high and low bars for all orientations, and the usual denizens of such places. This little bit of social engineering would have worked if the Zone had no neighbors, but in cities everything touches everything else. The Zone's neighbors were Chinatown, New England Medical Center, and Don Bosco Technical High School. Both the Zone and Don Bosco were within the geographical jurisdiction of Boston Municipal court. At various times, almost all civil cases and jury-trial appeals of criminal cases came to the BMC from the eight courts in Metropolitan Boston and its neighborhoods.

Because of its proximity to public transportation, Don Bosco attracted boys from all over the Archdiocese of Boston, from all over the city and the suburbs. Its full name was Don Bosco Technical High School, although one of the reasons the school eventually closed is that it did not keep up with computers, the "technical" study most in demand these days in Boston. In my later years as a judge, the Zone pretty much disappeared as well—wiped out by urban renewal in downtown Boston.

§ § §

Timmy O'Leary was a sophomore at Don Bosco. His cousin, Michael McCarthy, was a junior. They both lived on the South Shore, Timmy in Quincy and Michael in Scituate. Timmy O'Leary was suing the Massachusetts Bay Transportation Authority (MBTA) for negligence.

Timmy was about six feet three inches tall, 170 pounds, pale with short-clipped red hair. He seemed a happy kid. Michael was shorter, more graceful, with long, straight black hair. He was dark and looked more Italian than Irish. He looked moody and sultry. They both wore jackets and ties to court, not a common occurrence. They were very courteous and respectful, perhaps the result of the Salesians.

Timmy and Mike testified similarly. One February day, late leaving school, they caught a bus that took them to the Red Line at the Broadway MBTA Station in South Boston. Timmy and Mike got on the bus carrying their green book bags with yellow lettering and wearing, as they were required to, ties and dress shirts and dress trousers, as well as winter coats to keep them warm. They went down the fifty or so steps at the Broadway Station to the toll takers, went through the gate with their passes, and passed both the toll taker in his booth and the inspector outside the booth, who was chatting it up with the toll taker.

They then went down another fifty steps or so to the lower platform to wait for the Quincy train. There are two trains on the Red Line, one—the Ashmont train—ends up in Dorchester, and the other ends up in Quincy, a smaller city just south of Boston. They wanted the Quincy train.

They stood with about twenty of their schoolmates on the platform for no longer than a minute when a horde of youths, probably thirty or forty kids, came running down the stairs, having leapt over the toll booths, screaming "Get Flaherty! Get Flaherty! Get O'Brien and Flaherty!"

Patrick Flaherty, known as Paris because he was so debonair, was one of the Don Bosco students. His friends, including Eamon McGuire, surrounded him. Timmy O'Leary was back about five feet from this group and leaning against a pillar. His cousin, Michael McCarthy, was about five feet behind him.

The vandals managed to pull Paris Flaherty away from his protectors and tried to push him into the subway pit, which had a third rail—the very dangerous electrified third rail. Eamon McGuire tackled the principal brute, who was trying to pull Paris over to the rail, and himself got stomped. Paris got slugged a few times.

But the worst was to happen to Timmy O'Leary. He was sucker punched from the right, and his nose "splattered across his face." He crumpled over. Michael McCarthy picked him up off the ground.

The marauders ran back up the stairs, shouting as loudly as they had coming down. A minute or so later, according to Timmy and Mike, the Transit Authority inspector came down to the platform nonchalantly smoking a cigarette, which is illegal in subway stations. According to the Transit Authority inspector himself, he came down "in the course of his duties being unaware of any commotion having occurred."

The inspector went over to Timmy because he was the most obviously hurt, being bloodied and bowed. Just then a train pulled in, and the inspector told Timmy and Mike to get on the train and get off after two stops at the JFK Station. The inspector told Timmy that an ambulance would be there waiting for him.

The inspector got on the train with the boys and traveled as far as the next station. In the course of the one station ride, the inspector acknowledged to Timmy and Mike that there had been a lot of fights and that "those little bastards, the Tynan Devils, had been raising hell at the Broadway Station."

Timmy got off at the JFK Station with his cousin and waited for ten minutes for an ambulance that never came. Fortunately, they saw a girl they knew who was picking up someone else at that station, and she gave them a ride to Timmy's house.

Both Timmy and Mike said the fight in the subway station was over a girl—one Helen from South Boston. The weekend before there had been a party in Dorchester, and Patrick "Paris" Flaherty, who is from Dorchester, had put the moves on the South Boston girl, which was not appreciated by those Tynan Devils of South Boston who were at the same party. Timmy O'Leary and Michael McCarthy had nothing to do with this courtship. They just happened to be wearing the same uniform as the would-be suitor and were at the wrong place when vengeance was sought.

After Timmy eventually made it home, his mother took him to the

Quincy hospital where he was sewn up and had some minor plastic surgery on his nose. He lost four days of school, and he hasn't breathed well since, according to his mother, a very pleasant, short, redheaded woman who was the third witness.

During Timmy's testimony, his lawyer asked if I would look at the scar on Timmy's nose. It wasn't easy to see because the light came from the windows behind Timmy, and I am blind in one eye. Also, it was slightly embarrassing because Timmy had to get very close to me, almost as if we were going to kiss. But I had to do it because if I found for Timmy, I had to put a dollar value on his particular injuries. Scars have value, particularly for women.

Because the Tynan Devils were not an "incorporated entity," because it was unlikely that any of them had any money, and probably because no one wanted to identify any of them for fear of further revenge, the lawsuit was brought against the MBTA. The MBTA had the money—the "deep pockets," as plaintiffs' lawyers say. Needless to say, the MBTA disclaimed any responsibility.

However, this case was not the usual negligence suit brought against the MBTA, such as the mother of five falling to the floor when the bus stopped abruptly or the portly man caught in the subway door. This complaint alleged that the MBTA had a "duty of care" to these boys as they waited for the train in the MBTA station, that they had a duty to keep the MBTA station safe from "the tortious acts of third parties," that the MBTA violated that duty, and that the plaintiff, Timothy O'Leary, suffered damages as a result.

The MBTA sent a detective to inquire of Timmy O'Leary four or five days after the incident. Unfortunately for the MBTA, Timmy said then substantially what he testified to in court, always a fortunate coincidence for plaintiffs. The only major difference was that whereas he now said there were thirty or forty vandals, he had said fifteen to twenty during his earlier interview, according to the investigator. This did not seem to me to be an important discrepancy.

The Transit Authority lawyer put the MBTA inspector, who Timmy and Michael claimed had been derelict in his duty, on the witness stand. I do not think that the lawyer had interviewed the inspector beforehand. The inspector not only appeared to have been derelict, he must have been deaf and blind. I wondered if he were not one of the Tynan Devils himself.

"Yes, I was at the tollbooth when the Don Bosco boys came by."

"I was there for a little while after they went downstairs."

"No, I hadn't heard any commotion going on before I, myself, went downstairs."

"Nobody jumped over the toll gates."

"I did see a few young men running up the stairs, but that wasn't unusual."

"Yes, there may have been more than twenty."

"I never told Timmy O'Leary that an ambulance would be coming. I helped Timmy O'Leary get on the subway, but I didn't do much else."

"Yes, I do smoke cigarettes."

"Yes, I had been smoking a cigarette that day."

"I do know the people in the neighborhood. I am from South Boston myself. I have heard of the Tynan Devils, but I do not recall seeing any of them this day."

When asked to define his job, he said he was a "troubleshooter." The first that he knew of "the melee" (his words) was when he was alerted to it by a dispatcher who had been alerted by a guard on a train that there was a "little scramble" on the platform. Until he walked down to the loading platform and heard some noise, he didn't realize that there had been any serious trouble.

In short, his testimony was not credible.

Nor was the testimony of the captain of the MBTA police, the next defense witness to testify, of much assistance to his employer. First of all, for some unexplained reason, the captain wore his captain's hat while testifying. Men never wear hats in court, just like they don't wear hats in church and probably for the same reason—out of respect for the institution. Court officers make them remove their hats. (On the other hand, in the old days, women, especially women lawyers, were supposed to wear hats in court. That custom bit the dust a while ago.) Maybe the captain was bald, or maybe he had military fantasies as his hat was covered with braid, scrambled eggs, like a Latin American colonel's. Maybe the braid dazzled the court officers, and that's why they didn't ask him to remove it. Maybe he refused. In any event, the hat made it difficult for me, the fact-finder in this case, to examine the captain's demeanor and facial gestures as he testified. He was sitting in the witness box to my right, but a little below me, and I couldn't see his face beneath the hat.

The captain introduced a written policy statement from the previous August, a "directive number 9191 from the general director of the Massachusetts Bay Transportation Authority," which directed that subway stations near certain dangerous locations would be more closely monitored by MBTA employees, inspectors, and police.

The captain pointed out that Broadway Station was not included in this directive at the time the policy was enacted, although after "the melee" security at Broadway Station was "beefed up." The policy had been written based on statistics from the previous school year, prior to the February day on which this fracas had occurred. The captain's recitation of the policy hurt the MBTA more than it helped because it established that special measures could be and in fact were taken in other problem areas. The policy was laudable, but its implementation was tardy in this case.

By the time of the trial, Timmy O'Leary had graduated and was a chef at the Parker House (where the famous rolls come from)—*the hotel where I have lunch on ceremonial occasions*, I noted as testimony drew to a close. I hoped I wasn't going to have to recuse myself. I had never seen Timmy O'Leary there; it's unlikely that I would because I ate in the handsome old dining room, not in the kitchen. But if I found against Timmy O'Leary, I might not want to go there again.

As fate and small-town Boston would have it, a year after the trial I did see Timmy O'Leary on the Red Line platform at the Park Street MBTA station, the hub of the universe. How could one miss his red hair? They say that if you wait at the Park Street Station long enough, you will eventually see everyone you ever knew. Timmy was headed toward Quincy or Ashmont, and I was going to Harvard Square. He did not appear to recognize me. That's not unusual; taken out of context, I look just like one of a hundred thousand middle-aged Irish guys in a tie who ride public transportation around Boston.

He, on the other hand, had his chef's clothes on, a double-breasted white cotton tunic and black-and-white checked pants. And of course he was still six foot three and topped by a flame of red. I couldn't see the scar on his nose across the tracks.

My findings read, in part:

> The MBTA was negligent and did not fulfill its duty to the plaintiff, a passenger on a common carrier, to protect him from harm which was foreseeable. The MBTA knew that there had been fights in the Broadway Station recently, but paid no special attention to the safety at that station even though it had a policy in practice to do so at other stations serving students and even though paying attention to trouble spots was consistent with the nature and operation of its business. In addition, the MBTA inspector, a "troubleshooter" in his own words, was negligent by doing nothing to stop this melee either before it occurred, as the vandals came over the turnstiles, after they came over the turnstiles screaming, once they began the battle, or when they fled back up the stairs. That the MBTA inspector, the "troubleshooter," in his own words, did not see or hear any of this melee is not credible.
>
> Therefore, the court finds for the plaintiff, Timothy O'Leary.
>
> A hearing on damages will be scheduled for one month from today.

{ viii }

THE MARGIN OF INDIFFERENCE

A judge can put off deciding a case for a while and call it "reserving judgment," or "taking the matter under advisement," but at some point a decision has to be made. Judges cannot remain indifferent forever.

After some trials I have thought, *How am I ever going to decide this case?* Fortunately, the law has created burdens of proof to guide me. If the plaintiff in a civil case does not convince by a "preponderance of the evidence," she loses. In a criminal case, the burden of proof for the prosecution is "beyond a reasonable doubt."

Although one can visualize a preponderance of the evidence as being 50.0001 percent, or that grain of sand that tips the scale, it is not so easy to define beyond a reasonable doubt. When I get to the language about reasonable doubt in jury instructions, I sometimes say to myself that the jury is never going to get this concept. Yet when I was a member of a jury, I was happily surprised that jurors wrestled intelligently with this and other difficult concepts.

I gave the instructions with more confidence thereafter.

BOOSTING

She'd get it for you less than wholesale

§ § §

I was a graduate student in government at the time. We had been discussing a concept called "the margin of indifference." The concept is that most people, even decision makers like legislators, are indifferent about most things. As a result, they can be led by people who are really interested in the subject at hand. Hitler's takeover of the German Reichstag in the thirties serves as a good example of the consequences of the margin of indifference.

I was pondering the theory as I walked along Brattle Street in Harvard Square about ten o'clock in the morning on a Saturday in August. There weren't many people around. It had been a hot summer. Anybody who could get away from the city did get away, and that included a lot of the usual denizens of Harvard Square. The others hadn't gotten up yet, it seemed.

I was on the right-hand side of Brattle Street going out of the Square. A car pulled up alongside of me, crossed the intersection, and parked ahead on Brattle Street, at the far corner of Church Street. I was about two doors down on the other side of the corner.

Out of the driver's-side back door came a young, good-looking muscleman wearing a light blue tank-top muscle shirt. I watched him as he headed back toward me. He crossed the street and walked over to the front of a women's clothing shop on the left-hand side of the Gropius-designed building that formerly housed Design Research, later Crate and Barrel.

Superman stood outside the clothing shop, crouched down, and looked into the store, which was about four or five steps below street level. Made curious by his actions, I leaned back into a doorway across the street and watched. Superman then went into the store, but not into the main part of the store. Rather, he went to the right, into a storeroom. (I could see clearly into the well-lit store through the large front display windows.) Shortly thereafter, he came out of the storeroom and out of the store carrying four long, corrugated-cardboard boxes piled on top of each other. There were clothes on top of the boxes. He had taken them from the storeroom.

Superman walked speedily, diagonally across the street back to the parked car. The trunk of the car sprung open as he approached. He put the boxes in the trunk, slammed the trunk shut, and jumped in the back seat. The car took off.

The driver of the car was a woman, and another woman sat in the front seat. There was also another man in the back seat.

All I could think of was that years before some wag like Cleveland Amory had written that one could detect people's class by the position of couples in a car. If both men were in the front seat, they were lower-class. If a man and his wife were in the front seat, it meant they were middle-class. If a man and the other man's wife were in the front seat, they were very sophisticated and upper-class. I guess it was the whiff of adultery that made them sophisticated. I don't recall what he said about two women in the front seat, one driving. I don't think it entered his mind. And of course, it had nothing to do with anything, either when Cleveland Amory had written it or now when I saw it. But that is what went through my sun-addled mind as the car drove away. Was I planning to describe them in Cleveland Amory's snotty terms? Was my inability to categorize them the reason I did not call the police? I doubt it.

I stood there astonished, saying to myself, *I just witnessed a crime!* In retrospect, I had known that was what was going on from just about the time Superman crouched down to look in the store. However, I did not note the license plate or anything else identifiable about the car or its occupants, except that there was a muscleman in the back seat.

What was my responsibility? Should I say something? Should I say nothing? To whom should I say it? Should I just go on my way? After my nit-picking, it was too late to do anything, I decided.

I went on my way, wondering whether I had just exercised the margin of indifference.

This two-minute experience came back to me years later in court as I read the police report for the crime for which Lady Diana Spencer (honest) had been convicted a year and a half before.

She was in front of me today for the first hearing, called the probable-cause hearing, before a probation revocation. The probation officer claimed that Ms. Spencer had violated the terms of her probation by committing two new crimes. She had not yet been convicted of those new crimes, but conviction was not necessary to revoke the earlier probation. The probation officer only had to show by a preponderance of the evidence, the civil standard of proof, that it was more likely than not that Ms. Spencer had committed the new crimes in order to have me revoke her probation and send her to jail for two years, the sentence that had been suspended after the earlier conviction.

According to the police report, the facts of the case for which Ms. Spencer had been convicted and was on probation were that she had been the driver in a scheme very similar to the one I had seen years before. Her "boosting," as it's called on the street, had occurred at the Versace store on Newbury Street. The thieves had stolen twenty-six silk shirts, seven baroque-patterned pillows, and sixteen silk scarves.

Unfortunately for Lady Diana, two witnesses recognized her hair, particularly her golden braids, and the car, and they also noted its license plate number. She was caught within the hour on Massachusetts Avenue sporting one of the scarves, which went nicely with her gold-braided hair.

Because of her then lengthy record, Ms. Spencer had been given a two-year sentence to be suspended for two years during which time she was to be on probation. If she didn't behave during the two years after the sentence, she could go to the House of Correction for two years.

The new charges triggering the probation surrender were arson; malicious destruction of property, to wit, a car; and forgery, uttering, and larceny—in other words bad checks. Her lawyer assured me that the arson-and-malicious-destruction-of-property case would "go away" because it wasn't Lady Diana who lit the car on fire. "It was just that she was the driver while her sister torched the sister's fiancé's car." (A lot of the women who appear in front of us have "fiancés"; they never have boyfriends, and they never get married, which might be a good thing, but sometimes I am tempted to ask, "Have you set a date?")

The sister's fiancé had been beating up the sister and, worse than that, had moved in with somebody else, so the sister took her revenge. But Lady Diana knew nothing about it, had not even seen the car go up in flames, and just drove away when the sister returned from the conflagration. Again, two witnesses noted her license plate number. Lady Diana Spencer was stopped within two blocks, unfortunately (or fortunately, depending on whether she would beat the case), in the driver's seat. This time she had golden curls, according to the witnesses.

The second case for which Ms. Spencer was being surrendered was more problematic, involving an elaborate check-bouncing scheme. Lady Di was one of the check cashers. She deposited a $4,000 check in a bank one day and drew a $3,000 check from the account the next day. However, Lady Diana had been helpful to the prosecution in that case by revealing who put her up to her shenanigans, so I was being asked to allow her to serve six months on the bad-check charge concurrent with the two years for the probation revocation. That would be it. In her defense, Lady Diana had only received $250 for her efforts, according to the prosecutor. How he knew that, I was not told.

At least the prosecutor had not asked for a sidebar, like prosecutors often do, to make this request. Thus I could say aloud in open court what I usually said in an Irish whisper to the assistant district attorney at sidebar, "I am not an agent of the prosecution. If you want to make a deal, don't drag me into it. You have the power to dismiss any of these cases on your own, and you know it. If you want to *nul prosse* [dismiss] an arson case, then do it." I suppose the reason the request was made in open court was that we were in one of the tiny courtrooms, and everyone in the room, except for the probation officer and me, was in on the deal beforehand.

The day I saw her in court, Lady Diana again had golden braids woven into her hair. She was about forty and a little stouter than she had been in the mug shots taken after the earlier arrest. The absence of cocaine may have added to her weight, I mused. Her lawyer had told me that she had "confronted" her drug problem.

"What is she doing about her addiction?" I asked.

Well, Lady Diana Spencer did not like that, and she threw me a full teapot with one hand on the hip, the other pointing, and a scowl. She was "no addict," she told her lawyer loudly, and he told me the same.

"Why has she been convicted five times for possession of cocaine in the last eight years?" I asked. "Most addicts don't even get arrested."

"Only four convictions; the first was continued without a finding," her lawyer replied to her knowing smile.

"And all the recent charges with the exception of the sister's vendetta are consistent with supporting a drug habit."

She looked at me, angrier than before.

"So let me ask again, What is she doing about her addiction?

There was no response.

"Does the probation department have a request for bail?"

"Yes, we request bail of one thousand dollars," said a voice at my right. "Although she came in today, she has defaulted twenty-six times before; she uses twelve aliases, and she's been convicted fourteen times."

I said to the defense attorney, "You told me that she had 'confronted' her drug problem. What does that mean?"

"She doesn't do drugs anymore."

"As of when?"

He leaned over and asked her. She looked at me more angrily than ever. She had been told by somebody, probably the police, that nothing would happen today. She was cooperating with the police and believed that that would keep her from doing time. She did not realize that the probation officer and I were not in on the deal.

I set bail at $1,000. She was put in custody but appealed the bail and was released that afternoon after the bail appeal was heard by a Superior Court judge.

I did not see Lady Diana Spencer in person again. The final surrender hearing did not come before me. I thought no more of her until about a year later when I saw her on television. She had either beat the probation surrender, or she had defaulted and not been caught. Now she was part of an "all-girl team" of bank robbers. None had been caught, but the TV stations were flashing a photo of Lady Diana, complete with golden curls, from the bank's hidden cameras behind the tellers.

In the unlikely event the police did not recognize her, I asked the probation officer to call the police and tell them who we thought she was.

ATTORNEY O'LEARY

He said he just wanted the money for the bus trip back home

§ § §

Late in the morning, late in the week, a case was called in the first session, *Commonwealth v. John O'Leary*. Out of the holding cell to the left came a man who looked somewhere over sixty wearing a Burberry raincoat, a navy blue suit, and a dress shirt without a tie. He was bald and a bit hunched over. The daily duty lawyer, Mr. Malin, had interviewed the man earlier. Daily duty lawyers are private attorneys who work in the criminal sessions for the day at an hourly rate paid by the state. A new lawyer, albeit in his mid-forties, Mr. Malin was exuberant and dedicated. He was like a five-year-old who likes school so much he just can't wait for the next question so he can raise his hand. He was a treat, frankly, because he was still unjaded and appeared very happy to be doing what he was doing, unlike a few of his comrades in the appointed defense bar who were burnt out at an early age—causing everyone to suffer as a result, including clients and judges.

Mr. Malin had been a private detective; he was famous for finding people, according to a more experienced lawyer pal of his. He is also a black belt in karate, one of the court officers reported. You knew that he had worked with his hands at some point, and he relished wearing a suit these days. He was good-looking in a hearty Irish way, with a beard and a twinkle in his blue eyes.

Poor O'Leary, on the other hand, had no twinkle and hadn't had one in a long time. His clothes were still good, but overall he was shabby. Peering out of his raincoat, with his head hunched down, he looked like a turtle. His hands shook in the handcuffs. He had been arrested early that morning in the waiting room at the New England Medical Center, where he had gone because he thought he had sprained or broken his left wrist, which he was holding with his right hand. He was charged with disorderly conduct, not a major felony. Because he was so well dressed, I asked the probation officer whether he was indigent. The probation officer said, "Well, he's a lawyer, Judge, and he says that he has offices in Worcester and in Boston."

I am originally from Worcester. I was practically raised in the Worcester County Courthouse, where my father regularly sat as a judge and where one of my most doting aunts worked in the Clerk of Courts Office. My grandfather had been a lawyer there, my brother and sister-in-law are now lawyers there, and I have a couple of cousins who practice law there as well. Thirty years earlier, I had been an assistant district attorney for the so-called Middle District, Worcester County. So I inquired of Mr. O'Leary what the name of his office was in Worcester. He said, "O'Leary and Crowley."

Now, I happen to know O'Leary and Crowley, because it's an insurance agency, and it's been my family's insurance agency for almost three generations. In fact, Phillip O'Leary, its current president, may well be a cousin of mine—if not by blood, then by courtesy. His mother is my brother's godmother, and my father was his sister's godfather. Phillip and I were in law school together.

Phillip O'Leary runs the insurance agency with his brother and a cousin. He no longer practices law, because of a case to which my father appointed him. Shortly after he got out of law school, he was assigned to represent a man vegetating in Bridgewater State Hospital who had been committed as a sexually dangerous person some eighteen years before. Phillip worked very hard on the case, and on account of Phillip's efforts the inmate was released. Two weeks later, the man pulled a little boy into his apartment from a window, molested him, and killed him. Phillip was so horrified he never practiced law again.

All this came back to me as John O'Leary told me he was from the law firm of "O'Leary and Crowley." To the best of my knowledge, O'Leary and Crowley did not exist as a law firm. In any event, I let him go on and asked him where his Worcester office was. Now I had not lived in Worcester for quite a while, so there were a couple of generations of lawyers there I didn't know so well, and O'Leary was five years younger than I, according to the complaint. He could have fooled me, but I took the risk. He said Elm Street. A law office could very well be on Elm Street, and I wouldn't have known its name. I asked him where his Boston office was, and he said State Street. That's where most law offices are; thus the local saying "You need a State Street lawyer to figure that out."

Given the opportunity to speak, Mr. O'Leary decided to tell me his woes of the previous night. He was walking down Tremont Street when he was attacked; someone twisted his wrist, and he then fell on the same wrist. He went to the New England Medical Center emergency room to have the wrist taken care of. Once there, he was treated most brusquely and impolitely by the security guards, who had him arrested before he was seen by the doctors. They must have mistaken his wincing with pain for intoxication, he offered.

According to the record, which I am required to look at before setting the terms for releasing an arrested defendant, it appeared that Mr. O'Leary had a problem with drink. The record reflected two convictions for operating under the influence of intoxicating liquor. I asked Mr. Malin if he would take Mr. O'Leary to the organization called Lawyers Concerned for Lawyers to see if we could get some help for him. I told Mr. Malin that it was down in Haymarket and gave him directions to get there. He said he'd be happy to take Mr. O'Leary during the lunch hour, and Mr. O'Leary was released on personal recognizance to Mr. Malin. That is supposed to mean that Mr. Malin would make sure that Mr. O'Leary came back, but nobody would hold Mr. Malin to it.

My session continued into the afternoon. Mr. Malin returned, and I asked him how the trip to Haymarket went. He said, "We took Mr. O'Leary down to Lawyers Concerned for Lawyers, and we talked to a very nice woman there. We set him up with counseling. They gave me ten dollars, and we hailed a cab and sent Mr. O'Leary to Boston City Hospital for his wrist."

I called my friend at Lawyers Concerned for Lawyers when I had free time later in the afternoon. She said, "We were able to set up a great program for Mr. O'Leary, and he seemed very interested. He will come to our noontime meeting tomorrow and once a week will see Jane McMahon, one of the counselors. He doesn't want to go to detox, although I think he needs it. We put him in a cab to go to City Hospital to have his wrist looked at. Maybe they will detox him as well. I called a social worker over there, and he'll keep an eye out for him. He seemed eager, but I'm not sure about him. I don't think that he has had a practice for some time. He said that his wife left him ten years ago and that she took all the money. I don't know if any of that is true, but we'll do what we can. He really needs some help."

Then I called my friend Phillip O'Leary. He returned my call the next morning. I said, "Phil, who is John O'Leary?"

"Oh my God, have you seen John O'Leary?" he asked. "I grew up with him, and he's always claimed to be a member of my family, but he's not. He did go to high school with my brother. He's a couple of years younger than me." Now as Phil always kept in shape and never drank, to my mind the contrast between Phil O'Leary and John O'Leary was startling.

I told Phil what had happened the day before. Phil said, "It doesn't surprise me, but he's not a lawyer. He's never been a lawyer. He did work as a real estate broker for a while but not for a long time. He pretends to be a lot of people. As you know, our office here is right near the Worcester courthouse. Two years ago or so, he appeared in our office. He said he had to come to court in Worcester for an eviction of one of his tenants and that he had left his Mercedes down in Kelly Square and was just short of cab money to return to get the Mercedes. Could I give him ten dollars for cab money?

"I was on to him so I said, 'Better than that, I'll drive you down.' I did drive him towards Kelly Square but he jumped out at the shopping mall on Main Street, saying he had to go in and collect the rents. He thanked me very profusely. Of course, there was no Mercedes, and there were no rents. He owns nothing. John's father had been the principal of the junior high school, and his mother's still alive, but he is far gone. I think that she has a restraining order on him. He's not a lawyer, and he never has been a lawyer, but I guess he wanted to be a lawyer."

"Didn't we all!" I said.

I was recounting this story to a couple of my judge colleagues later in the day, and one of them, who lives on Tremont Street, said, "Oh, yeah, that guy" and described him perfectly, down to the black wing tips. "He's always on Tremont Street, panhandling, and he's always kind of neat, and he always gives the story that he's a lawyer from Worcester and that he forgot his money."

§ § §

Two months later on a bright sunny day, I was walking down Tremont Street on the way to my eye doctor at the New England Medical Center. John O'Leary approached and stopped, wearing the same raincoat he had worn to court. I stopped, too. He asked me for $1.37 so he could get the bus back to Worcester. I gave him fifty cents because it was loose in my pocket, and I did not want to open my wallet on a busy street. He had no memory of me or, for that matter, anything else.

It seemed inevitable that we should have met again, but I was still surprised.

GUNS

Sometimes there's no question about what to do

§ § §

I rush to say that the facts that he looked like the recent abortion-clinic killer and that he came from New Hampshire like the abortion-clinic killer did not influence me in any way.

I was sitting in Room 379, a kind of sterile courtroom, albeit in the historic, quirky Old Building. Someone had painted the room all white, even the oak woodwork and there were too-bright fluorescent lights that couldn't be shut off. Above my head was one of the many portraits of Elijah Adlow, our colorful chief justice in the fifties and sixties. He would regale the spectators' section with his wit, sometimes at the expense of the people appearing before him, saying things we could never get away with today. There were no tape recordings of our sessions then.

The defendant, Billy Shedd, was brought down from the first session dock, right through all the people in the corridor, in shackles. He was in his late twenties, sallow-skinned, five eight or nine, and skinny; he had wild, straight black hair that stuck out everywhere on his head, and was dressed in blue jeans and a sweatshirt. He never looked up.

Billy was represented by Alice H. Hummock, one of the more aggressive and anti-authoritarian public defenders. For me, she was dangerous because she would say things like, "But Judge, of course you can't do that," and my rebellious Irish self would say, *Just watch me*. So I had to constantly watch myself not to jump at her bait.

This hearing required me to decide a motion to suppress evidence that had been seized from Billy Shedd's car, to wit, a shotgun and three handguns plus over a hundred rounds of ammunition. Billy

Shedd did not have a firearms identification (FID) card for any of these weapons; thus they were illegal. On a tip from an unnamed citizen, the police stopped Billy's car, searched it without a warrant, and "seized" the weapons to be used as evidence against him at trial. I had to decide whether the so-called "automobile exception" to the constitutional mandate that all searches and seizures of evidence be made with a warrant allowed the stop, search, and seizure in this case. The automobile exception, as it existed at that time, went something like this: because automobiles were mobile, they could be searched if the officers who stopped the car were in danger or reasonably feared that they were in danger. In Billy Shedd's case, the question was whether his situation as the driver of an automobile was so "exigent" that the requirement of a warrant before a search could be waived.

Evidence is presented in layers. Sometimes the layers overlap, sometimes they seep through, coloring and strengthening the layer above or beneath. One layer might extend over the previous one. If a lawyer is trying to make a particular point strongly, she may use another witness or a piece of evidence to make the earlier evidence glow.

In this case three policemen testified for the Commonwealth. The testimony of each layered over and supported the others, but around the edges were differences that reflected the individual officers' ideas about their jobs more than they revealed different facts. Officer no. 1, Patrolman Joe Slack, had been on the police force twenty-eight years. He'd been stationed in Area A, basically downtown Boston, for the last fourteen. Area A is one of the police patrol areas covered by my court, although I had never seen Officer Slack before despite having been a judge for a while at that time.

Officer Slack testified that he was approached by The Citizen, and that's the way Officer Slack referred to him, with shades of the French Revolution, who walked up to him while he was parked in a marked police car, about eight o'clock at night in the Faneuil Hall area, a big tourist attraction. The Citizen said, "That man in that black car over there is loading a pistol."

Officer Slack replied, "Which man in which car?" and together they identified Billy Shedd's car.

The Citizen walked away to a green station wagon containing a woman and three young kids. Officer Slack pulled his cruiser down the street a little closer to the car driven by Billy Shedd, the man allegedly with the gun, pulled over to the side to park again, and made a radio call for help. Officer Slack was in uniform and in a marked cruiser, so it was not easy for him to hide. Billy Shedd's car, a black sedan, was then about one hundred feet away.

Officer Slack waited. Two or three minutes later, Billy Shedd got out, looked around, looked directly at Officer Slack in his car, got back in the car, and slowly drove away. Mr. Shedd took a right. Officer Slack, a very cautious man, kept his distance but noticed that the car had New Hampshire plates with the motto LIVE FREE OR DIE. It also appeared that Billy Shedd did not know where he was going because he hesitated at every intersection.

By this time, two other cruisers had arrived to assist Officer Slack. They blocked the traffic at the intersection of Congress and New Chardon streets, creating a traffic jam. When Billy Shedd drew up to the intersection, his car got stuck in the jam, and he was approached by Officer Bravo. Uninvited, Mr. Shedd got out of the car. Officer Slack did not hear all of the conversation between Officer Bravo and Billy Shedd.

Officer Slack was approached again by The Citizen, who pulled up in the station wagon with his family and said, "Oh, you got him." Again Officer Slack failed to obtain any identifying information, not even The Citizen's license plate number, nor was he too specific about what The Citizen looked like.

Cross-examination of Officer Slack by Billy Shedd's attorney, Alice H. Hummock, did not help Mr. Shedd. Officer Slack did manage to say, "I did hear Mr. Shedd say that he decided to leave after he spotted me near Faneuil Hall," which to a fact-finder, me in this case, indicated consciousness of guilt. However, the defense attorney violated the first rule of trial lawyering—*Never ask a question to which you don't know the answer*—by asking Officer Slack *the* essential question for the prosecution: "Were you in fear for your safety?"

The assistant district attorney had neglected to ask this question although he had performed pretty well otherwise. Officer Slack had testified that he had not taken his gun out when he approached Mr. Shedd's car, perhaps indicating that he was not afraid for his safety. According to the automobile exception, the car could only be searched without a warrant if the police officers feared for their safety.

Officer Slack now replied, "Well, we were notified there were guns in the vehicle, and we hadn't found any guns yet. Of course I was in fear for my safety. I've got a wife and three kids. I've been shot at before. Of course I was in fear. After Mr. Shedd was frisked and we didn't find any weapons on him, I wasn't in fear, but I wasn't going to let him get back in the car. There could've been guns there."

Ms. Hummock, the defense attorney, had just made the Commonwealth's case. Officer Slack testified further, "I did not hear specifically what Officer Bravo said to the defendant, but I think he asked him if he had a firearms identification card, and I heard Mr. Shedd say, 'No, I have a constitutional right to bear arms.'" Officer Slack also noted that Billy Shedd received the Miranda warnings. Contrary to usual police testimony, Officer Slack recited them—that Billy Shedd could remain silent, that anything he said could be used against him, that he could have a lawyer present at any time, that a lawyer would be appointed if he could not afford one, and that he could stop the questioning at any time.

At the end of cross-examination, the assistant district attorney jumped up and said, "A few questions on redirect examination, Your Honor." No questions were really necessary because Attorney Alice H. Hummock had done his work for him. I guessed that the prosecutor felt it was essential that the same questions come out of his mouth so I would know to which side the answers should be credited. *Does he think that I've been asleep?* I wondered. *Should I show him my notes, with all their stars, arrows and exclamation points?* I didn't care where the truth came from.

Mindful of the cautionary advice, given new trial judges by their older colleagues, to employ non-verbal gestures when your words are being recorded, I made a pained face but said for the tape recorder, "Go ahead."

"Why did you call for backup, Officer Slack?" the assistant district attorney asked.

"I called for backup because if he was loading the weapon I had heard about from The Citizen, I didn't want to approach the vehicle myself."

"That's all, Judge. Thank you, Officer Slack."

Whereas Officer Slack was a seasoned veteran and had successfully avoided making arrests and appearing in court, the next witness, Officer Bravo, was a young, aggressive, smart, and brave police officer in his late twenties who I had seen in court frequently. I liked him. He was straightforward and unassuming. I particularly liked the way he introduced himself.

It is my experience in court that many police officers, most lawyers, and even judges introduce themselves by their title. When asked, "What is your name, sir?" they say, "My name is Officer John Jones" or "My name is Attorney John Jones" or "My name is Judge John Jones."

Officer Bravo always said, "My name is Joe Bravo."

He identified Billy Shedd's car as a dark-colored or black 1993 Ford Crown Victoria, and added "like an unmarked police car." Officer Bravo approached the car from the front on foot and told the pedestrians within a hundred feet to move away, that a dangerous situation existed. He had his gun drawn. Once at the car, he ordered Billy Shedd out and to the side of the cruiser.

As Mr. Shedd exited the car, Officer Bravo asked him, "Do you have weapons in your vehicle?"

Mr. Shedd replied, "I do."

At that point, Officer Bravo, as they say, Mirandized him. The policeman then asked Billy Shedd to step back toward the cruiser.

"Do you have a firearms identification card or a license to carry a weapon?"

Billy Shedd replied, "I don't need one. I have a constitutional right to bear arms." He repeated that twice.

Officer Bravo asked another policeman on the scene, Officer Bridge, to search the driver's side of the car. As soon as Officer Bravo reached the passenger side, Officer Bridge shouted, "I've got it!" and pulled a pistol out from under the driver's front seat. He waved it in the air. Officer Bravo then looked in the rear seat and saw a .38-caliber automatic on top of a newspaper. Officer Bravo also removed from the back seat a 12-gauge shotgun that was loaded. The .38 automatic was loaded as well.

In the trunk, one hundred rounds of ammunition were found as well as a blue light and a strobe light. When asked about the latter, Billy Shedd told Officer Bravo that he was a part-time policeman in East Alstead, New Hampshire.

Billy Shedd was handcuffed after the recovery of the second weapon and put in the back seat of the cruiser.

Officer Bravo knew how to testify in a case like this. He said, "Based on the information that weapons were involved, I was fearful for my safety and the safety of the public. Therefore, I took the weapons out. Basically, when I first saw Billy Shedd, I told him that I had information that he had weapons in the car. He said, 'Yeah, I do.'"

The defense attorney again leapt in to fill the breach for the Commonwealth.

She asked, "If Billy Shedd had produced a firearms identification card, what would you have done?"

Officer Bravo said, "If he had produced an FID card, the whole thing would have been over. I would have let him go." That was the correct answer for this hearing, although I am doubtful that it would have happened in reality.

On redirect, the assistant district attorney asked, "Did you ask

[Mr. Shedd] why he had blue lights and a strobe light in his car at this time?"

"Yes, Mr. Shedd said he was going to use them to help solve a case in North Carolina, which is where he was headed."

The next witness was Officer Bridge, who was maybe thirty-eight years old. He had caught my attention early on because he had an eye patch. He mentioned that he had just had an operation for a detached retina. I had had two such operations in the right eye the previous year. He rushed to say that he did not have the eye patch on the day of this arrest, lest we think that his vision, thus his testimony at the hearing, was impaired. As for me, I wanted to ask him who his surgeon was and wanted to compare ophthalmological notes. None of my surgeries had restored my sight, which is why I had to turn excessively to watch him on the witness stand to my right.

Officer Bridge had seen Officer Bravo approach the defendant on foot and then heard Officer Bravo say, "There's a weapon in the car." He went on, "I looked inside. I opened the door and looked down inside and saw a .38 revolver on the floor of the driver's side, partly sticking out, wooden handle under the driver's side. I retrieved the gun and shouted, 'I've got the gun out of the car!' It was loaded. Then Officer Bravo stood up while searching the front seat and said, 'I found another gun.' The bullets in the brown bag were found in the back seat after a third gun was found in a dirty bag on the floor with a couple of boxes on the seat. Another officer found the shotgun in the trunk and found more bullets.

"I didn't have conversation with the defendant but the defendant was talking a lot, talking to all of us about his 'constitutional right to bear arms.' I heard that a couple of times."

On cross-examination, Officer Bridge acknowledged that there was no warrant to search the car.

That was the end of the testimony. Although Billy Shedd could have testified for the limited purpose of an inquiry about the stop and the search, it would have been risky to put him on the stand. Judging from what the police reported he had said at the scene, he was probably a loose cannon. Attorney Hummock wisely chose to rest her case.

In her summary of the testimony of the three police officers, Ms. Hummock listed the names of hopefully pertinent cases, some of which I knew, some of which I didn't. She didn't give me citations, nor did she give me copies of the cases, which signified to me that she didn't want me to be guided by them. I would say that she assumed I knew the cases, if I didn't happen to know that she was just showing off. In any event, she argued that there was neither "probable cause" nor the "exigent circumstances" that would have permitted such a search of Billy Shedd's car, and there was certainly no "consent to the search"—all buzz words for the defense.

The assistant district attorney did not even invoke the recently adopted automobile exception to the constitutional requirement that you have to have a warrant to search. He simply said, "The motion to suppress is defective because there is no affidavit with personal knowledge in support of it."

He was correct. Attorney Hummock had submitted an affidavit signed by her, but the rules require an affidavit from somebody who has personal knowledge of the situation, someone who was present at the time of the incident. There was no such affidavit. I was off the hook. I did not even have to decide if the search was illegal—fortunately, because the case presented a close constitutional question.

The assistant district attorney did not rest on that leg alone. He argued, "The tip from a concerned citizen gave rise to suspicion, that allowed a threshold inquiry, and the officer never lost sight of the vehicle. The police had an 'articulable, reasonable suspicion' to stop the car. There were 'exigent circumstances' which allowed for 'the search and seizure.' The defendant's answers, both before and after being given the Miranda rights, gave rise to probable cause and a justifiable search."

In my mind there was still the problem of "the tip," The Citizen in the green station wagon with his wife and three kids. Officer Slack had not asked his name. He wasn't in court. There was no way to check on him to see if he was reliable. There were a whole series of U.S. Supreme Court and other appellate decisions about "unreliable" and invented informants. The reliability of "The Citizen" who occasioned the stop of Mr. Shedd in the first place, still concerned me.

After taking the matter under advisement, I overcame my concern a few days later and denied the motion to suppress, citing both the lack of an affidavit and the "exigency" of the situation. The denial was appealed. The decision was sustained on appeal. I suspect the Appeals Court was just as alarmed by the number of guns and the amount of ammunition as I had been.

The case did not come to trial for almost six months, which was unusual in our court. We could usually give someone a trial within three months of arrest, particularly if the person was in custody. Billy Shedd, who could not provide the high cash bail that was imposed, was kept in custody until trial, an outcome he may have welcomed as defendants often don't want trials right away because they can earn credit for time they will have to serve.

The trial was held before another judge. Questions were raised regarding Mr. Shedd's competency and criminal responsibility, and he was sent for a mental examination. The results of the examination indicated that he was a paranoid schizophrenic. He had been hospitalized often both in New Hampshire and in North Carolina for his mental illness.

Mr. Shedd was civilly committed for a year, unless he became competent to stand trial before the year ended. If he did not become competent, the matter would be reviewed at year's end, and he could be committed again.

JURY DUTY

The judge is put on the jury, incognito

§ § §

In Massachusetts, jury service lasts one day or one trial. Everybody has to serve and that includes judges. Whereas there used to be many exemptions—young mothers, the aged, doctors, lawyers, judges, lighthouse keepers, members of the Ancient and Honorable Artillery, to name a few—now there are none. I've been called three times since I became a judge.

The first time the prosecutor challenged me peremptorily (i.e., for no reason that she had to explain), and I was out the door. I saw her do it.

The third time I was seated as a juror despite the fact that I knew both the prosecutor and the defense lawyer. They both had appeared in front of me. As a matter of fact, I had talked to both of them before the trial, not knowing that I would be called for their trial, of course. (The courthouse cafeteria was next to the jury room, and I spent most of the time waiting to called schmoozing in the cafeteria.) In response to the question, "Do you know the parties, the witnesses, or any of the lawyers in this case?" I raised my hand, was brought up to the sidebar, and told the judge and the lawyers that I knew both of the lawyers. Nonetheless, I was selected to serve. On the second day of trial, however, the prosecution's chief witness, the victim of the assault, failed to show up, and the judge declared a mistrial.

The second time I was called for jury duty was the most interesting. I reported for jury service to the building I worked in as a judge. I could have been called for a case in my own court. I wasn't, thank God. After lunch, by which time we all thought we were not going to be called at all, those of us who had not been impaneled in the morning, having been divided into panels of about twenty-four each, were called up to a courtroom. Six panels were called, leading me to believe that it was a very serious case. Why else would a judge tie up over one hundred potential jurors to select fourteen jurors (the twelve jurors and two alternates)? I was in one of the last of the six panels and believed that the earlier panels would have been exhausted before they got to me.

I answered yes to the statutory question from the judge, "Do any of you know the lawyers in this case?" and approached the bench.

I knew both of them. They both had tried cases in front of me. At the sidebar, I told the judge, "I know both of the lawyers, and I believe that I can be impartial."

The defense lawyer blurted out, "But Judge, you hear cases like this."

I had no response. I did hear cases like this, and I was curious why this case was being heard in the Superior Court rather than in my court. I knew the judge too and liked him. He had a reputation as a very kindly man. He had sat in my court for a short time, and our staff loved him.

The defendant, an African American man in his thirties, had the same last name as one of Boston's finest African American families. The name is to black Boston what Kennedy is to Irish Boston. For the purposes of this story, I'll call him "Jack Smith."

He was charged with breaking and entering in the nighttime with intent to commit a felony—to wit, larceny—over $250; possession of a burglarious tool, to wit, a screwdriver; attempted larceny over $250; assault with a dangerous weapon, to wit, a screwdriver; and possession of a dangerous weapon, to wit, a screwdriver.

I was surprised, first, that the call of jurors got up to my number, then, that I was seated. I found out after the trial that the defense attorney had run out of peremptory challenges, those for which the lawyer does not have to give a reason. So he tried to challenge me for cause, for a reason he had to explain, but the judge would not honor the challenge because I had said that I could be impartial. It is just as well that I did not know that beforehand. I think that I can easily let go of petty slights, but who knows?

These were the facts: Rosa Lopez had just bought her first car, a red Toyota. She parked it in back of her apartment and could see it from her living room window. Because it was her first car and because she was proud of having been able to buy it, she looked out at it often. The back lot was lit from her building. About 8:30 PM she looked out and saw to her surprise someone in her car. She screamed and then called 9-1-1. Within minutes a cruiser pulled up to the mouth of the alley behind her apartment.

Officer Renn got out of the cruiser and approached the driver's side of the car with his flashlight shining. He saw Jack Smith inside the car, digging at the radio in the dashboard with a big screwdriver. Officer Renn knew Jack Smith. (He wasn't able to tell us how he knew him, I knew. It was probably because he had arrested him before.) Jack Smith looked up at him, then wriggled over to the passenger's side and out the door. He ran down the alley a way and then jumped over a low fence to his left. Officer Renn, who is a little heavy, followed but could not make the fence. Fortunately, his partner, Officer Walkowski, fresh from the Marine Corps, had anticipated this route and picked up the trail just after Jack Smith cleared the first fence.

Jack Smith ran across the street and into another yard with Officer Walkowski in hot pursuit and gaining. Jack Smith stumbled after getting over the next fence. So did Officer Walkowski. Jack Smith still had the screwdriver in his right hand, and his hand was raised to the height of his shoulder. Officer Walkowski jumped on Jack Smith's back, bending him forward.

"Drop it!" Officer Walkowski said.

Jack Smith leaned down and plunged the screwdriver into the ground.

The case went on for two days of testimony. By the first recess, all the court officers knew that a judge was on the jury. It's not that I'm so important; it's just that in the tedium of the workday any novelty is appreciated. They did not let on, however. I may have gotten a nod that the other jurors didn't, but no one called me judge. And I never told any of the other jurors what I did for a living. As a matter of fact, we knew very little about each other. I knew only the foreman's first name and did not know anyone else's first or last name. That was to remain so throughout. Two women realized that they both were nurses, but that was as intimate as it got.

Rosa Lopez and the police officers were the only witnesses who testified. Jack Smith exercised his constitutional right to remain silent. The judge instructed us that we could not construe this fact in any way, that Jack Smith did not have to prove his innocence. The Commonwealth had to prove his guilt beyond a reasonable doubt.

The judge also instructed us that if anything became unclear, we should feel free to come back and ask him a question. I am not so generous in my instructions to a jury because often juries want to know more than has been presented, like where the fingerprints are. (There rarely are fingerprints for lower-level crimes in Boston.) I tell them that they have heard all the evidence they are going to hear, that there will be no more evidence, but that if they have a question of law, I will try to answer it. I do not invite questions as this more kindly judge did.

After the instructions, the judge picked the only African American man on the jury as the foreman. He was a young guy, in his late twenties at best. I knew nothing about him except the obvious and his first name. Judges, on the other hand, have the jury questionnaires in front of them and know more about each of the jurors than anyone else. It is not unusual to pick a minority person as foreperson when the person on trial is of the same minority. It guarantees that there will be minority representation on the jury, to make it appear to be a jury of the defendant's "peers." This practice seems fairly harmless as the foreperson carries no greater weight than any of the other jurors. The foreperson's duty is to keep the jury on track.

We were advised to talk about the charges and the evidence before we took a vote.

One court officer, a guy about my age who I remembered from the days when my father used to sit in Boston, seemed to be in charge of the jury. He gave us the nuts-and-bolts instructions once we were in the jury room. "The bathroom is behind you. Stop talking about the case when someone is in the hopper. Talk about anything else—baseball, sex, the horses, anything. Also, you can go outside the door into the hallway to stretch your legs, but you guys in here don't say anything about the case while somebody is outside the door. We'll bring you lunch today and coffee if you come back tomorrow. I'm sorry about the room, but it's all we have."

He had cause to apologize. The window was broken, and there was a draft at the same time that the heat was on too high. Depending on where you sat, you could boil and freeze all at once. The chairs were motley, the leftovers after the employees had taken the better ones. And there were only twelve chairs even though we numbered fourteen until deliberation, when the alternates would be excused.

I knew that there were some grand judges' chairs sitting in court officers' rooms tucked away in far corners of this building. I had once threatened to bring my feminist colleagues through one of our court officers' nooks that was plastered with *Playboy* pinups and Marine memorabilia. The women judges would have loved the naked ladies, I'm sure. The court officers' room also had a television, a microwave, and a refrigerator on one of the custom art deco tables made especially for this building in the thirties when it was built.

Following the judge's instructions, we went around the room talking about the case before taking a vote. Two men and one woman wanted to convict Jack of everything right away. One of the men simply said "guilty" when the discussion got to him. The woman, rather than talking about the facts, said, "I know he did it. I vote guilty on everything."

The rest of us had questions about some of the charges. Everybody agreed about the breaking and entering of the car, we knew the incident had occurred in the nighttime, but we had no evidence of the value of the radio that Jack Smith was trying to steal. The charge required us to find it to have been worth more than $250. Could we find him guilty if the value was less?

The radio was obviously worth something, but we had no evidence of how much. One juror said that she had just bought a new car radio for around $300. Another juror said he could get it for less.

"Yeah, from Jack Smith," yet another said.

We all laughed.

The first juror said, "No, from a discount house on the computer."

I said, "I don't think we can rely on our own experience. Someone should have testified to the value." This was the only time I talked.

"Let's ask the judge," said a woman on the other side of the table.

She drafted the question: "If no value was given for the radio, what do we do regarding the breaking and entering with intent to commit a felony and the attempted larceny over $250 charges?"

We buzzed the court officer and sent the question out. Then we waited for what seemed to be a long time. I knew that the judge was trying to round up the clerk, the defendant, and the lawyers who had probably gone out of the building. He would then discuss the question with the lawyers and try to get them to agree on what his response to us should be.

Finally, we were brought down to the courtroom.

"If you find that there was no credible evidence offered as to the value of the car radio but you find that there was a breaking and entering, you may find the defendant guilty of the lesser-included offense of breaking and entering with intent to commit a misdemeanor. And you may find the defendant guilty of attempted larceny under $250."

The notion of jury nullification had required the judge to say "may" rather than a stronger word such as "should" or "must." Some—not all—believe that a jury can simply let a defendant go even if the jurors believe the defendant to be guilty. That's called jury nullification. The fear of that power of the jury leads judges to be cautious and never to command a jury in a criminal case to do anything to the detriment of a defendant.

I knew that the importance of the charges really concerned sentencing. If the value of the radio was less than $250, the offenses were both misdemeanors, and the penalty for trying to steal the radio would be less. But it was not appropriate for me to tell the other jurors that.

I was grateful that the court employees were cool enough to keep from calling me "judge." They were pros, I realized, and had seen bigger fish than I. My fear was that the other jurors would find out what I do for a living and then lean on me to give them answers. The worst part would be that I would not know the answer. I worried that there would be an impasse once we got to the deliberations and that I would have to pull rank and assert my allegedly superior knowledge. I also fantasized that, having done that, some juror would say "So what?" and tell me to go screw myself.

When we went back up to the jury room, we took a vote on the breaking and entering and attempted larceny charges and voted to convict Jack of the lesser-included offenses.

Our next concern was whether Jack's raising his screwdriver up to shoulder level was assault with a dangerous weapon. Was the screwdriver a dangerous weapon? Was it a "burglarious tool" as well? Could it be both at the same time? It was charged as both.

The judge had instructed us that to convict Jack of assault with a dangerous weapon we had to believe that Jack had the "specific intent" to commit an assault, and the judge had given us some examples of specific intent, which weren't that helpful. I knew that they were the examples given in the prescribed instructions and that the judge was wary of wandering too far from those instructions. I would have been too. Some of us jurors weren't so sure what he meant, and the same woman who had earlier suggested that we ask for clarification from the judge asked that we do it again. This time the written request was, "We do not understand 'specific intent.' Please explain it again."

Down we went to the courtroom after a while, a shorter while than before. The judge read us what he had read us before.

There were two very strong analytic thinkers on the jury, a woman and a man, both in their late twenties or early thirties. I guessed that they were engineers. They had really listened to the judge's instructions, particularly the part about reasonable doubt—not an easy concept to explain or to grasp. The woman pointed out that Jack's carrying the screwdriver was subject to many interpretations. After all, he was ahead of the cop and did not brandish it at him. Furthermore, he put it down, plunging it into the dirt, when asked. Just because the cop feared the screwdriver did not make Jack's carrying of it dangerous. After all, Jack may just have wanted to make sure that the police did not get it and trace his fingerprints. Or it may have been expensive, and he didn't want to lose it. He must have thought that he could get away. Why else would he have run? Was that ambiguity of motive enough to defeat the charge?

"Yes," we all said, impressed by her analysis. That got rid of the assault-with-a-dangerous-weapon and the carrying-a-dangerous-weapon charges. Even the people who had wanted to find him guilty of everything at the beginning agreed. I think they were satisfied that we had found Jack guilty of the breaking and entering. Maybe they just wanted to go home.

Finally we all agreed that the fourteen-inch screwdriver was certainly a burglarious tool. We had pictures of the scrape marks around the radio and of the side of the radio sticking out from the dash. They were consistent with the tip of the screwdriver, which we also had with us.

The foreman took a final vote. Everyone was cheery. The foreman filled out the verdict slips, one for each charge. He pressed the buzzer. Our pal, the court officer, came in.

"You got a verdict? Good. But there'll be a little wait. The judge is taking a guilty plea in another case. It won't be long. Gather up your belongings. I don't think that you'll be back here in the Ritz."

He came back for us shortly, and we marched down single file, clutching our coats. We were not solemn; some of us were jolly, the two nurses still talking shop.

When I was a prosecutor, a smiling jury meant not guilty. I guessed that the lawyers here would know likewise. They would be only half right, and their theory would be diminished, but this was a verdict the defense could be happy with.

Everyone wants to be able to anticipate the actual verdict itself. I knew from my own experience that that was why judges asked for the verdict slips as soon as the jury returned to the courtroom. They don't like uncertainty and suspense either. When I first started hearing jury trials, I thought that I ought to wait to hear the actual verdict like everyone else. I soon changed my mind and justified this breach of egalitarianism by telling myself something like, "Well, I have to make sure that everything is in order. Sometimes the foreperson gets nervous and confused when announcing the verdict."

The defendant seemed happy with the verdict. I knew that he should be happy with the judge because whatever we had found, the judge was not a heavy sentencer. The prosecutor, a baby-faced young man but very experienced, did not seem too disappointed. The judge thanked us profusely and said that he would be happy to answer those questions he could for those of us who wanted to return to the jury room.

I never do that. I know that it is thought to be good public relations for the judicial system, but it seems like sucking up to me. Also I fear saying something I shouldn't. There have been judges who have gotten in trouble for their post-trial remarks. But I wanted to hear how this judge, whose temperament and demeanor I admired, would do it.

He did not disappoint. He thanked us again. He also told us that this was the third time that this case had gone to a jury. The two preceding cases had been mistrials. He did not know why there was no evidence of the value of the radio.

The assistant district attorney did, however. I ran into him a few weeks later. I told him that he had done a good job. He told me that although they had an expert testify at the first two trials about the value of the radio, the guy wouldn't come in this time. He was too tired of hanging around. The case had been tried in the Superior Court because the district attorney wanted to put Jack Smith away as a career criminal. He had a record a mile long for similar offenses.

Three or four months later, I was walking back from one of our sessions to the judges' lobby in my robe. On my left I could see a very "street"-dressed black man and two women who were dressed like street walkers sitting on a bench outside one of our jury courtrooms. As I came close, the man got up and approached me. He said, "Thanks, Judge. Thanks, Judge. Do you remember me?"

By this time the court officer escorting me had come between us. The man seemed friendly enough, and I was curious. I said, "I don't remember you. Why should I?"

He said, "You don't remember me? I'm Jack Smith. You was on that jury that let me go upstairs."

I remembered him.

"What are you doing here? I would have thought that you'd want to stay out of this place."

"No, no, I'm in no trouble. I'm just here with my girlfriends. I like coming here. You guys are good guys."

Oh, great! I thought.

ACKNOWLEDGMENTS

I especially want to thank Robert Coles for his appreciation and continued support of me for the past forty years, as well as for his interest in these stories and the idea of writing a book about the "lower courts" way back in 1970. Around that time, the then-young activist scholar, now law professor, John A. Robertson realized that it all happens in the "lower courts" and guided my career and interest that way.

My late father, the Honorable John Henry Meagher, Jr., aka "Black Jack," taught me both skepticism and a sense of justice. "Two wrongs don't make a right," he said as my brothers and I fought in the back seat of a station wagon in the forties.

The writers Joe Hayes (J. G. Hayes) and Andrew Holleran have been both inspirations and teachers. Michael Lowenthal, Johnny Diaz, and Joan Kenney helped me think about these stories in a larger sense. Judge Carol Ball, John Brennan, Martha Byington, Tom Fallon, Arianna Fucini, Ken Gaulin, Michael Joseph Gross, Maureen McGlame, Brendan O'Hara, Lavanya Sankaran, Constance Vecchione, and Robert Works were very helpful readers.

Albert LaFarge was an insightful and gentle editor of some of these stories at *DoubleTake* magazine in 2002. He has been a marvelous and effective agent for them more recently.

Judge Sally Kelly was my best pal at the Boston Municipal Court, and often my conscience and guidepost as well. Chief Justice William J. Tierney greeted me warmly when I became a judge in 1989 and took an early interest in my writing about the court.

My brother, Timothy J. Meagher, Ph.D., a great historian and a wonderful writer, has been a steady encouragement as well as an example. My brother Andrew C. J. Meagher, Esq., who has spent his career in the trial courts, helped to keep me in perspective and to track reality down. My sister, Mary Meagher, was a very helpful reader.

James Brink, director of the Social Law Library in Boston, very kindly archived a copy of most of these stories a few years ago, lest they be lost to posterity. Suzanne Hoey, chief librarian of the Worcester County Law Library, was a great help with research.

Lane Zachary, Colleen Mohyde, and Esmond Harmsworth encouraged me as these stories were written.

In 1989, Massachusetts Governor Michael S. Dukakis appointed me a judge. I remain very grateful.

The late Warren Presson, who found humor in everything, resolved one of my great fears about becoming a judge by telling me, "You look good in black."

Finally, my partner, the ever calming and even-tempered Renato Cellucci, has patiently seen me through the ups and downs of producing this book.